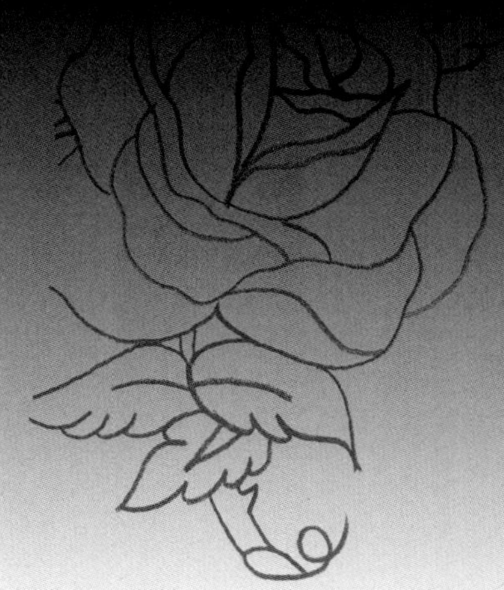

Traditional American Tattoo Design

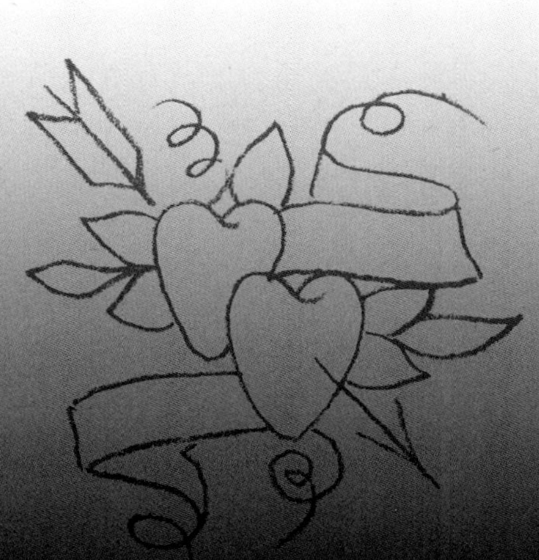

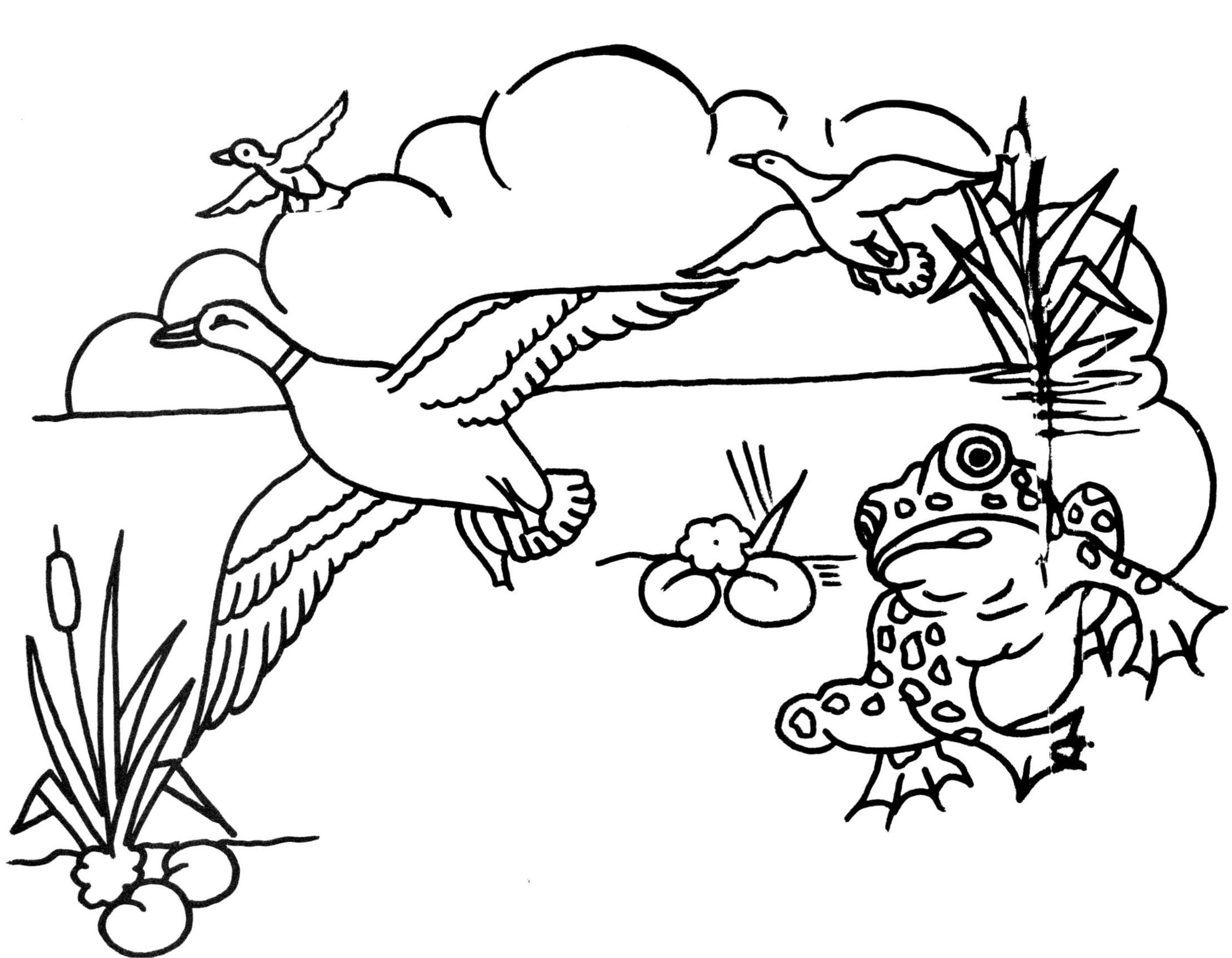

Traditional American Tattoo Design

Where It Came From and Its Evolution

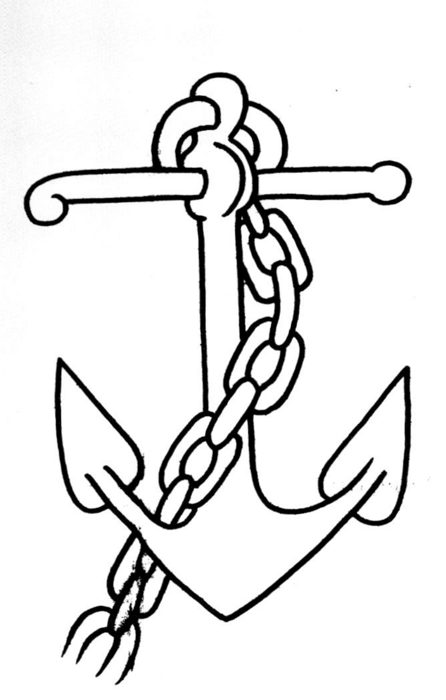

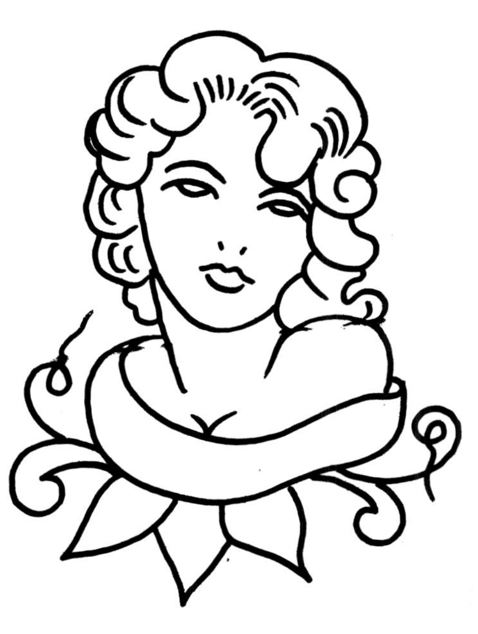

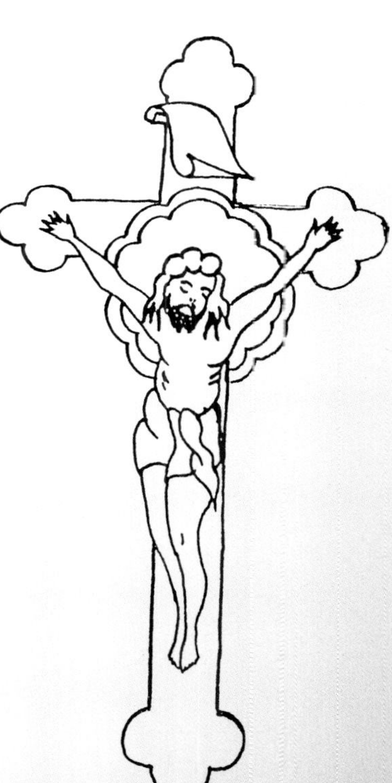

Jerry Swallow

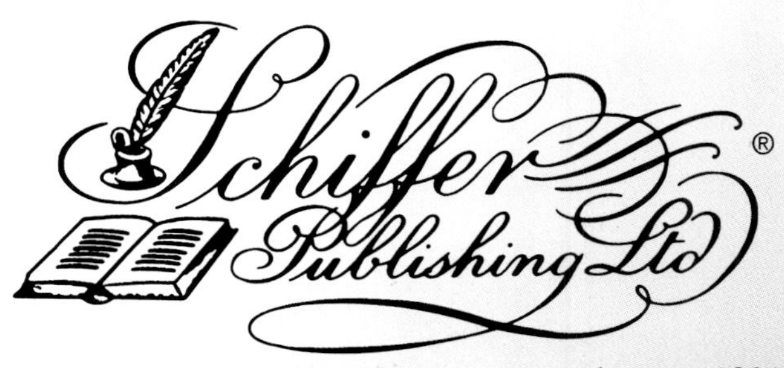

4880 Lower Valley Road, Atglen, Pennsylvania 19310

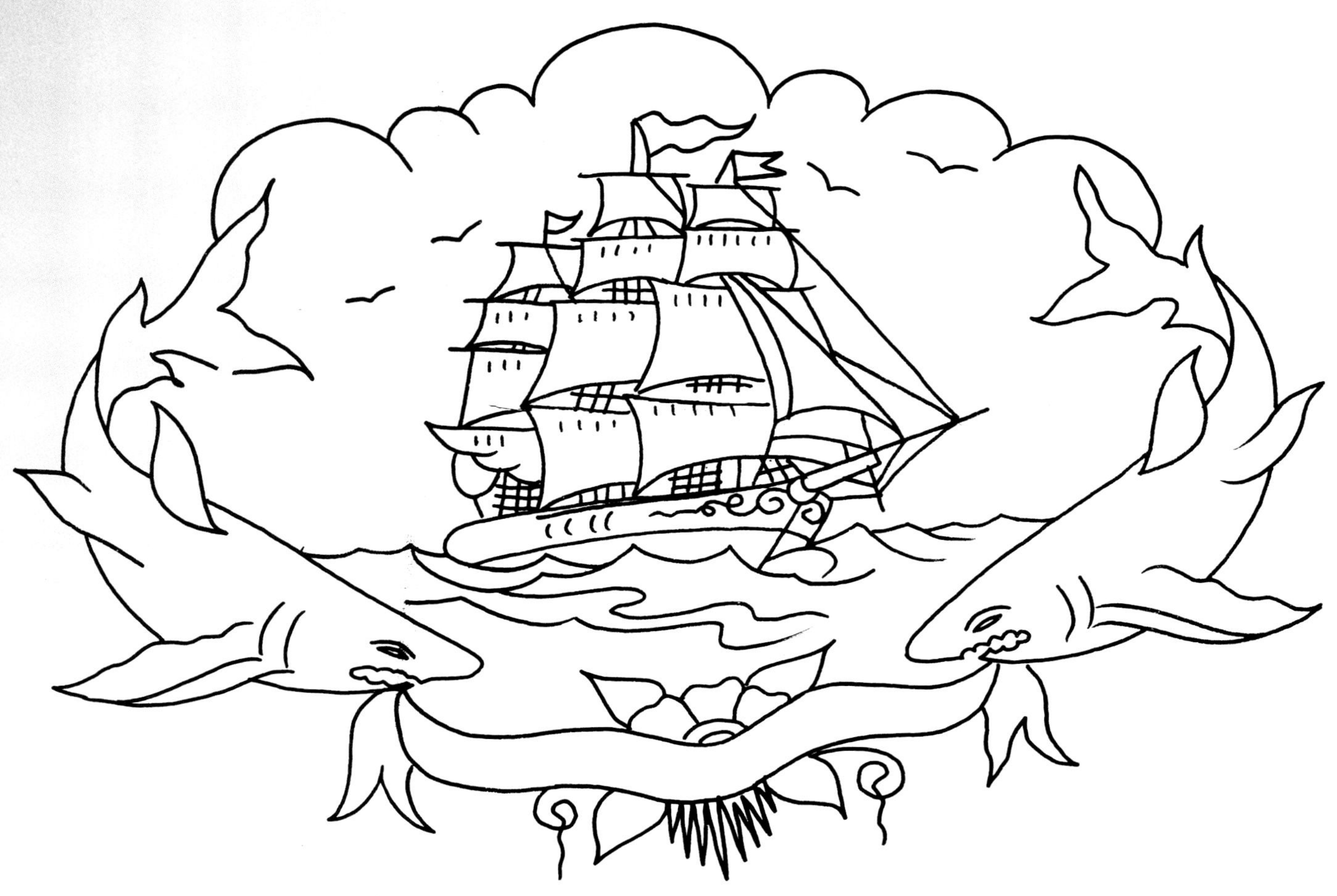

Other Schiffer Books on Related Subjects
Tattooed Women. Spider Webb.
Tattoo Road Trip: The Pacific Northwest. Bob Baxter.
Russian Prison Tattoos. Alix Lambert.
The Big Book of Tattoo. Spider Webb.

Library of Congress Control Number: 2007943190

Designed by Mark David Bowyer
Type set in GrekoDeco / Zurich BT

ISBN: 978-0-7643-2913-5
Printed in Serbia
5 4 3 2

Published by Schiffer Publishing Ltd.
4880 Lower Valley Road
Atglen, PA 19310
Phone: (610) 593-1777; Fax: (610) 593-2002
E-mail: Info@schifferbooks.com

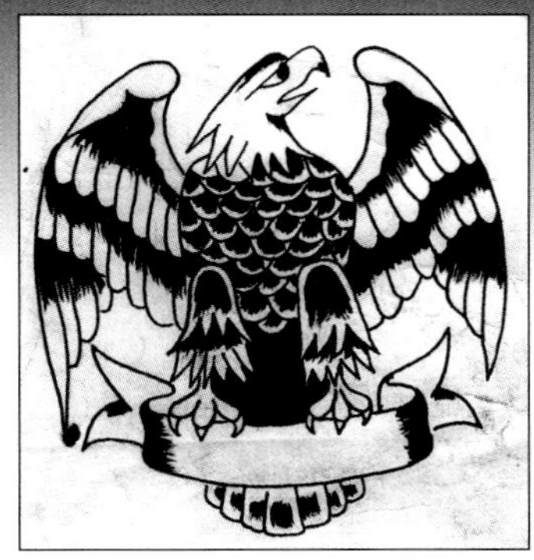

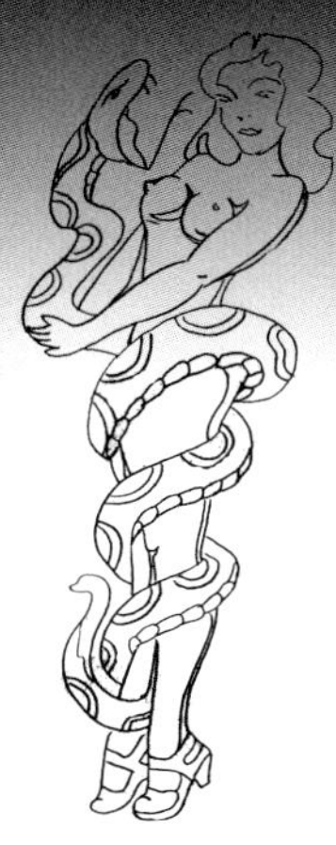

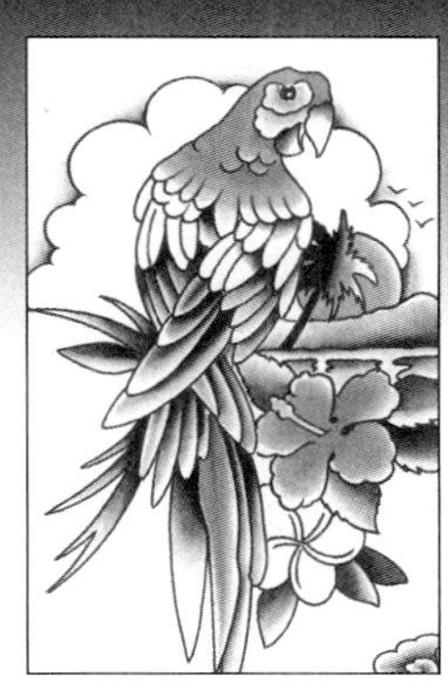

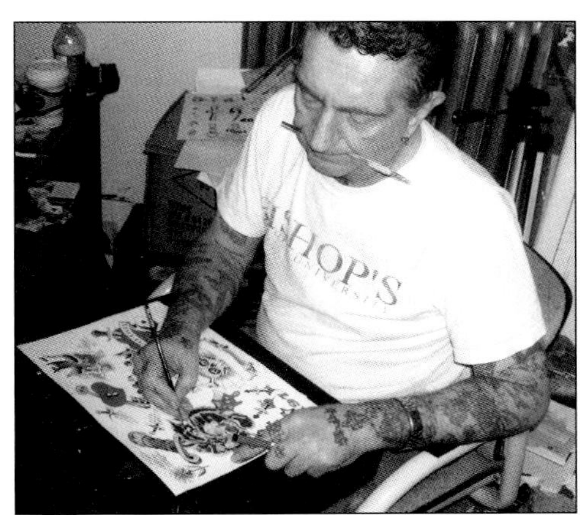

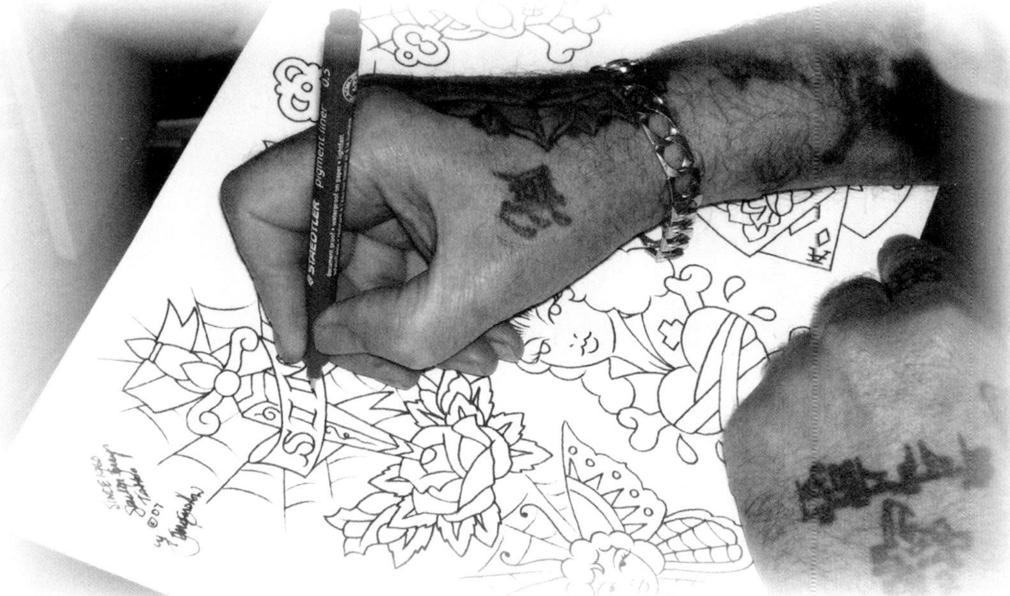
STAEDTLER pigment liner 0.5

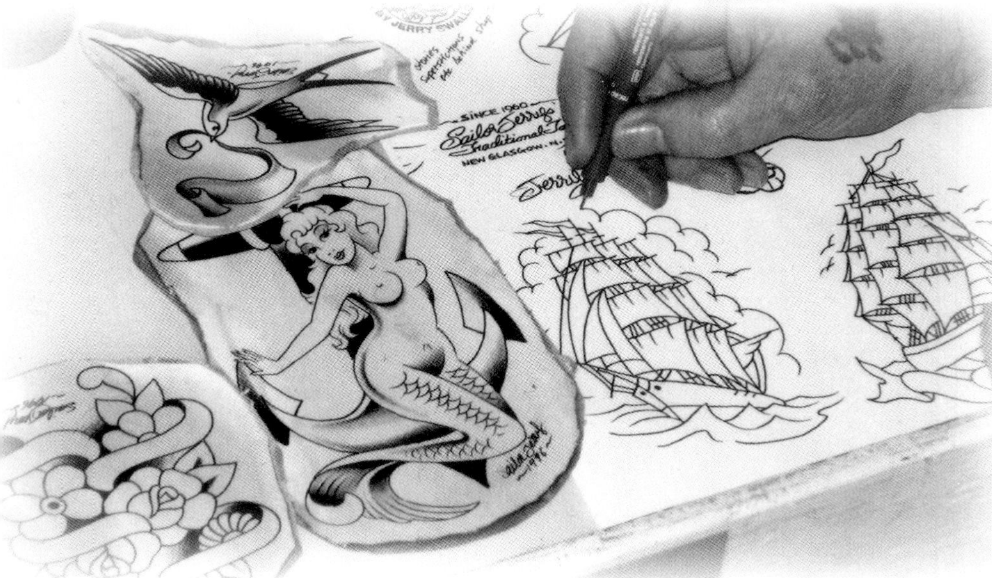
SINCE 1960
NEW GLASGOW

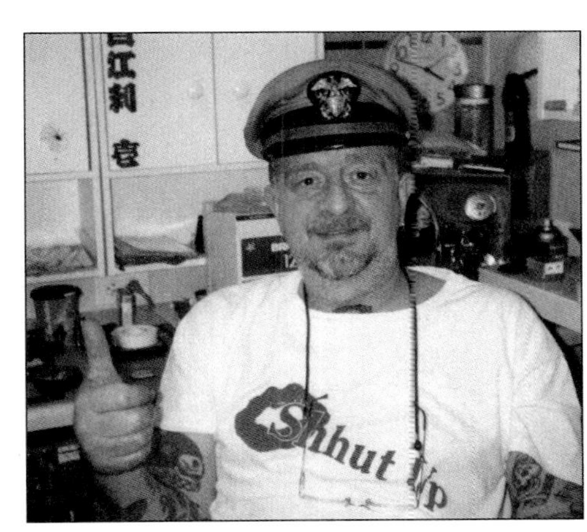
Shhut Up

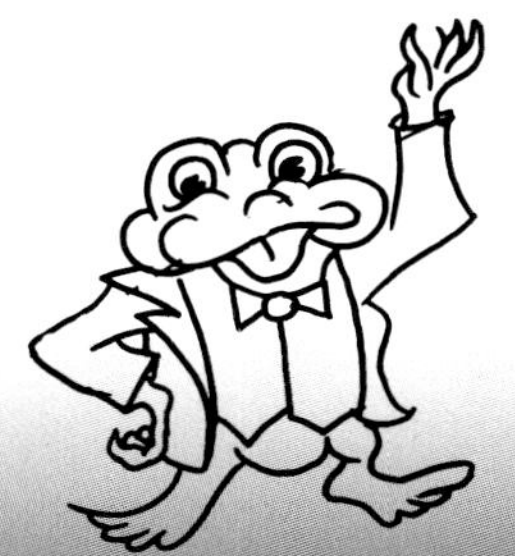

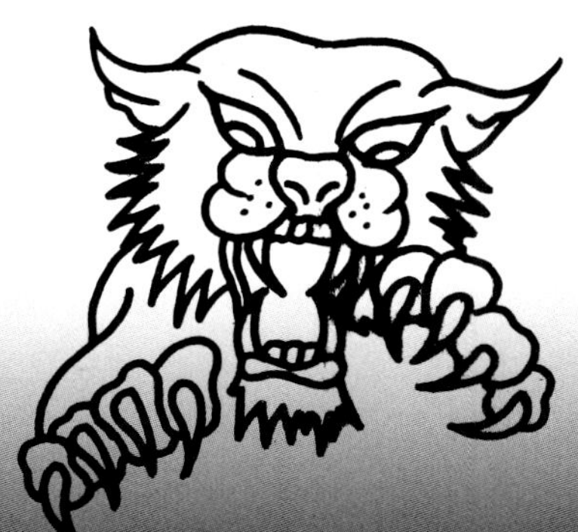

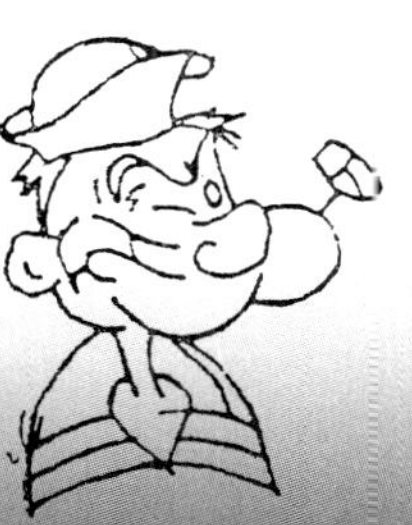

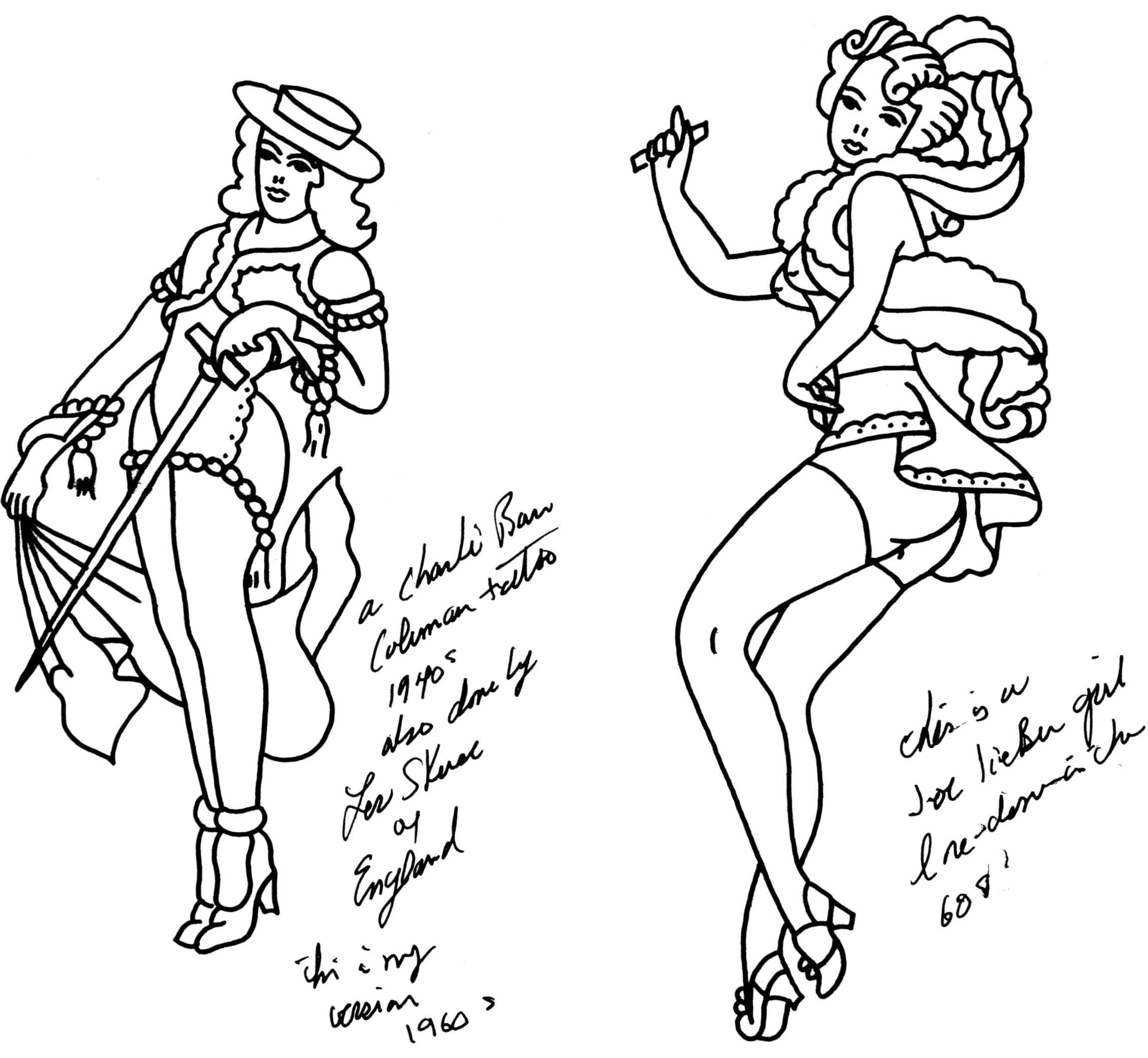
a Charlie Barr
Coleman tattoo
1940s
also done by
Les Skuse
of
England
this is my
version
1960s
this is a
Joe Lieber girl
I re-drawn in the
60s

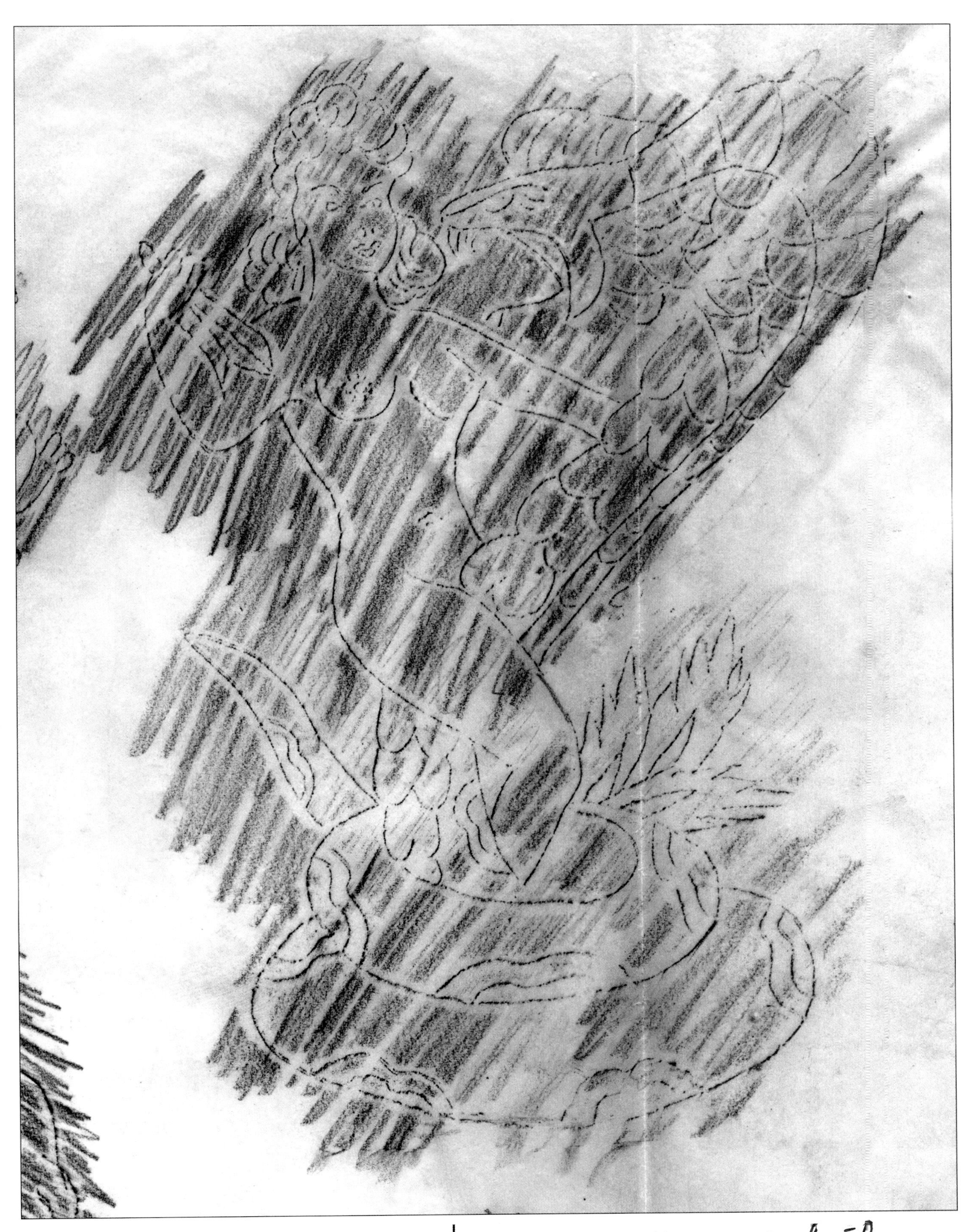

Joe liked girl and snake many tattooers took the design on their arm. reworked it some did it the same as Joe.

Standard design done by most tattooers -
So many lines, I like to open them up like Coleman did

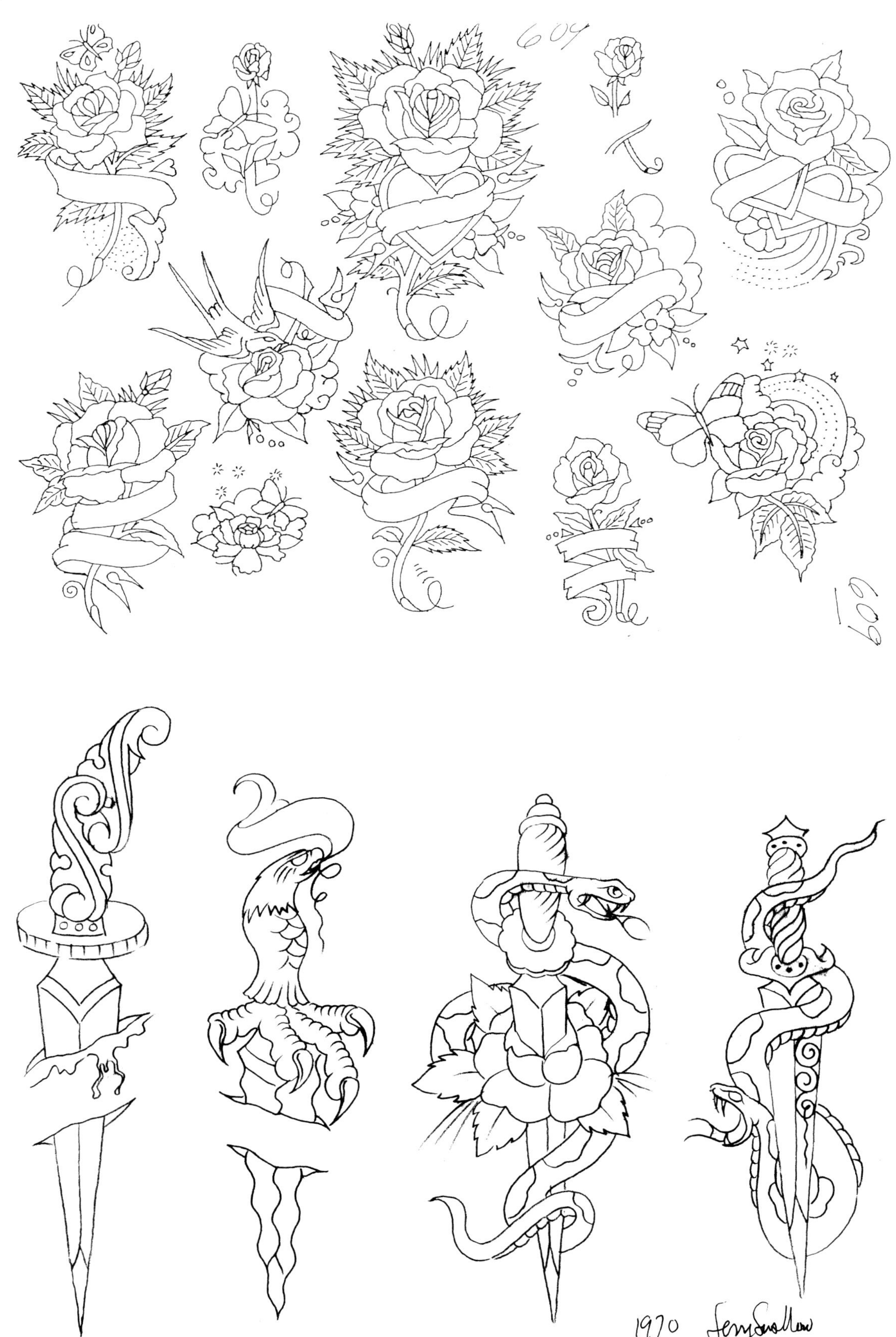

This is the style I liked to use
Bold open style tattoo

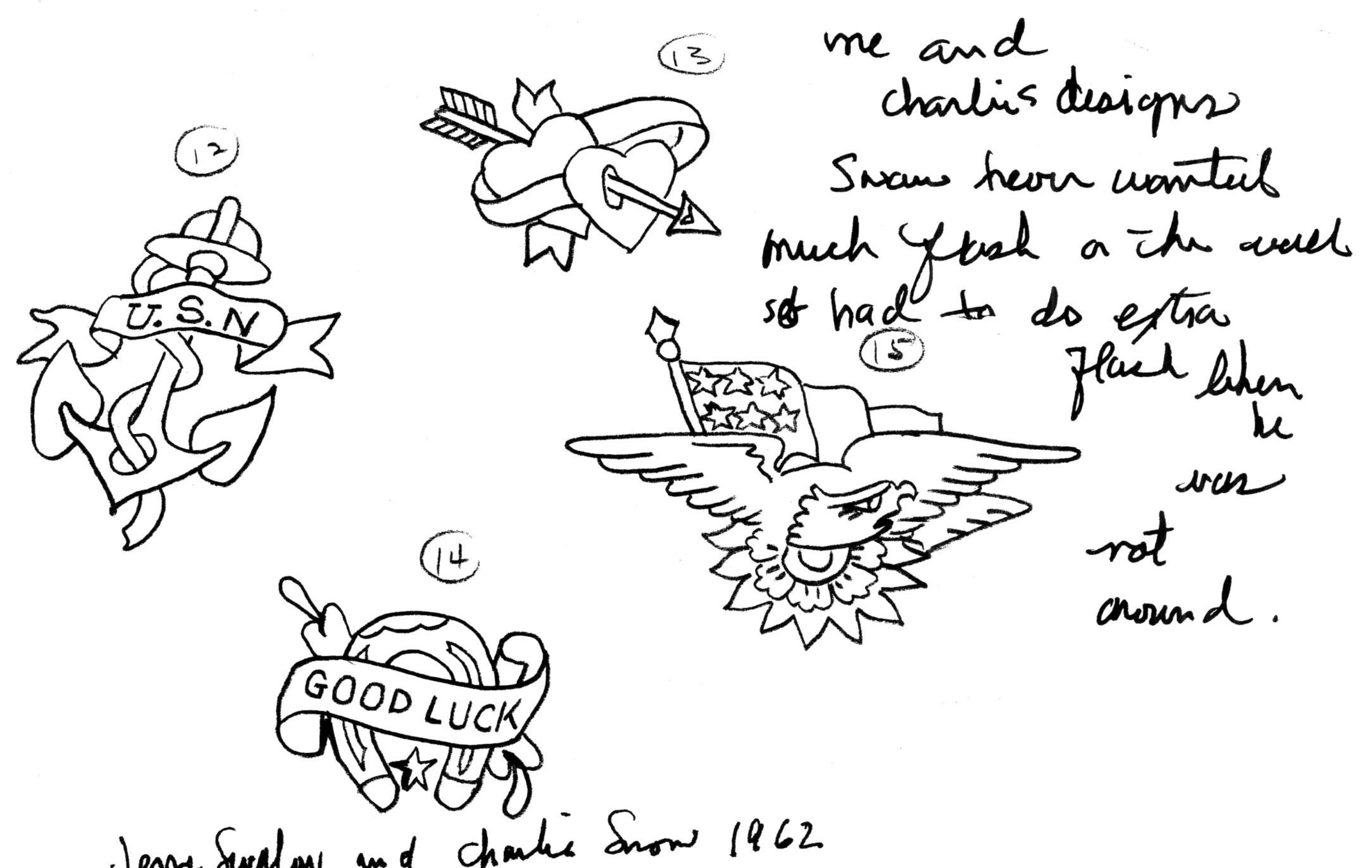

me and charlie's designs Snow never wanted much flash on the wall so had to do extra flash when he was not around.

Jerry Swallow and Charlie Snow 1962

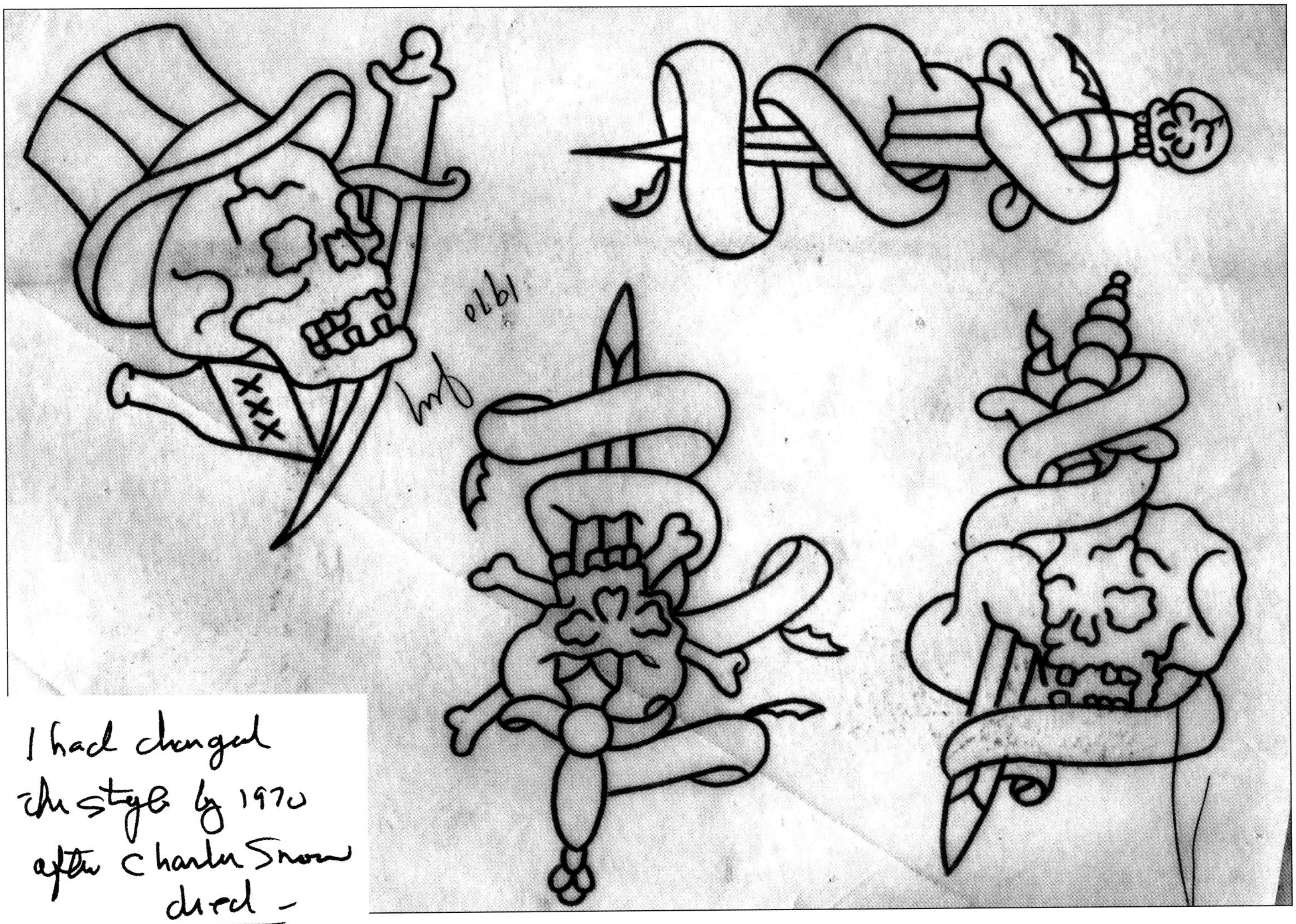

1970

Jerry

I had changed the style by 1970 after Charlie Snow died -

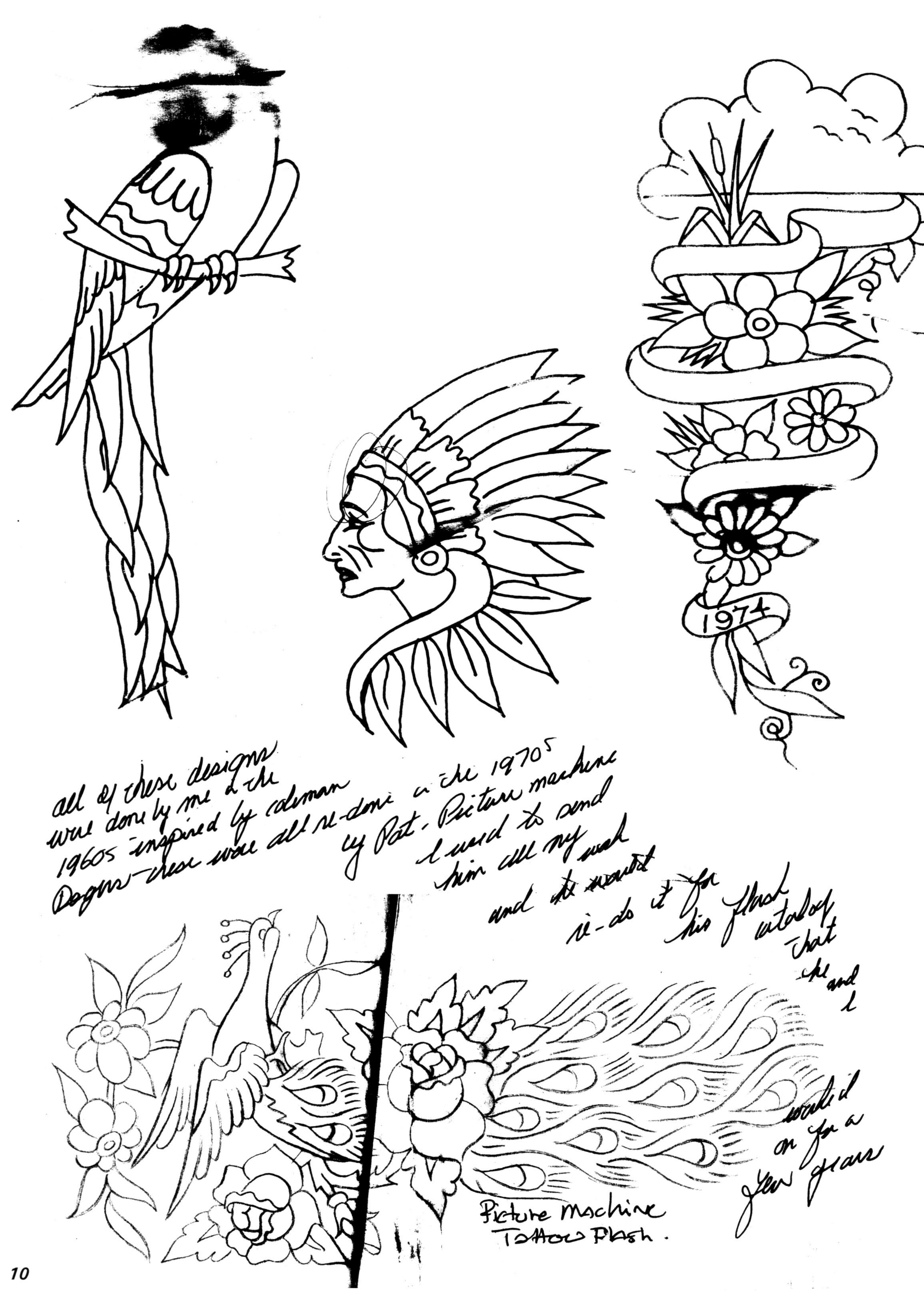
1974
all of these designs
were done by me in the
1960s inspired by coleman
Designs - these were all re-done in the 1970s
by Pat. Picture machine
I used to send
him all my work
and he would
re-do it for
his flash
catalog
that
he and
I
worked
on for a
few years
Picture Machine
Tattoo Flash.

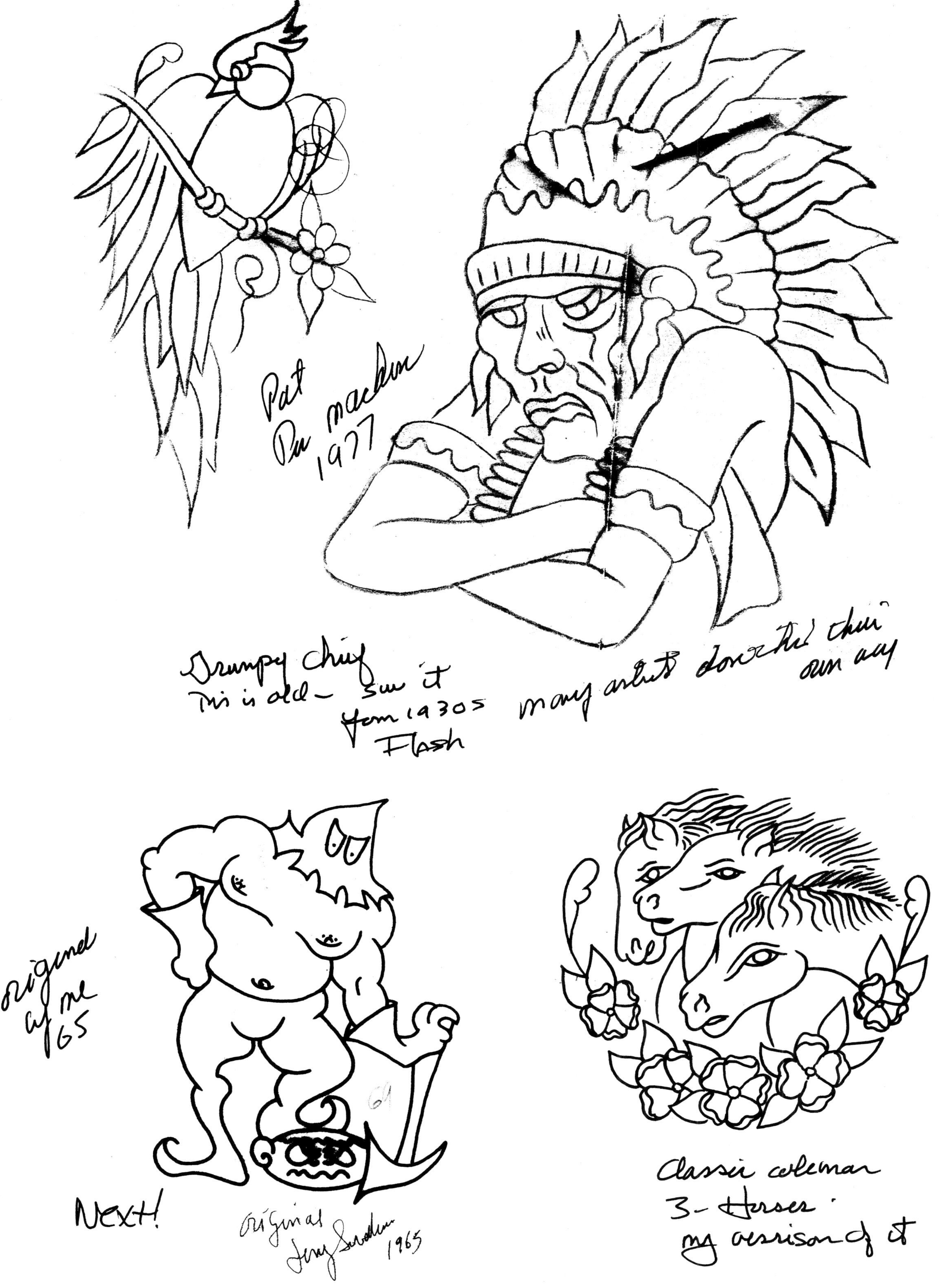
1977
Grumpy Chief
This is old - Saw it
from 1930s
Flash
many artists done their own way
original by me
65
NEXT!
original
1965
Classic coleman
3-Horses
my version of it

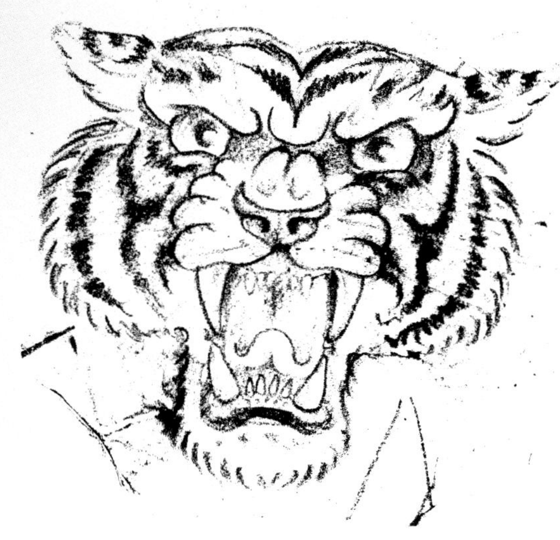

Special Request design I got in 1985

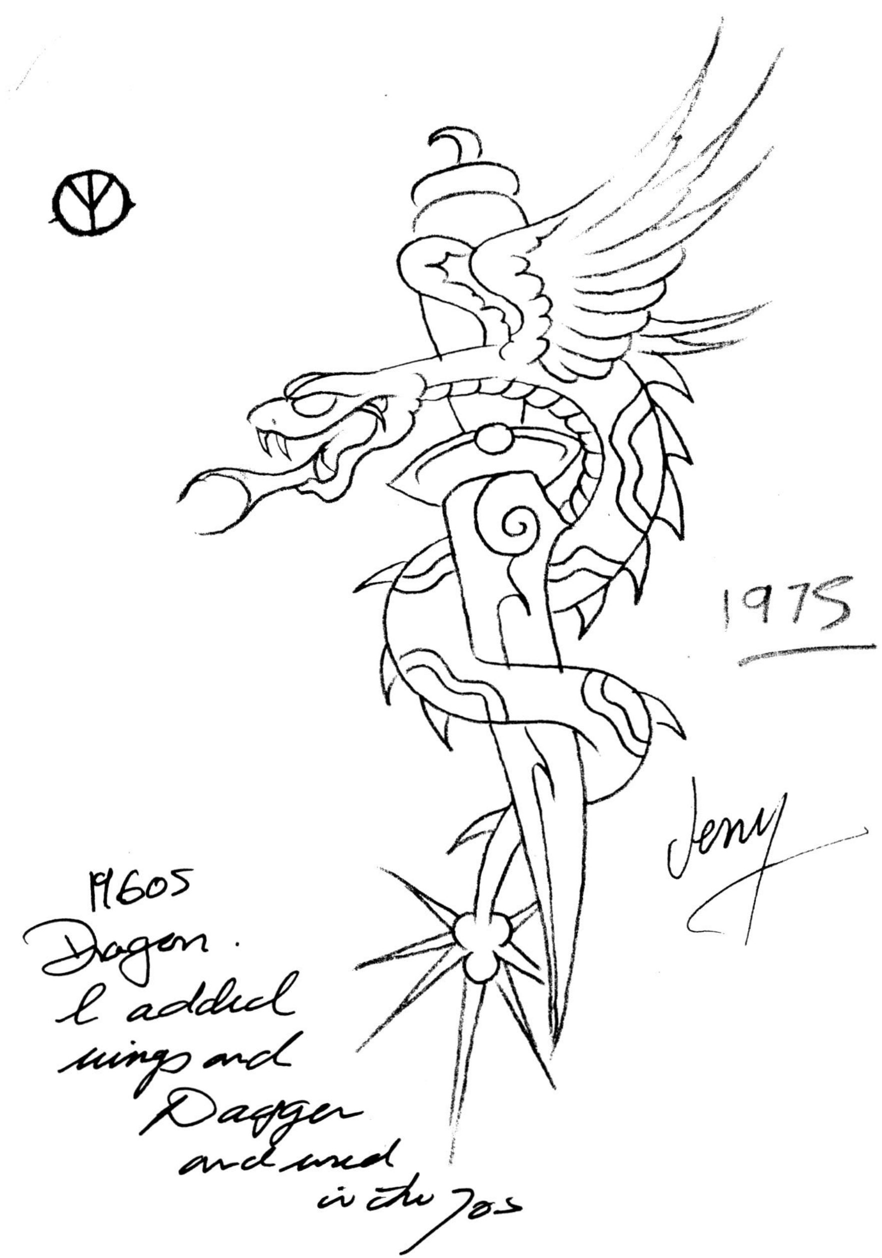

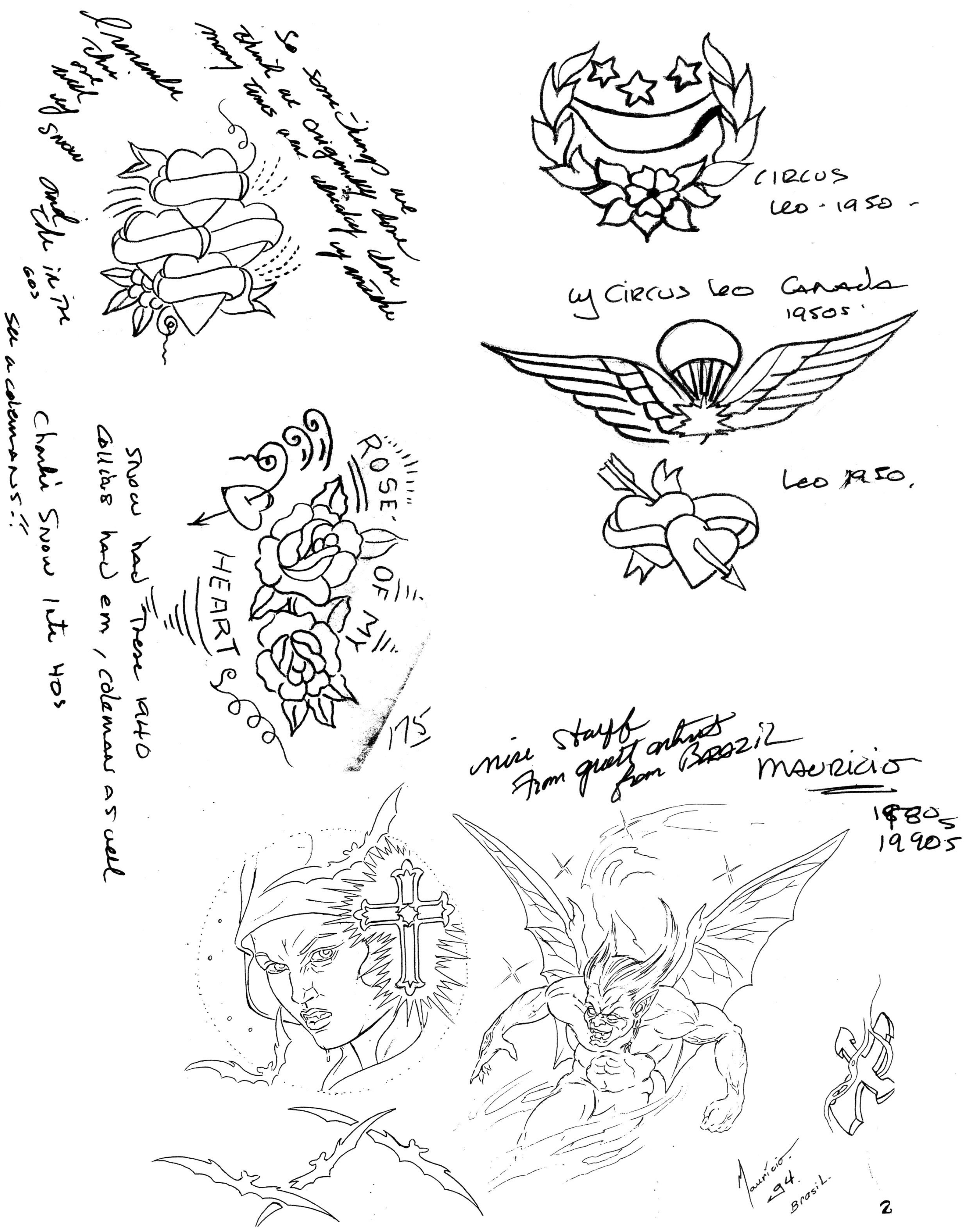
CIRCUS
LEO - 1950 -
ROSE OF MY HEART
175
MAURICIO
1980s
1990s
Mauricio
94
BRASIL
2

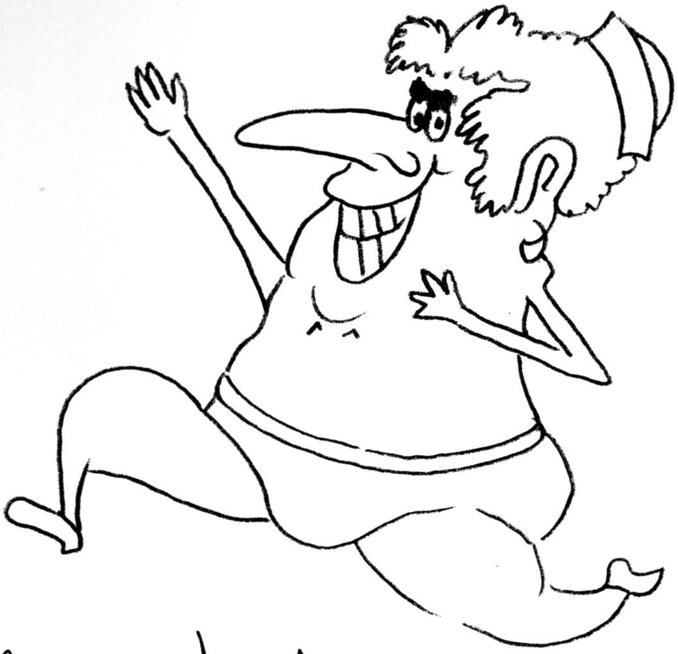

only God
Know why
Some Sailor
wanted this
1980s?

1975
Jerry Swallow

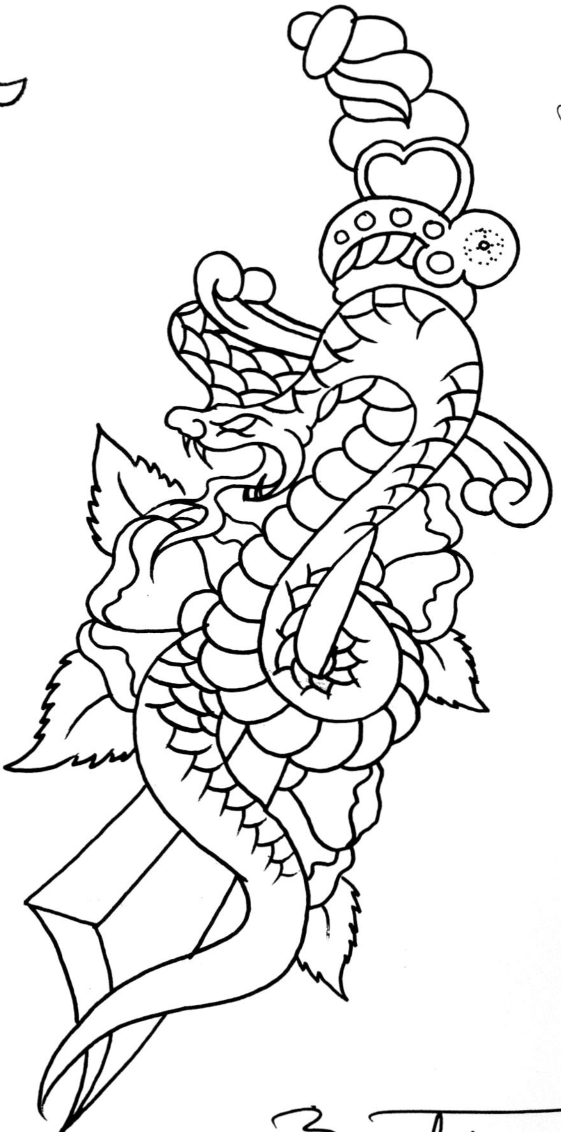

a 60s Beauty
worked For the 70s
60 yes! 70s They
looked like crap
But we had a different dictate then

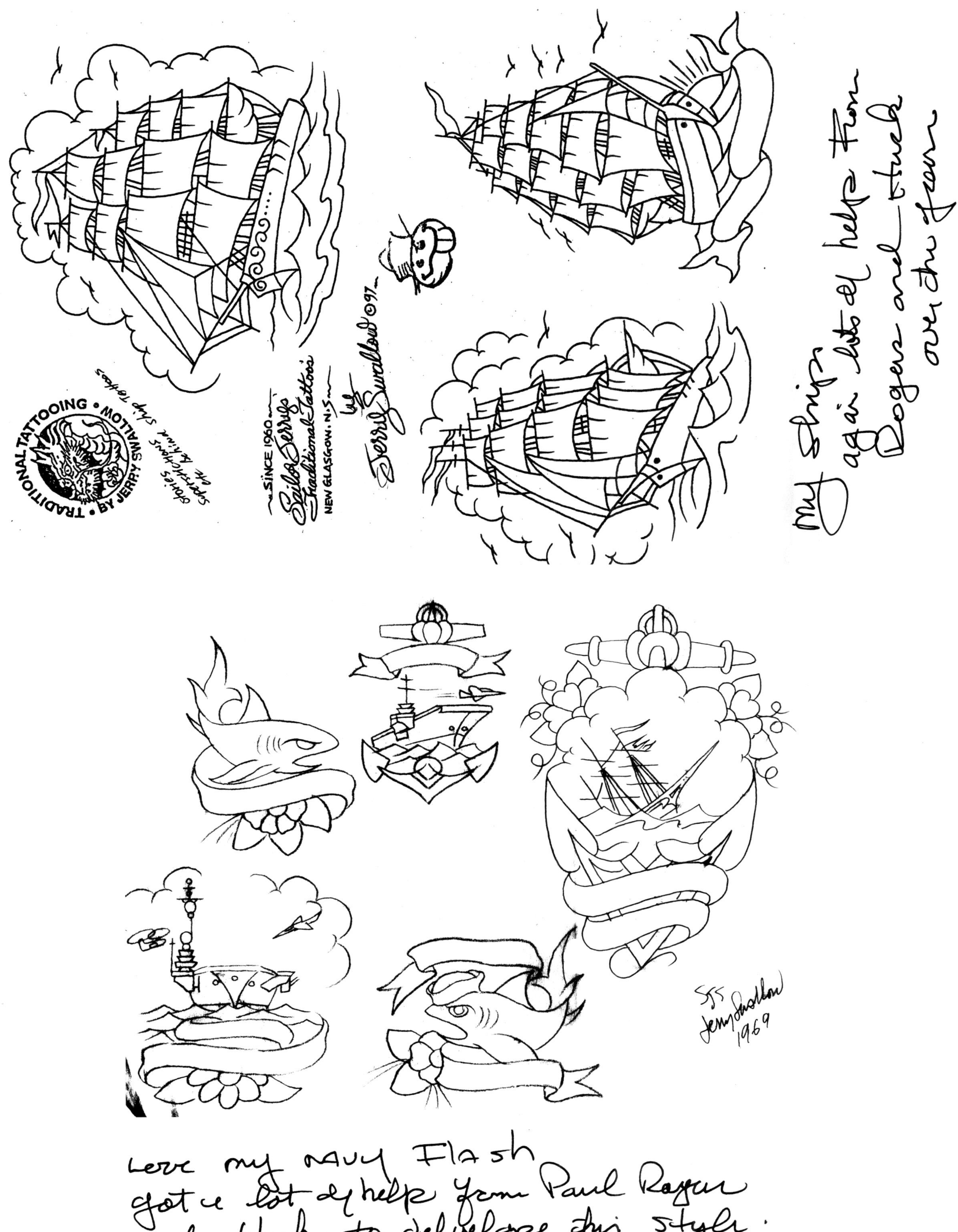

Love my navy Flash
got a lot of help from Paul Rogers
and Hutch to develope this style.

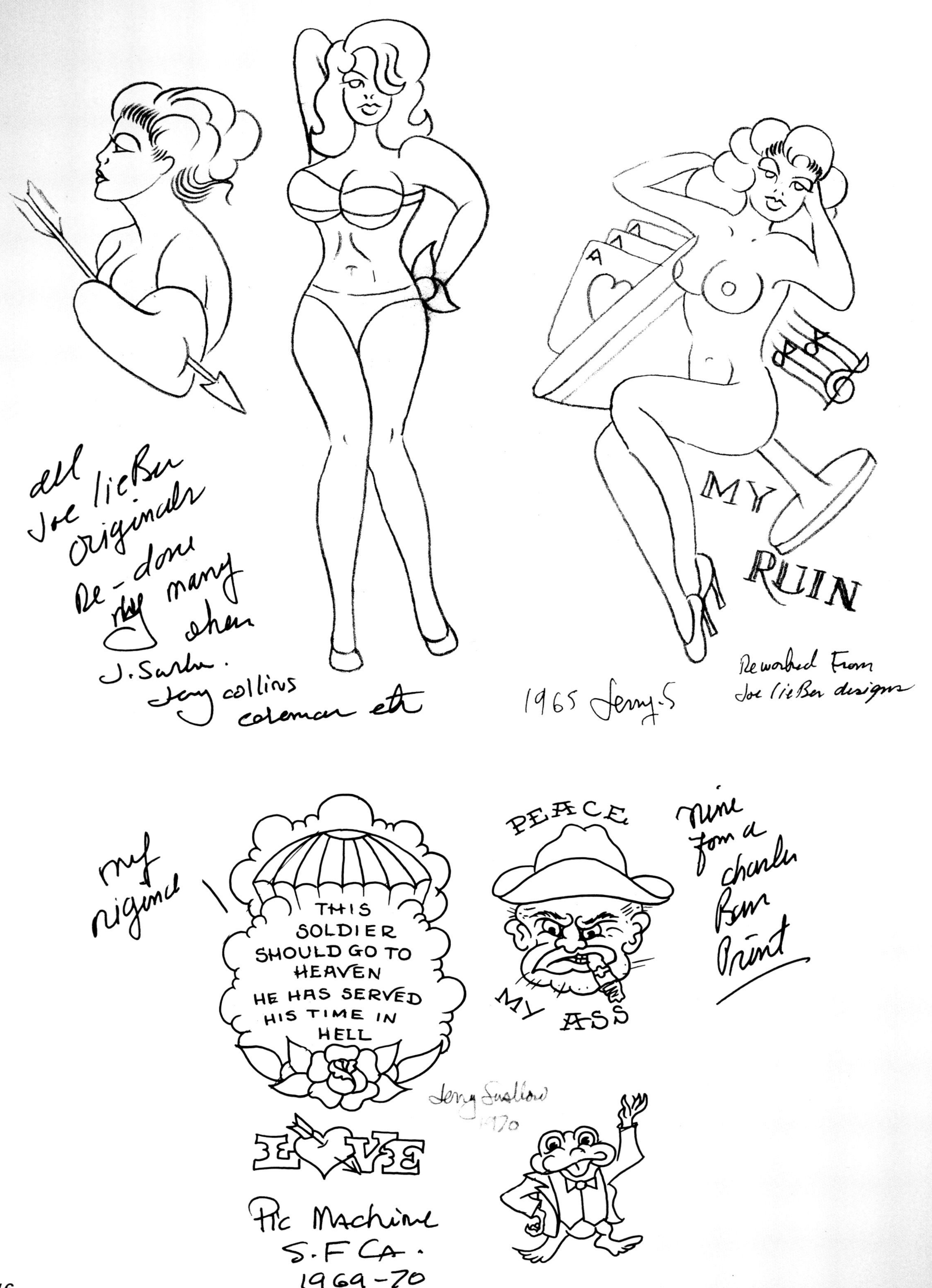
all Joe lieBer originals Re-done by many others
J. Sarlow.
Jerry collins
coleman etc
MY
RUIN
1965 Jerry S
Reworked From Joe lieBer designs
my original
THIS SOLDIER SHOULD GO TO HEAVEN HE HAS SERVED HIS TIME IN HELL
PEACE
MY ASS
mine from a charlie Barr Print
Jerry Swallow 1970
LOVE
Pic Machine S.F CA. 1969-70

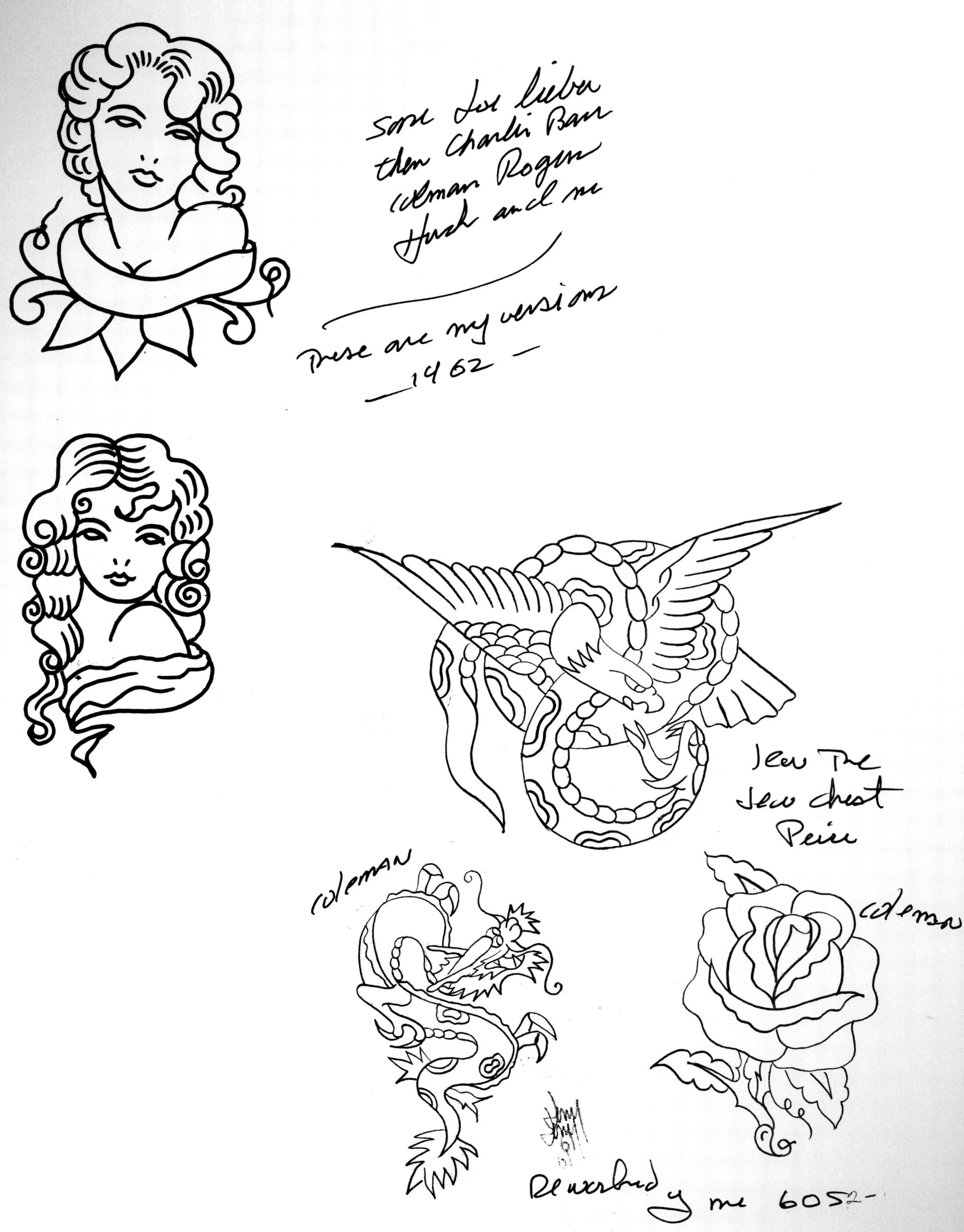
Some Joe Lieber
then Charlie Barr
Coleman Rogers
Hush and me
These are my versions
— 1962 —
coleman
coleman

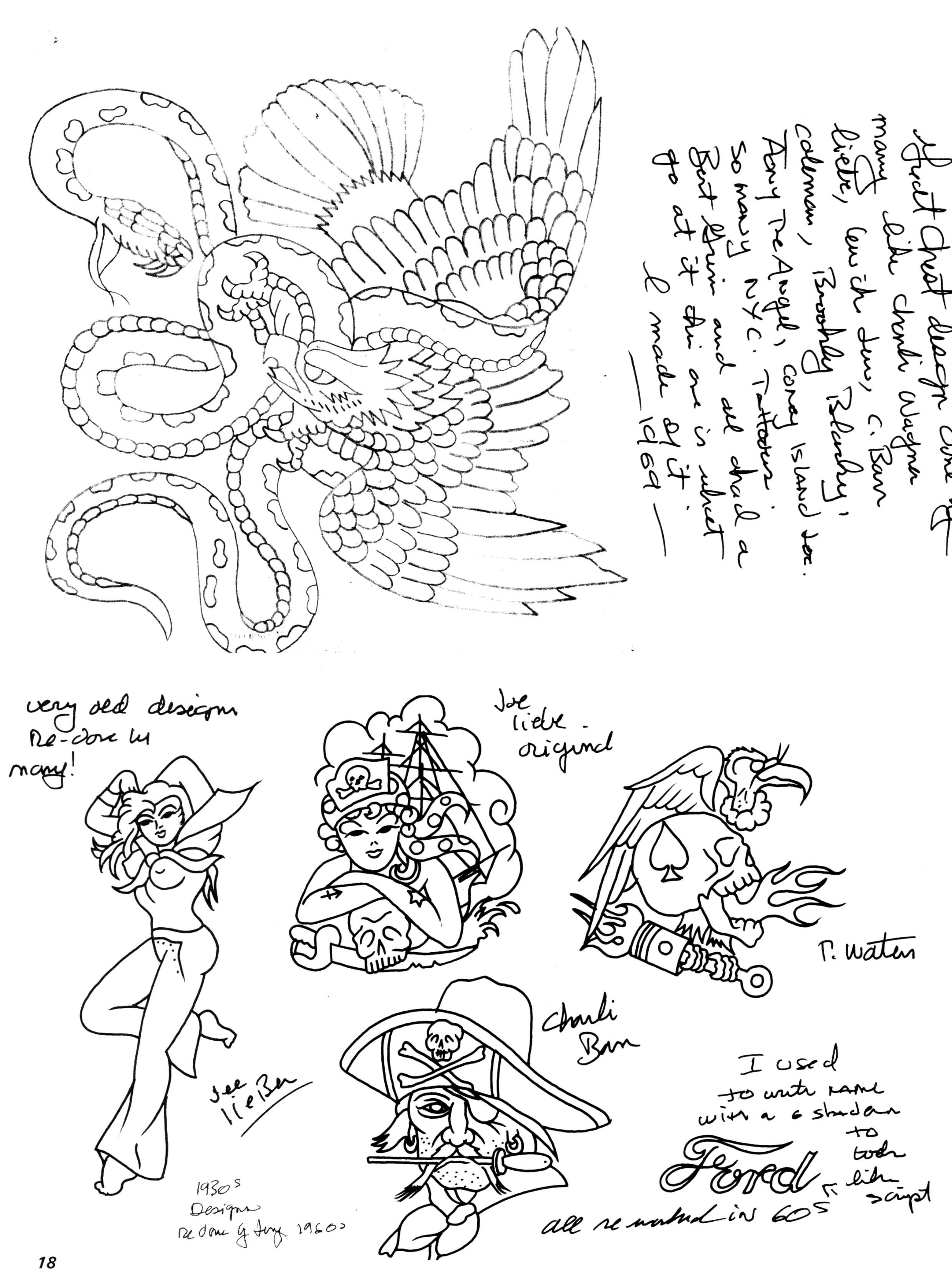
very old design
Re-done by
many!
Joe
Liebe
original
T. Waters
Charlie
Barr
I used
to write name
with a shadow
to
look
like
script
Ford
1930s
Designs
all re worked in 60s

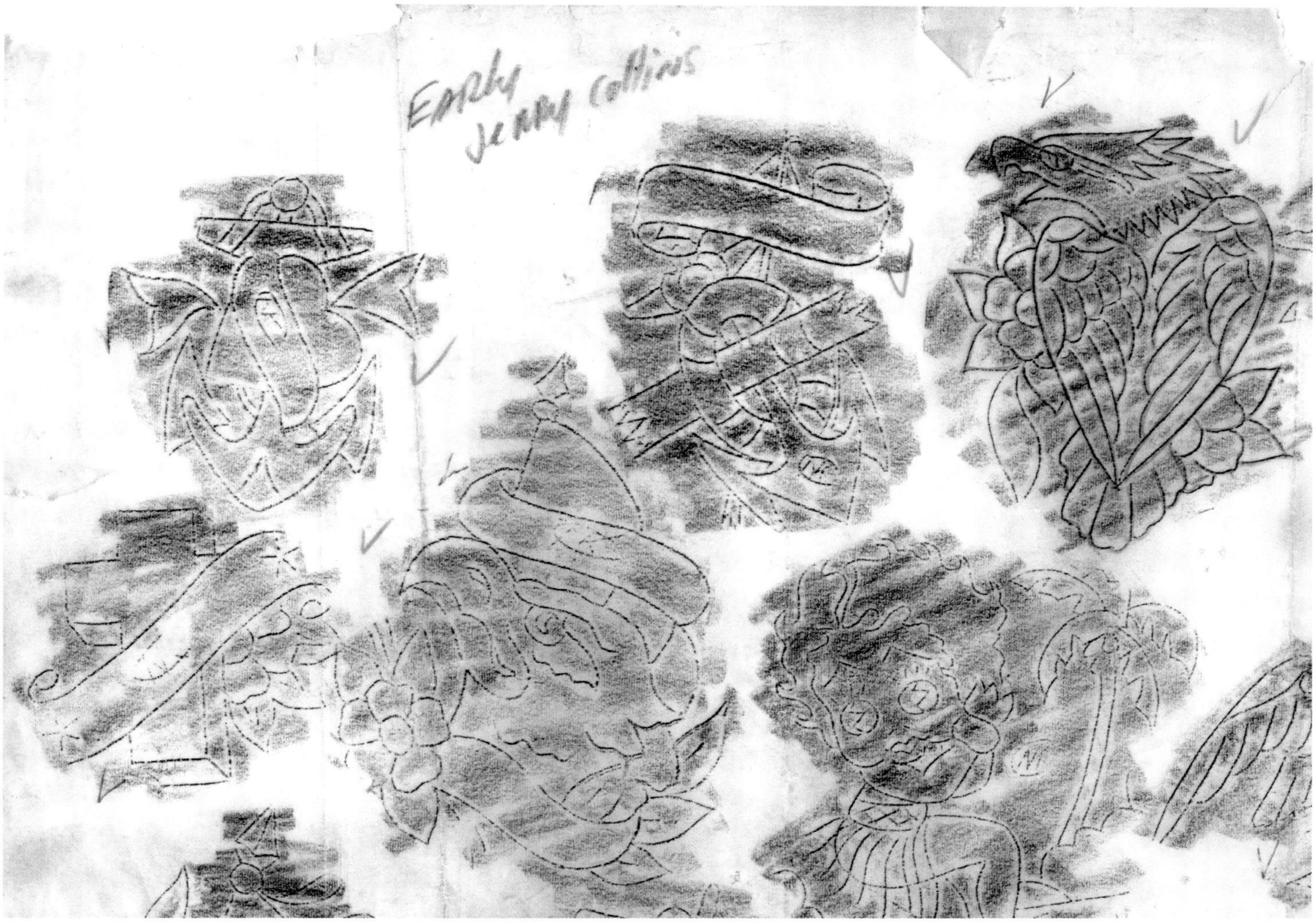

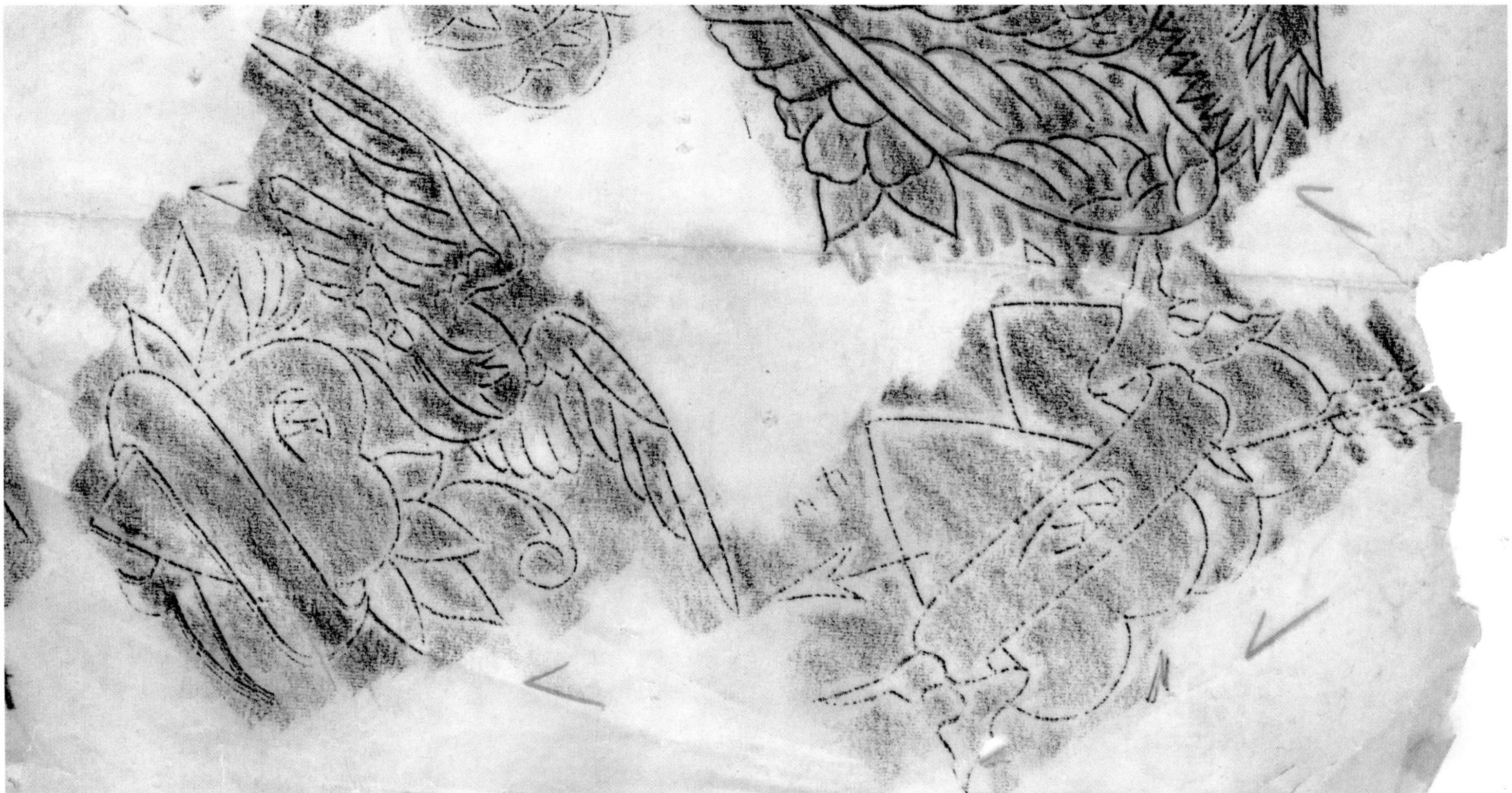

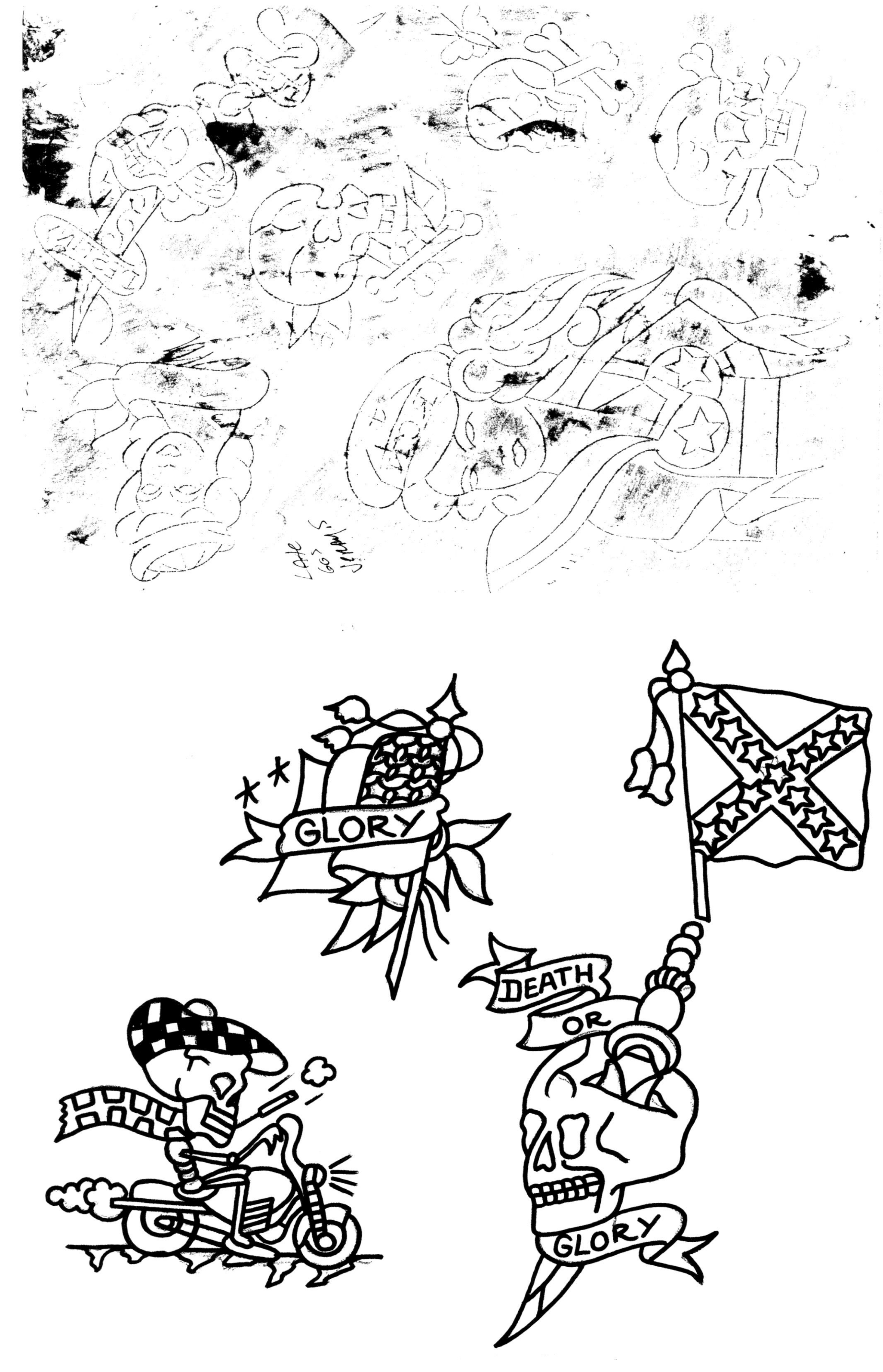
GLORY
DEATH
OR
GLORY

ZEEK Owen showed me how he drew dragon heads one night we spent the night at Hick's Place about 71.

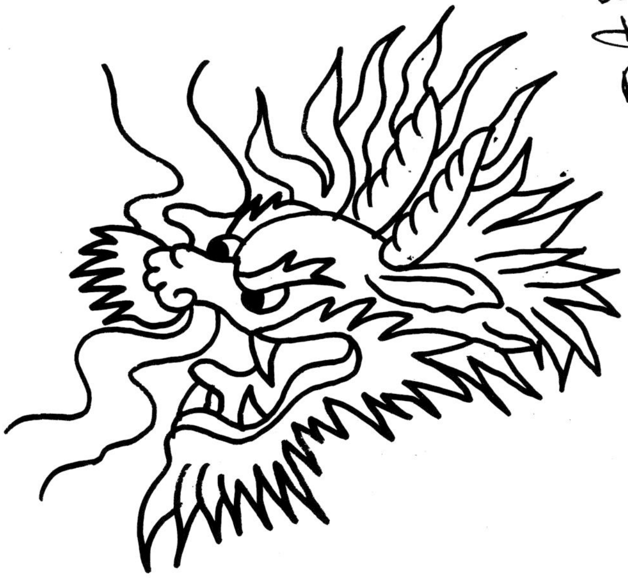

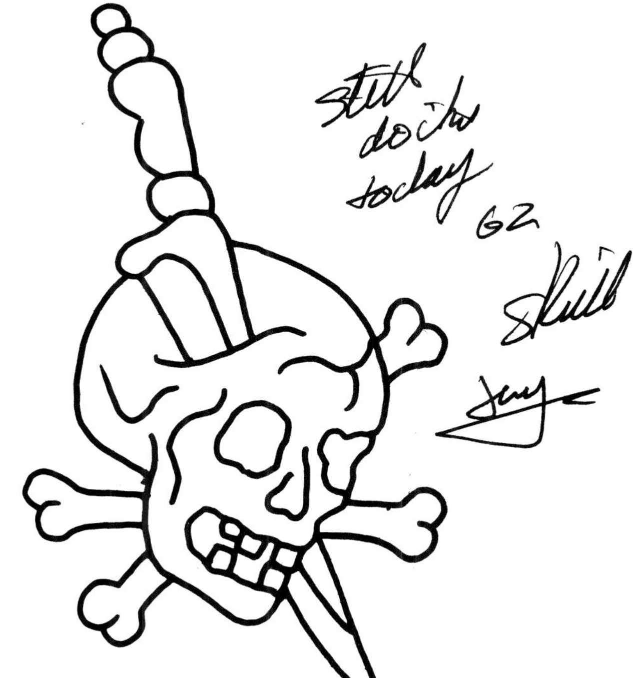

Coleman influence

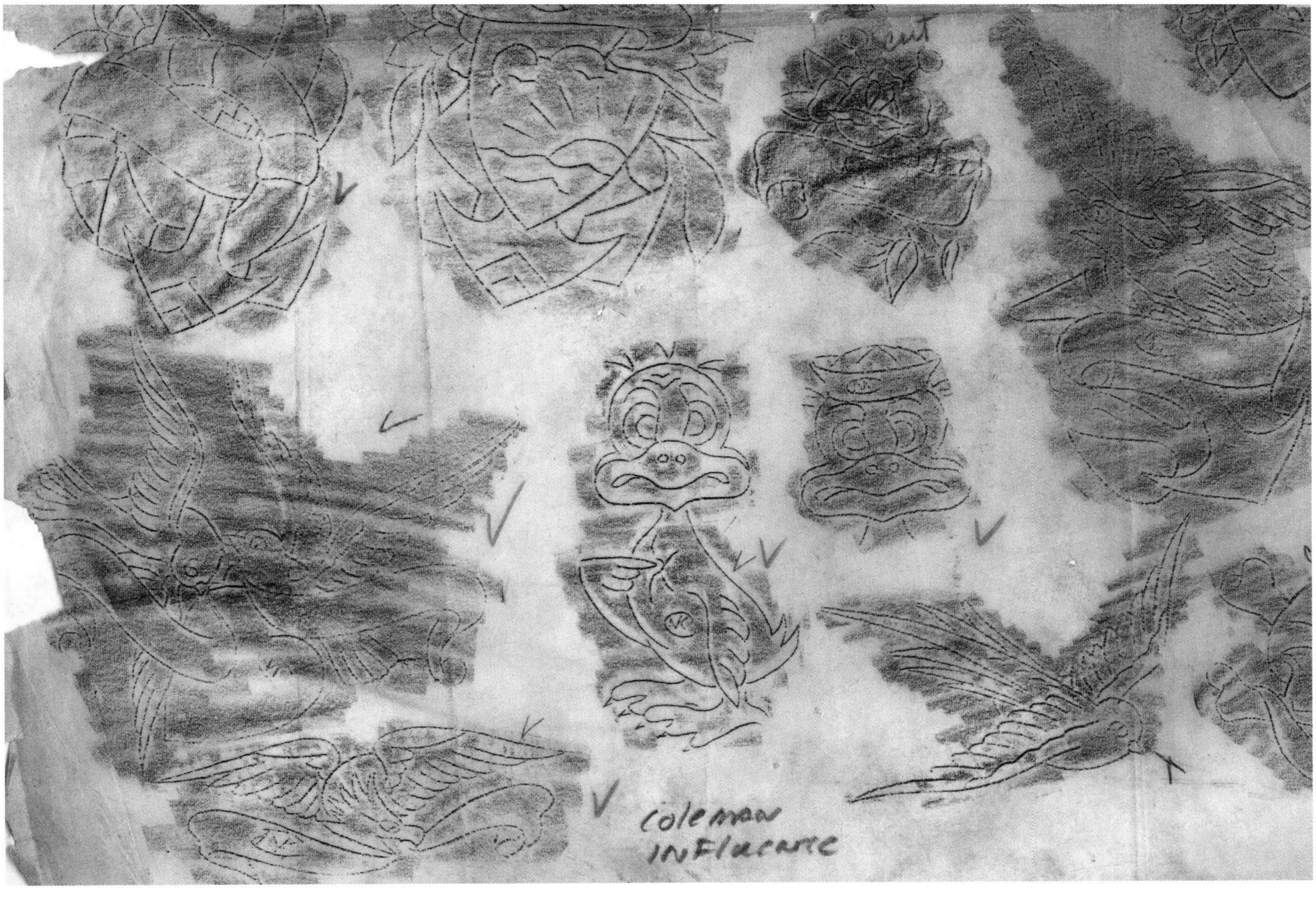

1960s Sailor Jerry Collins Everyone of these I have the originals from Charlie Barr and Joe Lieber.

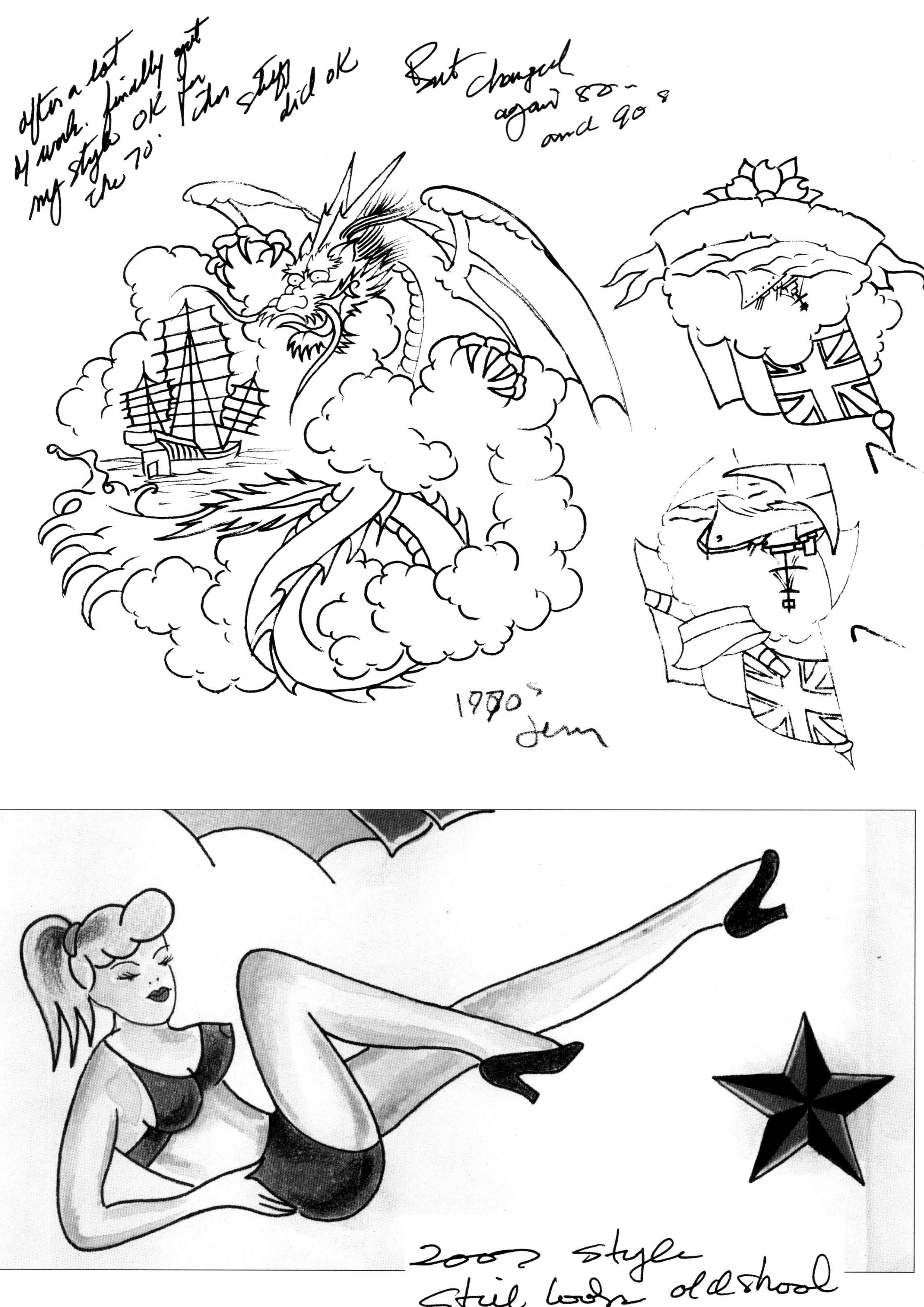
after a lot of work. finally got my style OK for the 70's. this stuff did OK
But changed again 80s and 90s
1980s Jerry
2000s style still looks old shool

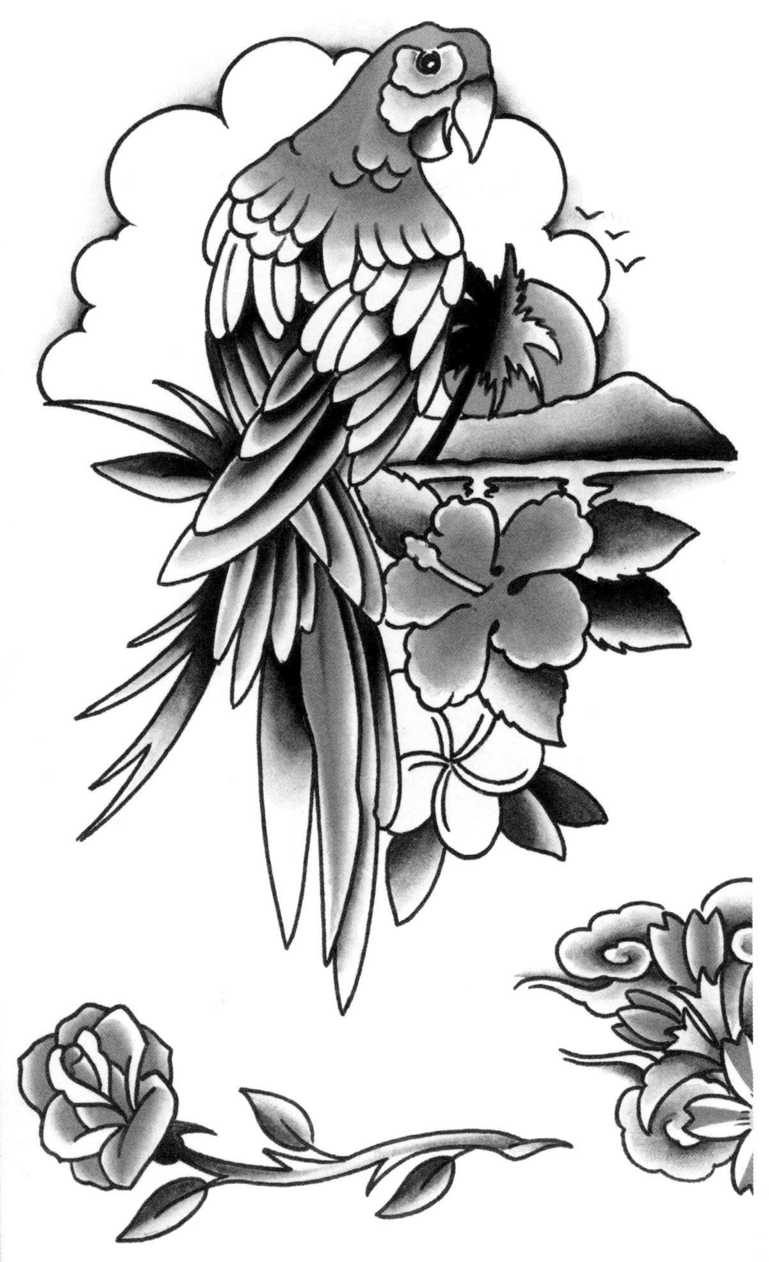

2007
Tattoo
designs
various artist's
given to me
as
gifts
See how the
old scool
styles are still
here!

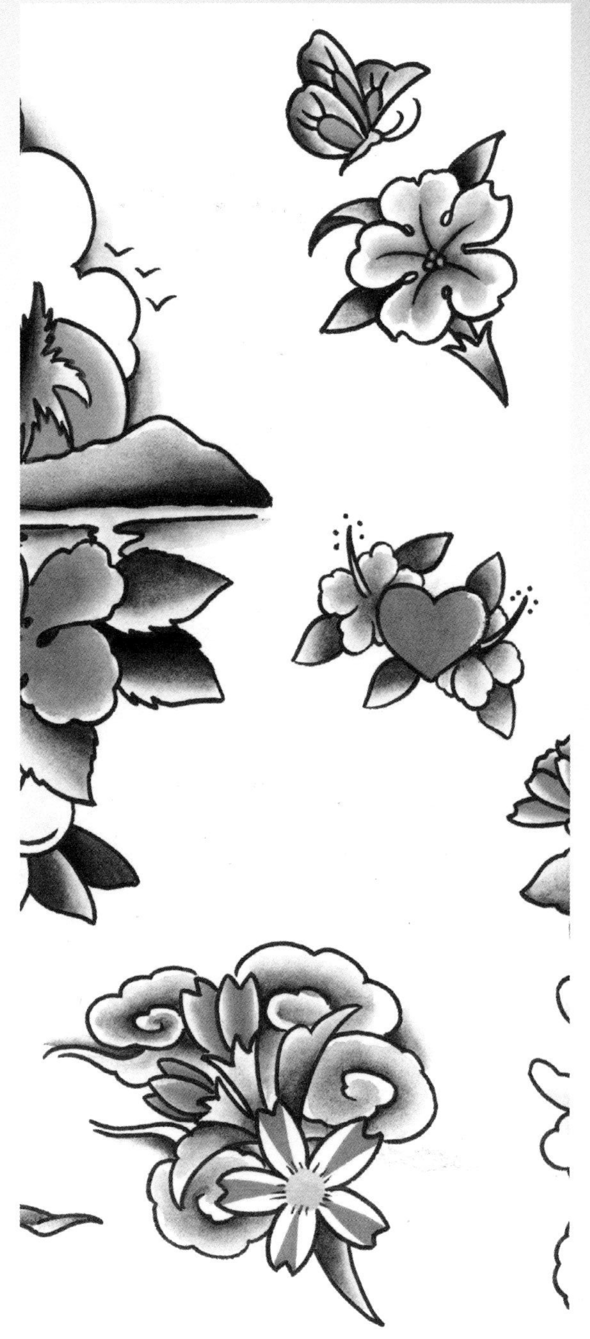

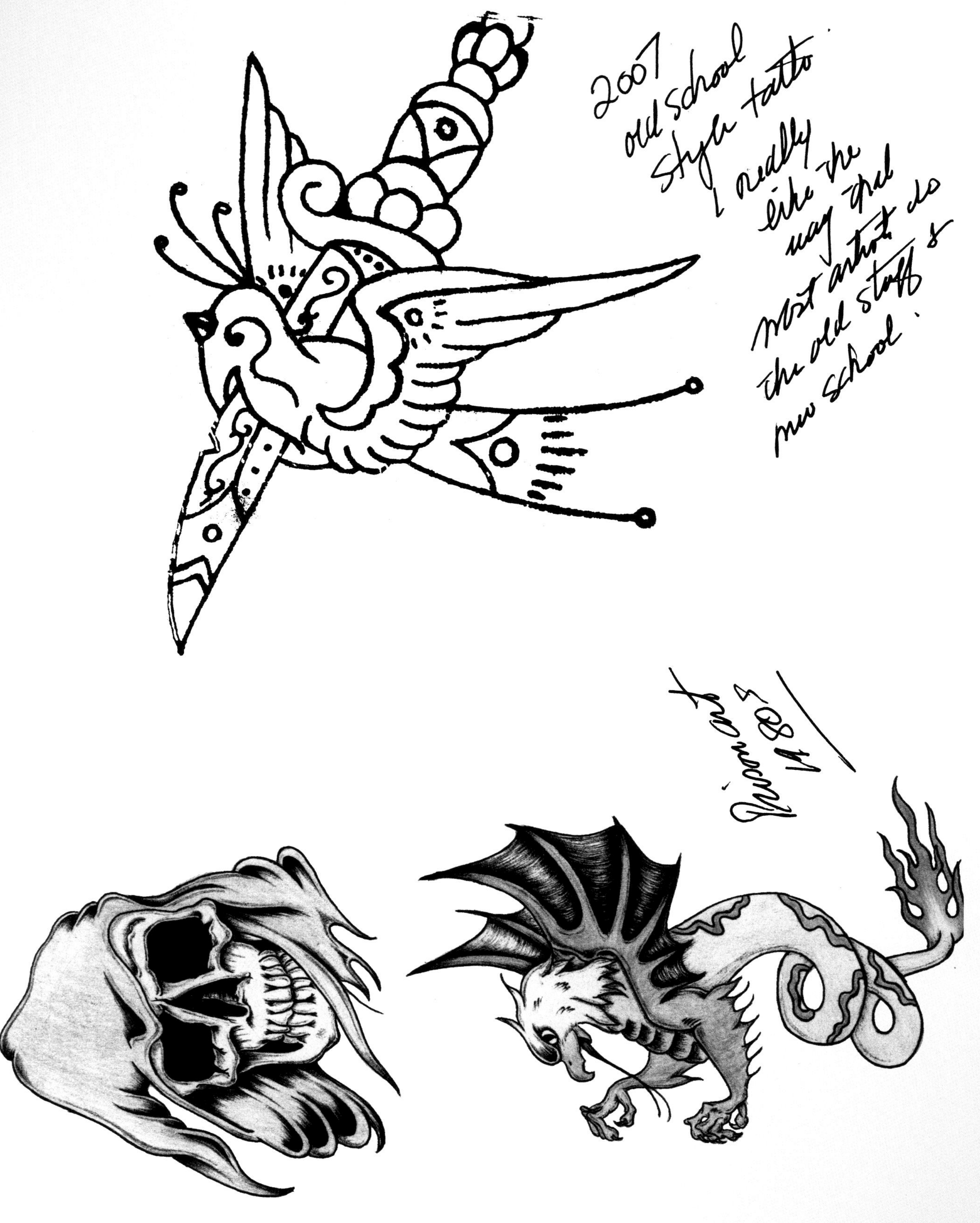
2007
old school
Style tatto
I really
like the
way that
most artists do
the old stuff &
new school.

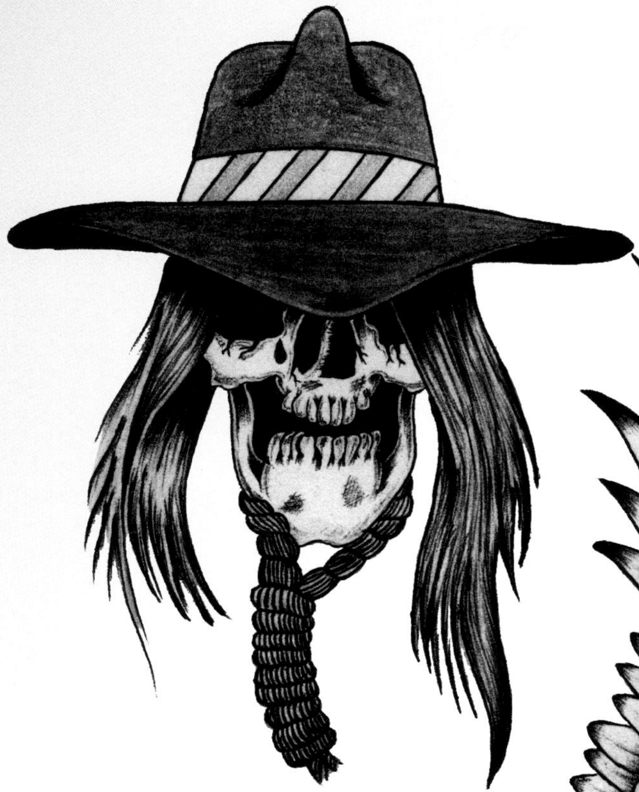

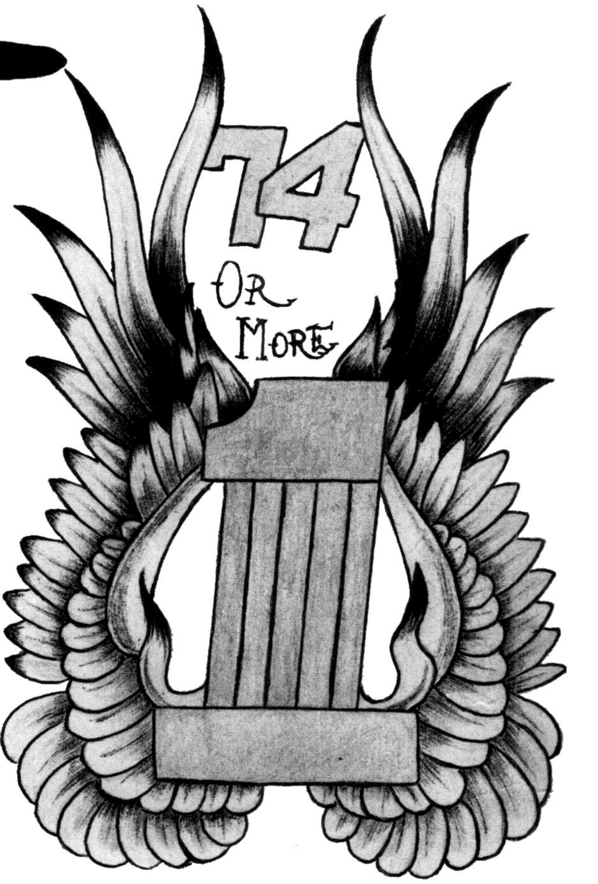

74
OR
MORE

Some design sent to me to look at from an inmate in
—Texas—

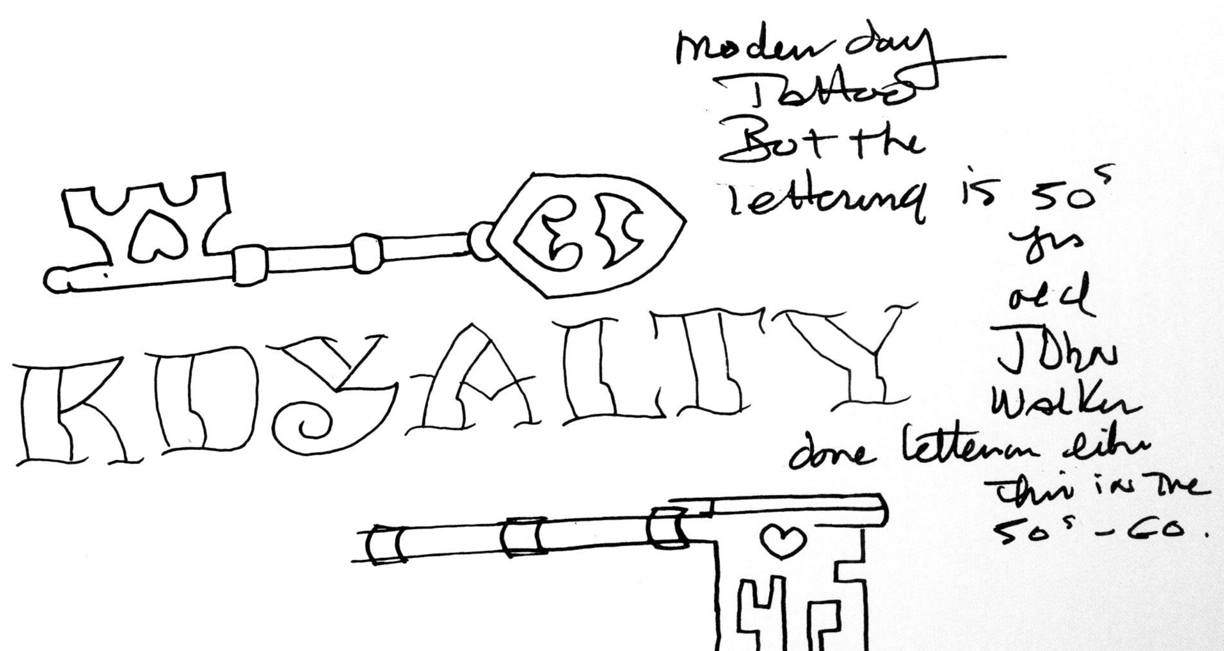

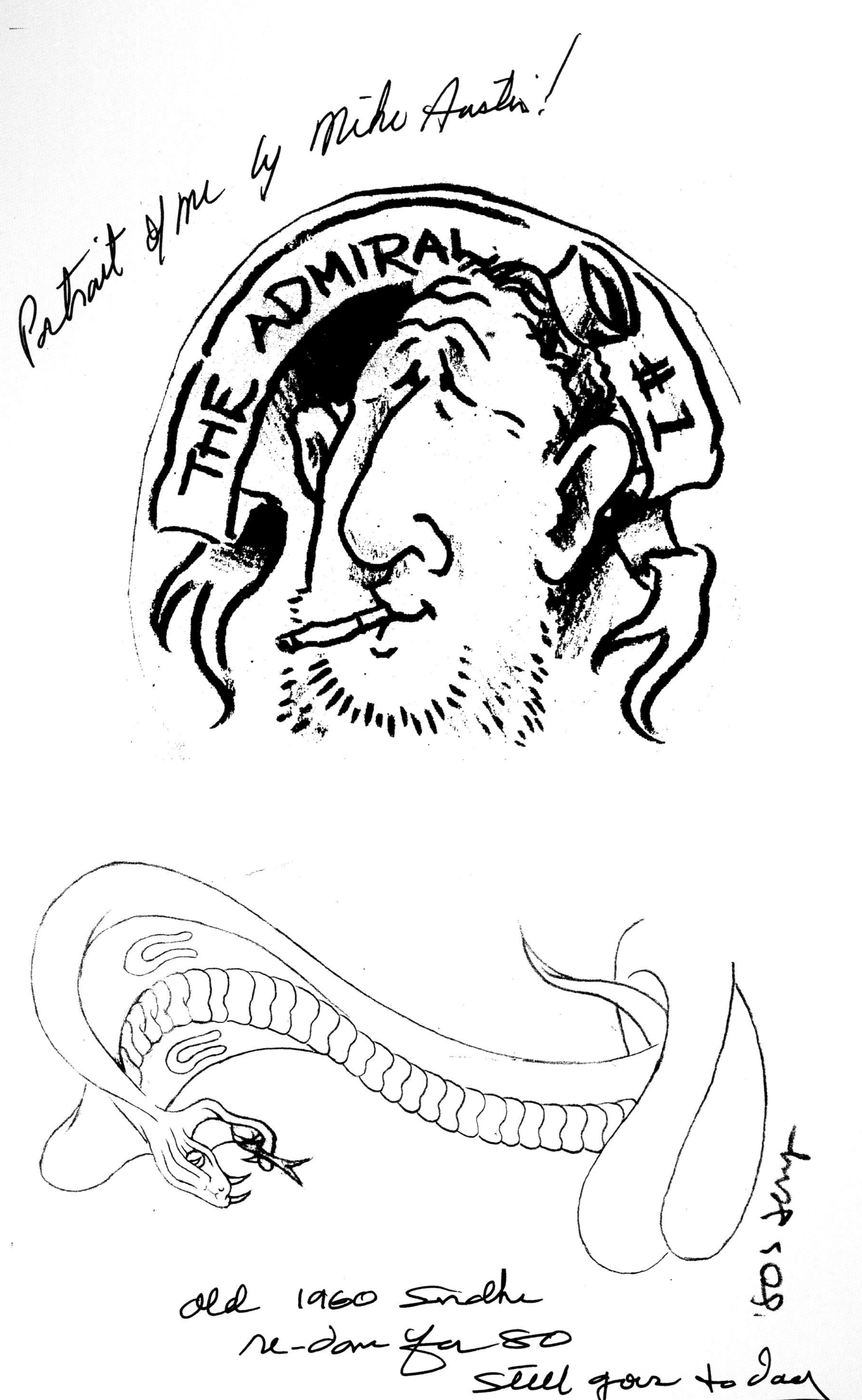
Portrait of me by Mike Austin!
THE ADMIRAL
#1
old 1960 sketch
re-done for 80
still goes today

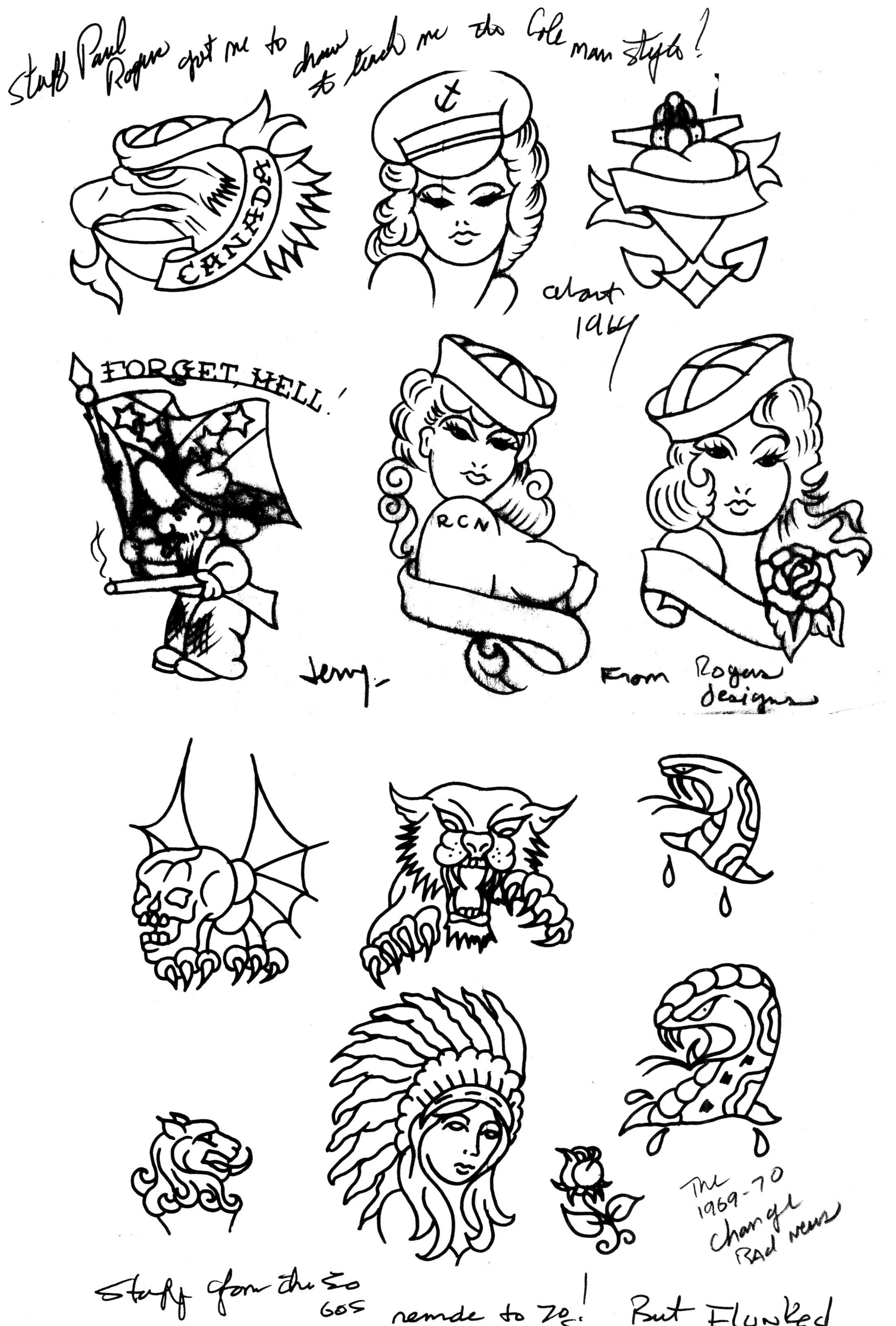
stuff Paul Rogers got me to draw to teach me the Coleman style?
CANADA
about 1964
FORGET HELL!
RCN
Jerry.
From Rogers designs
The 1969-70 change! Bad news
stuff from the 50s 60s remade to 70s! But Flunked

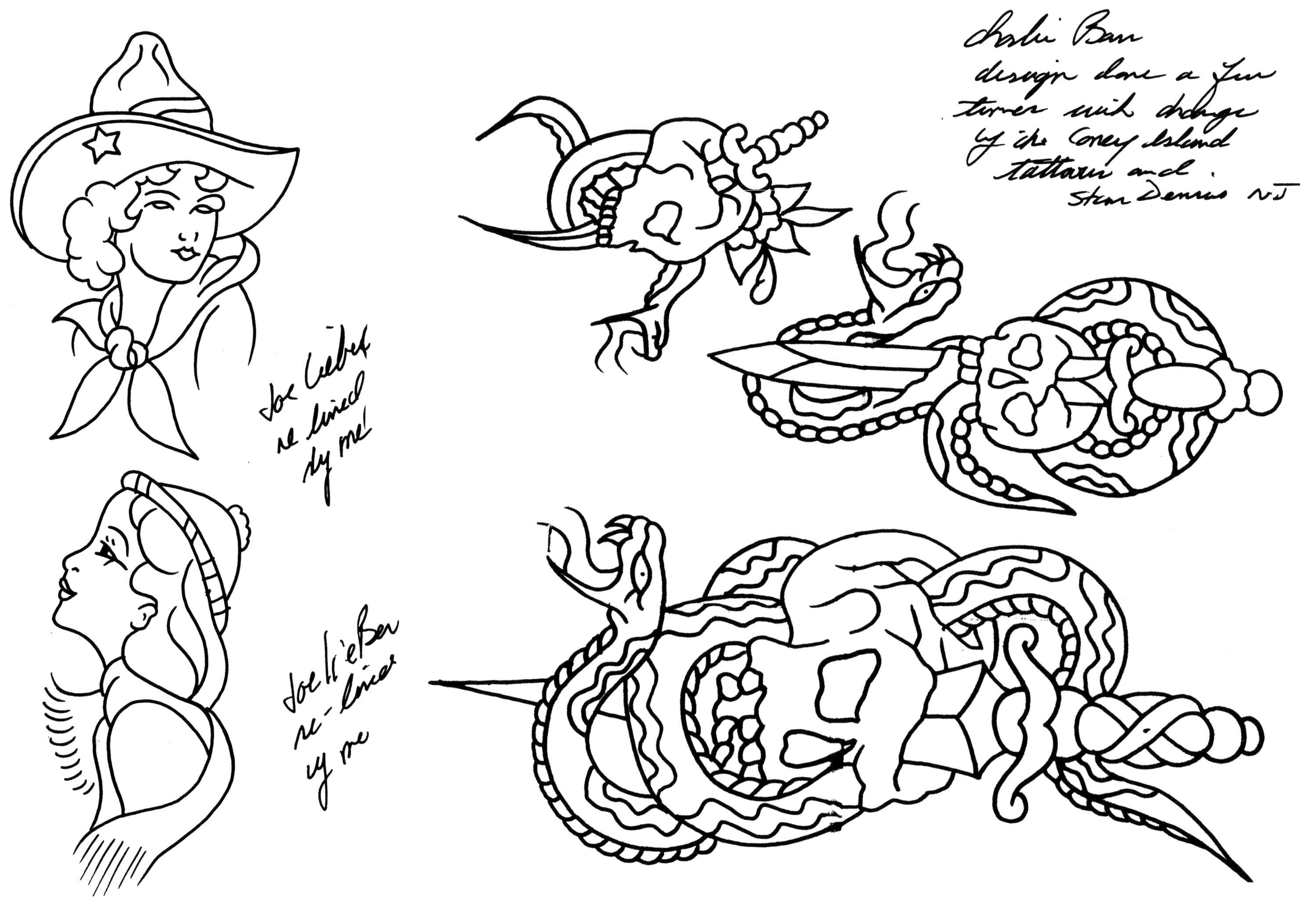
Charlie Barr
design done a few
times with change
by the Coney Island
tattooer and
Stan Dennis NJ
Joe Lieber
re-lined
by me
Joe Lieber
re-lined
by me

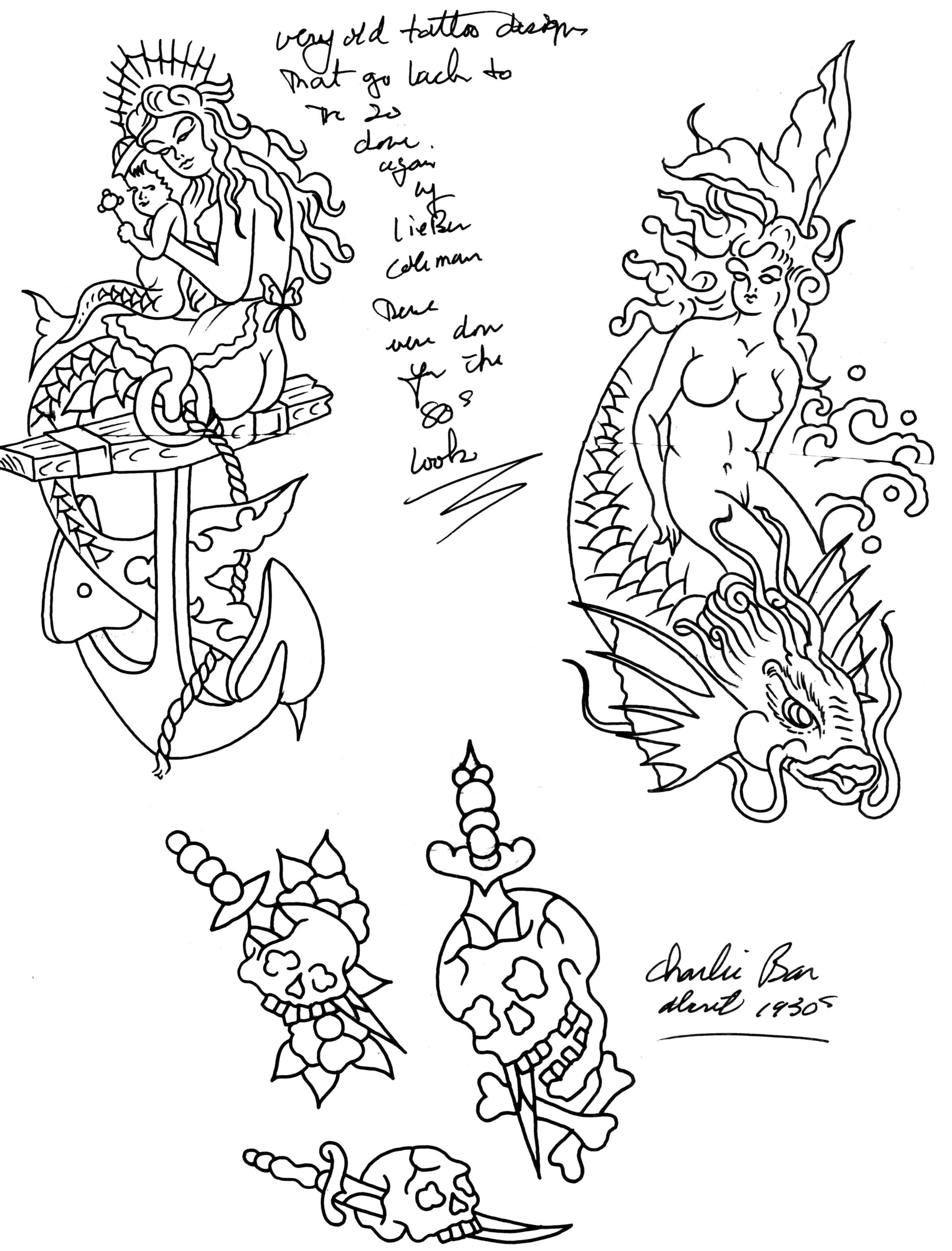
very old tattoo designs
that go back to
the 20
done
again
by
Coleman
These
were done
for the
80s
look
Charlie Barr
about 1930s

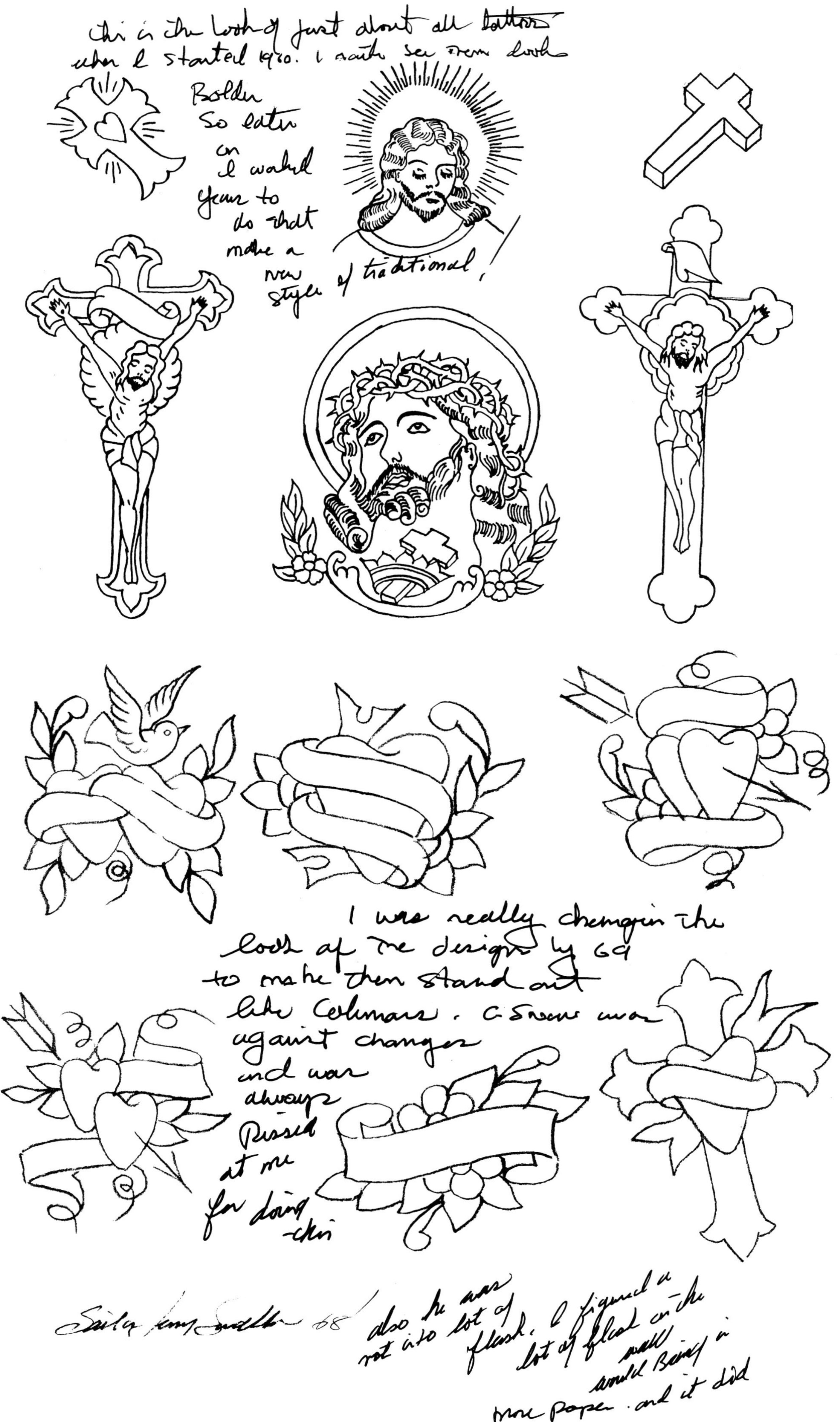
this is the look of just about all tattoos
when I started 1960.
Bolder
So later
on
I waited
years to
do that
make a
new
style of traditional!
I was really changing the
look of the designs by 69
to make them stand out
like Colmans. C Snow was
against changes
and was
always
pissed
at me
for doing
this
Sailor 68
also he was
not into lot of
flash. I figured a
lot of flash on the
wall
would bring in
more paper. and it did

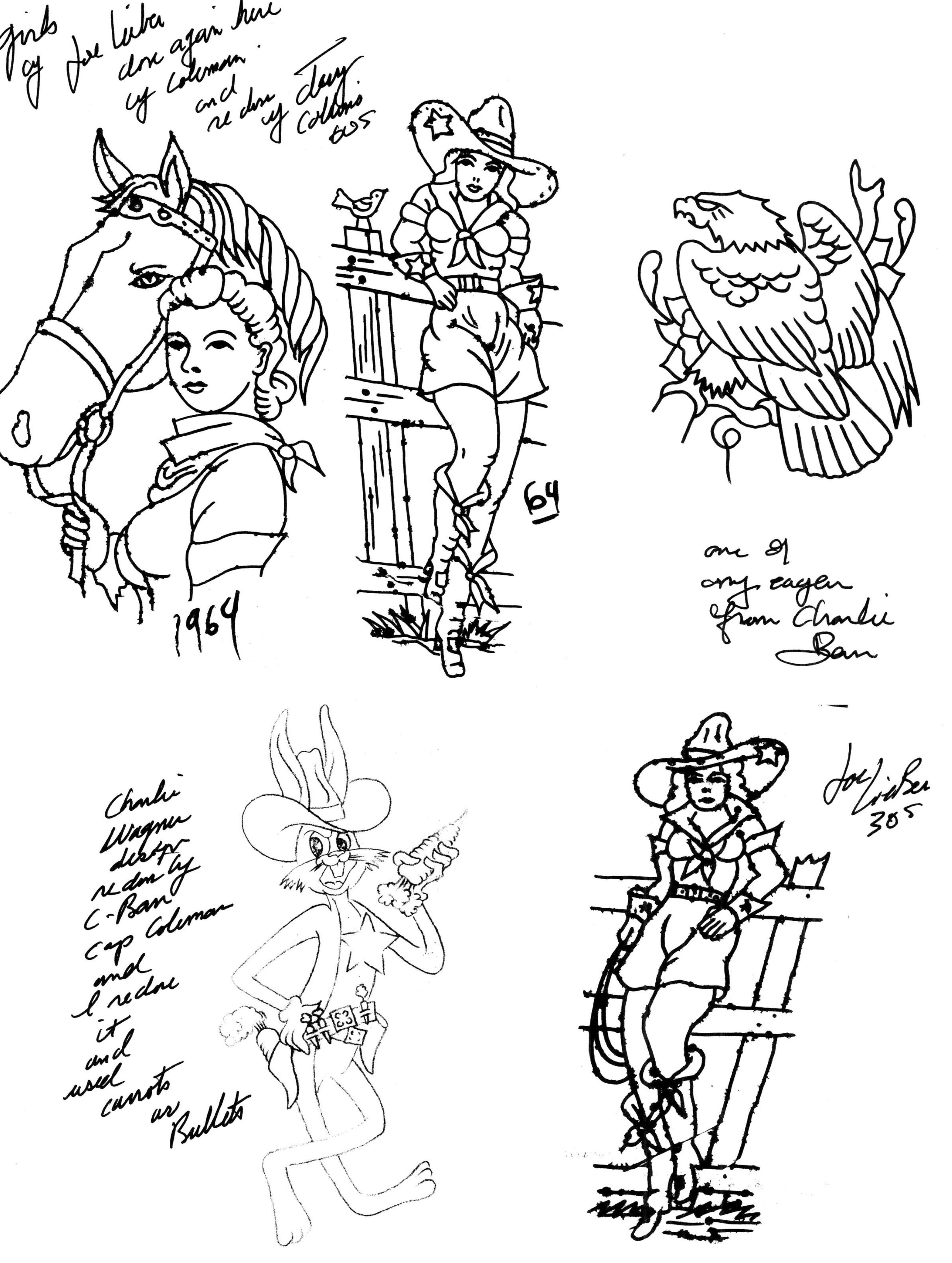
girls by Joe Lieber done again here by Coleman and re done by Tony Collins 305
1964
64
one of my eagles from Charlie Barr
Charlie Wagner design re done by C-Barr Cap Coleman and I redone it and used carrots as Bullets
Joe Lieber 305

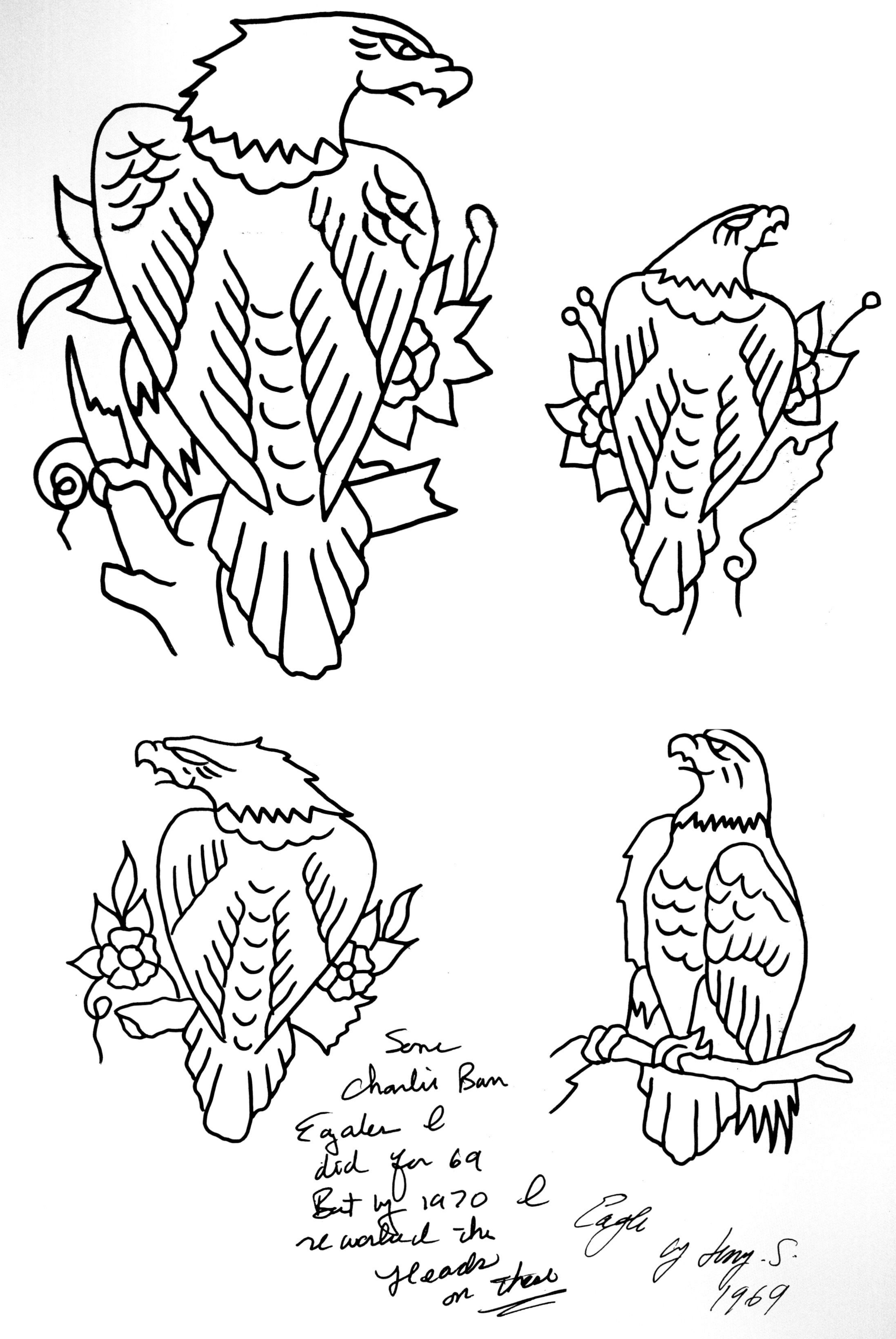
Some
Charlie Barr
Eagles I
did for 69
But by 1970 I
reworked the
Heads
on these
Eagle
by Huey S.
1969

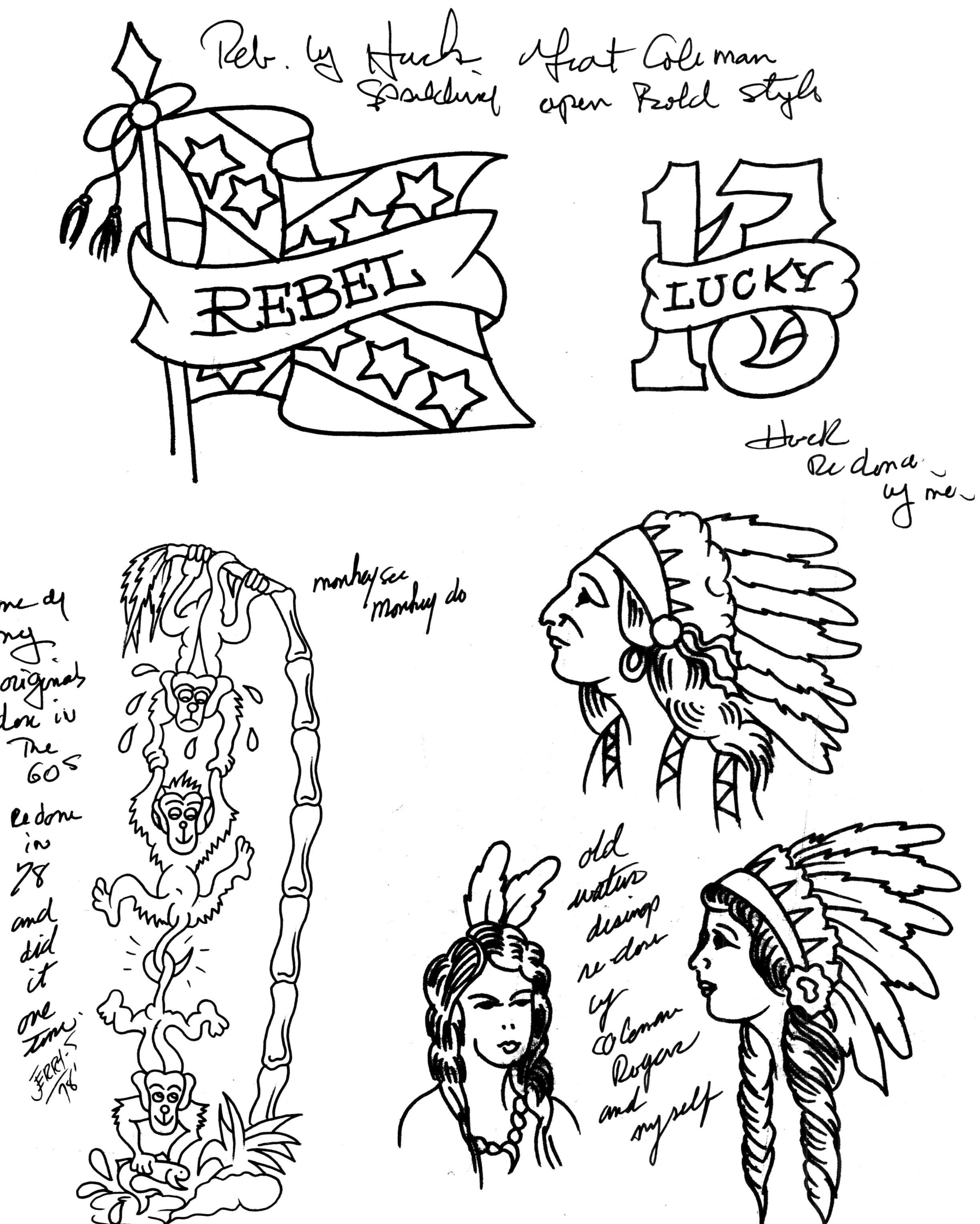
REBEL
LUCKY

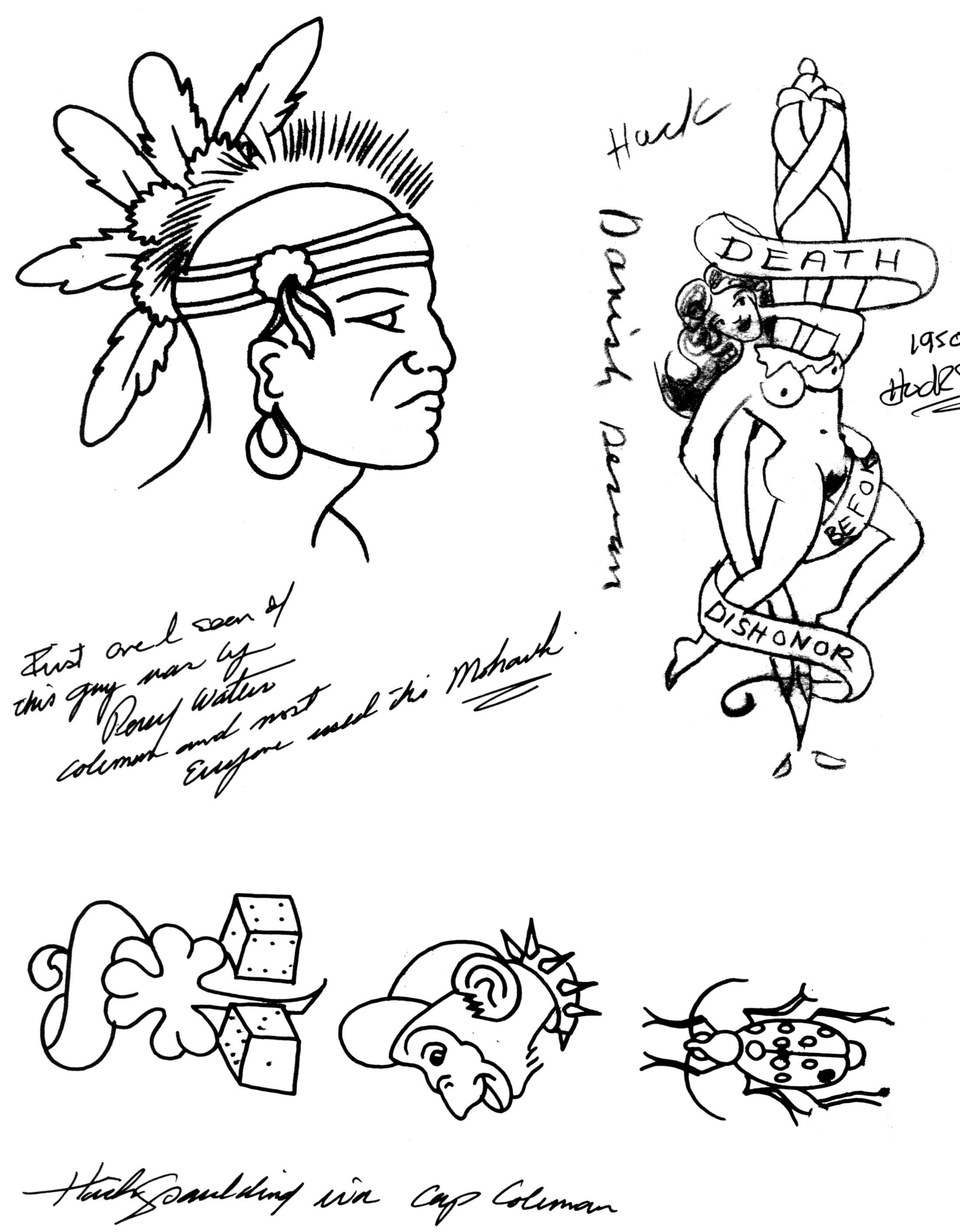
Hack
DEATH
DISHONOR
1950s
First one I seen of this guy was by Rooney Waters coleman and most Everyone used the Mohawk.
Hack Spaulding via Cap Coleman

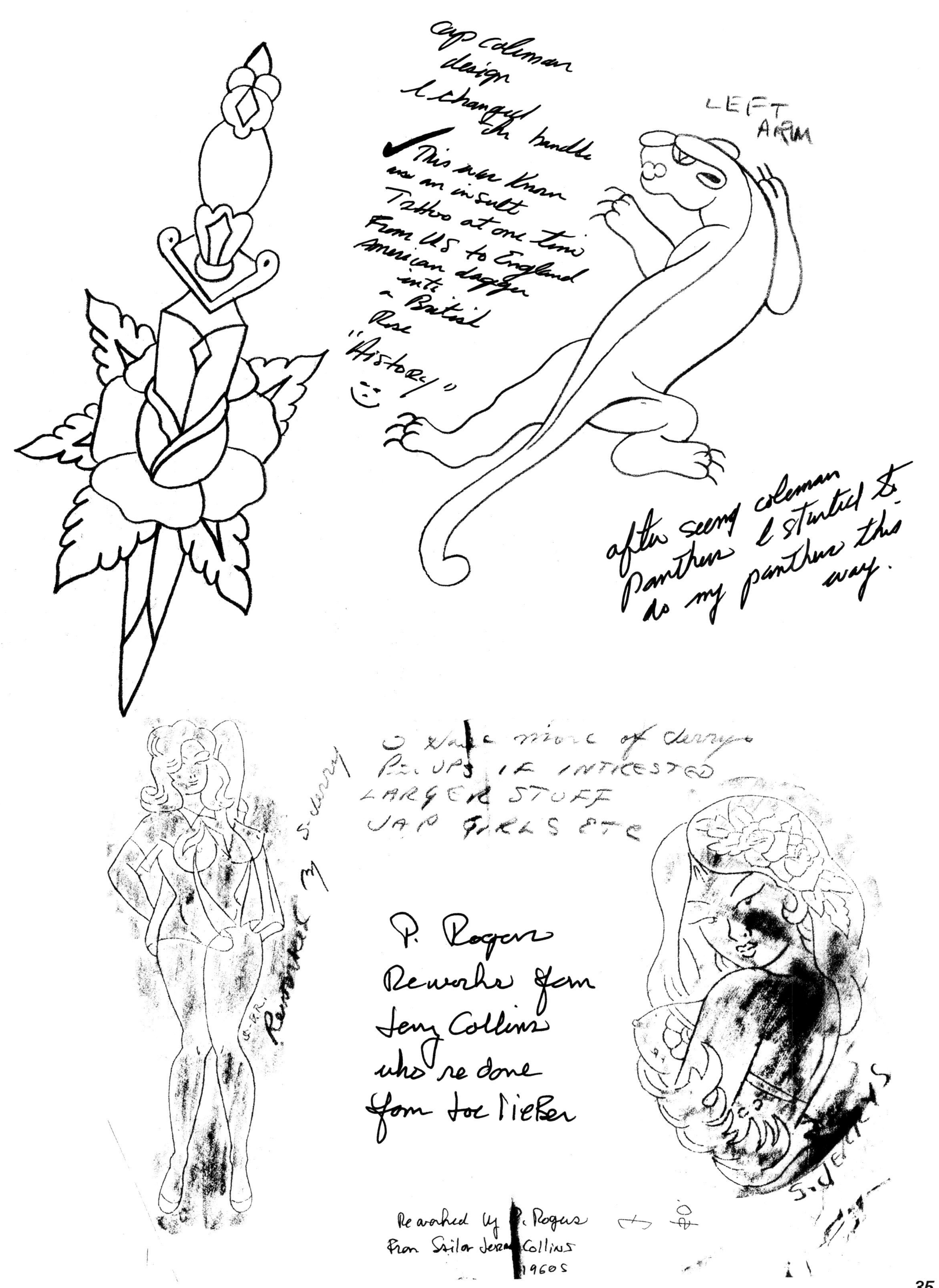
cap coleman
design
I changed
the handle
This was known
as an insult
Tattoo at one time
From US to England
American dagger
into
a British
Rose
"History"
LEFT
ARM
after seeing coleman
panther I started to
do my panther this
way.
I have more of Jerry's
PICUPS IF INTERESTED
LARGER STUFF
JAP GIRLS ETC
P. Rogers
Reworks from
Jerry Collins
who re done
from Joe Lieber
Reworked by P. Rogers
From Sailor Jerry Collins
1960s

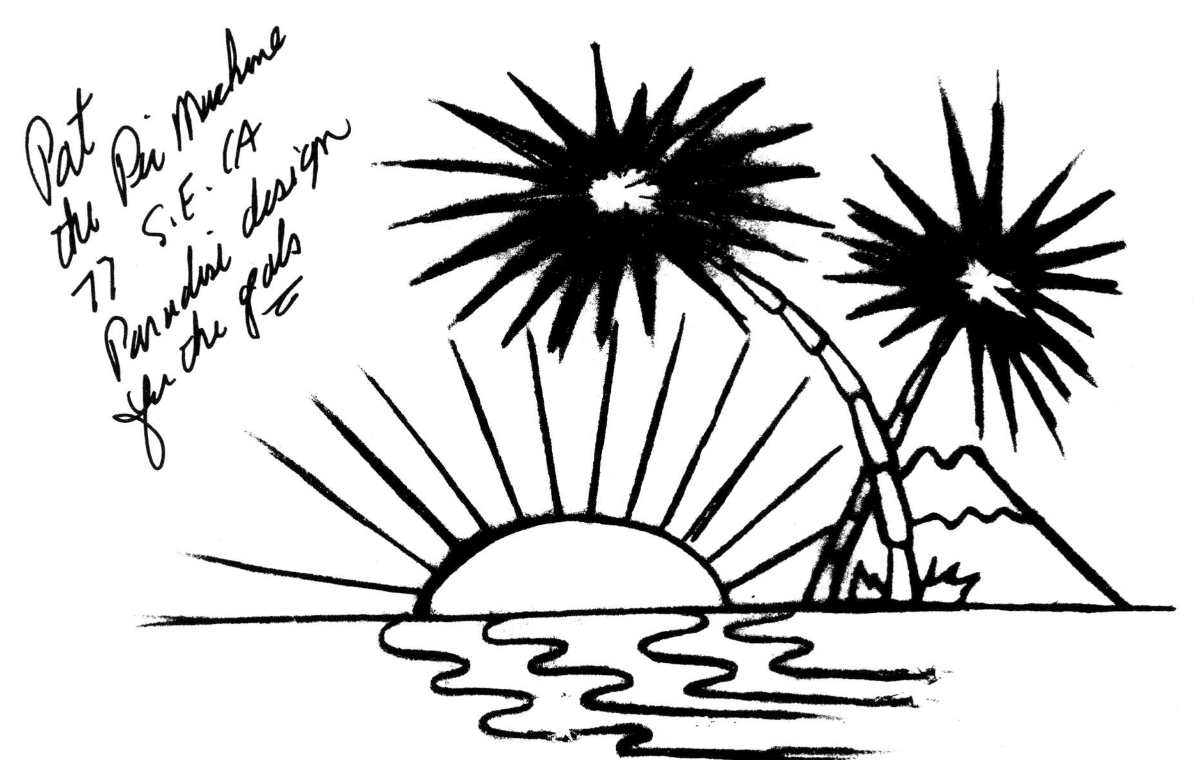

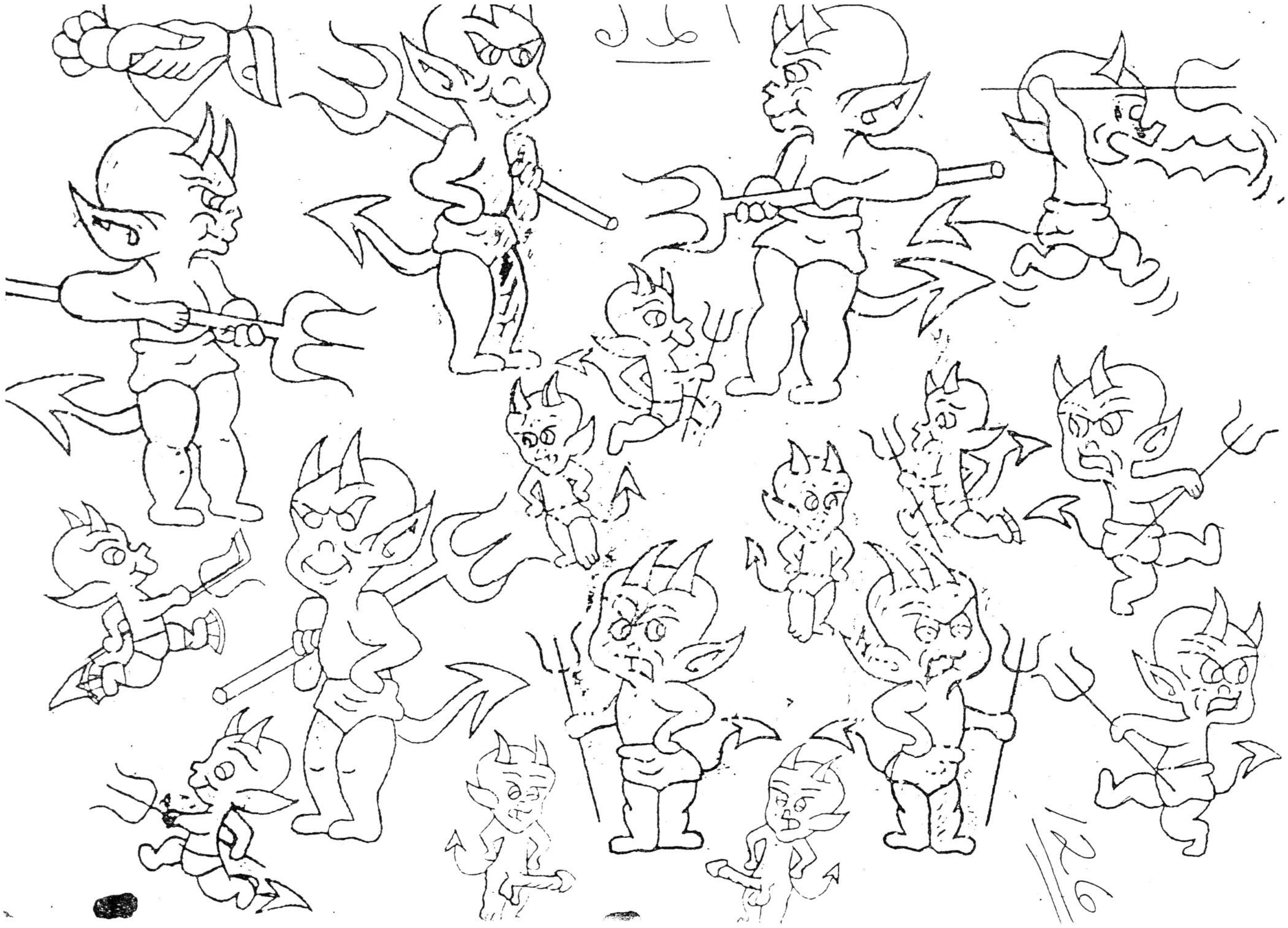

more devils by A. Newcome note the Hard On's on a few very old timer had a hand on tattoo Mickey Mouse Donald Duck. etc.

coleman sent these prints to some-one showing how he would color them

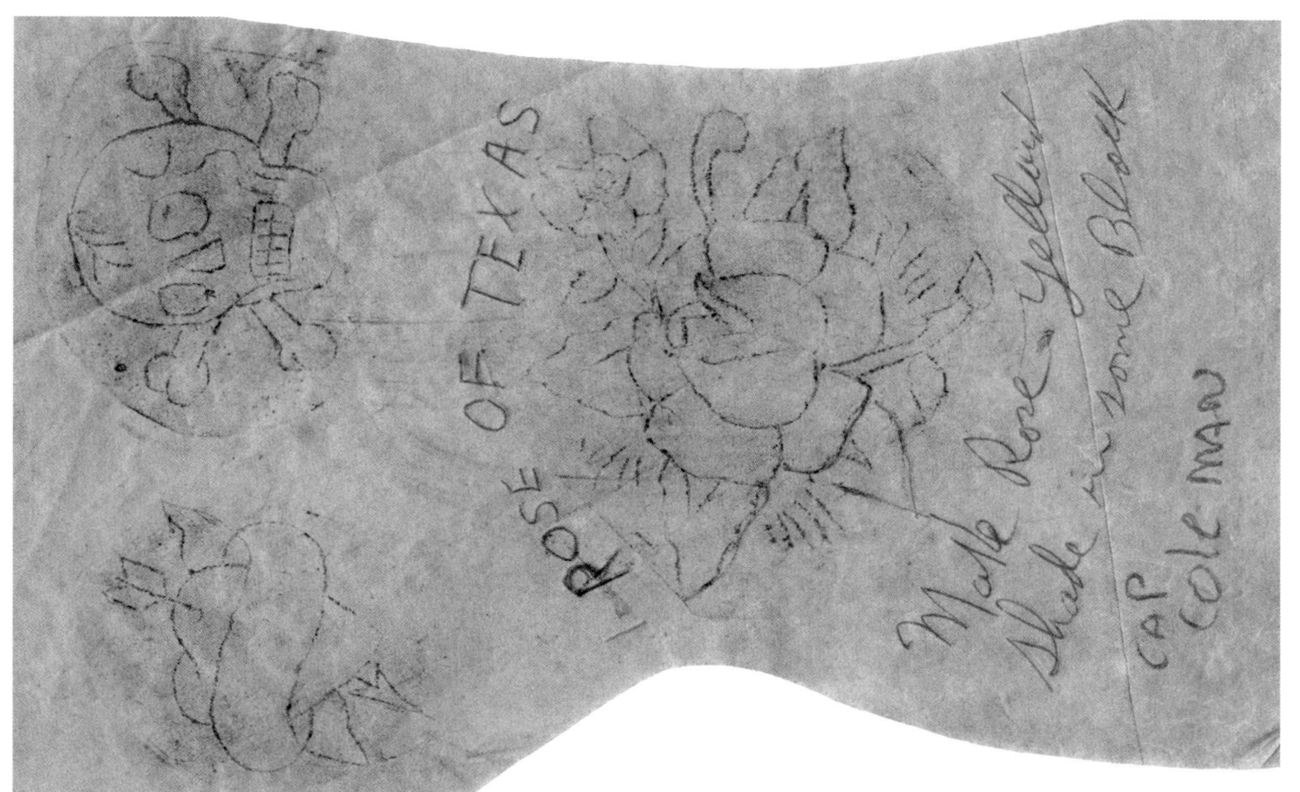

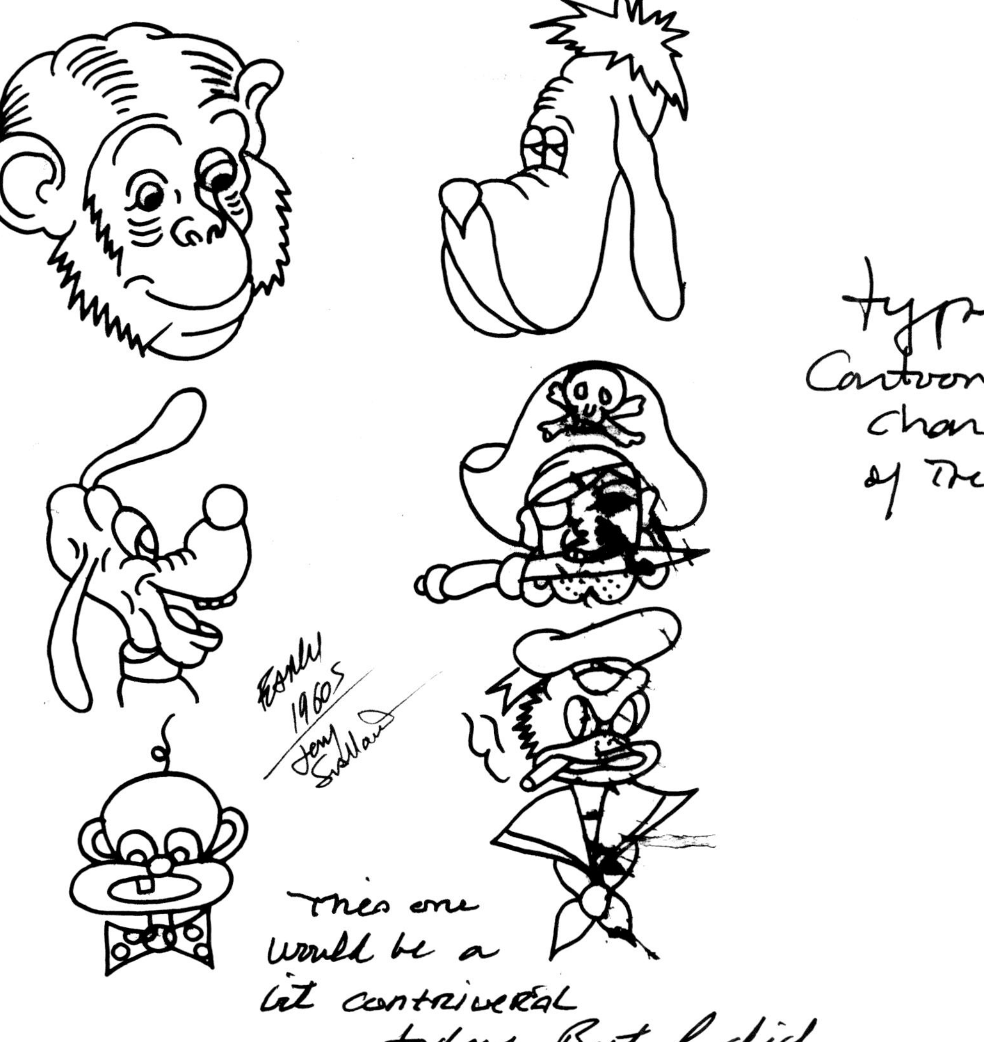

typical Cartoon characters of The 50-60s

This one would be a bit contriveral today But I did it many times in 60s and one time 1980.

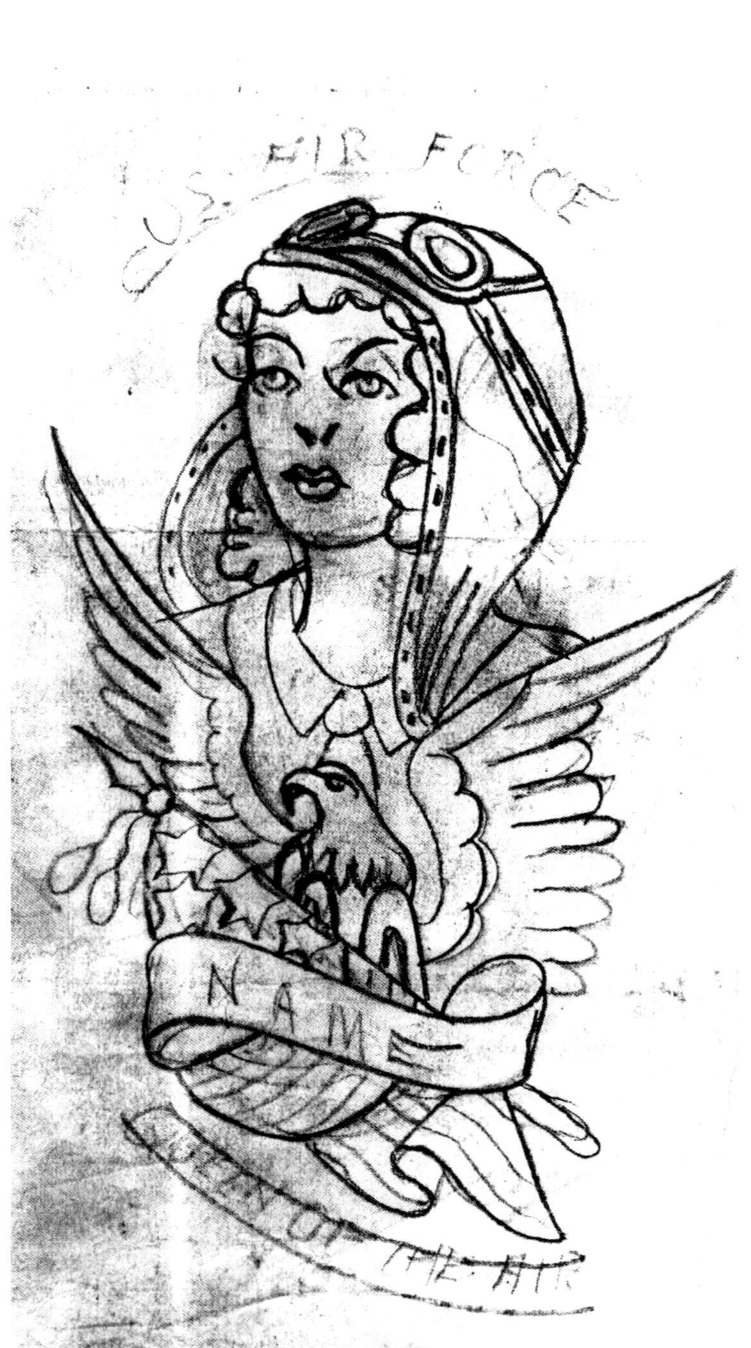

Lieber Design from the 30's. Some one worked it in the 40's as a wartime tattoo Liebers was done with-out the Flyer helmet on the chick!

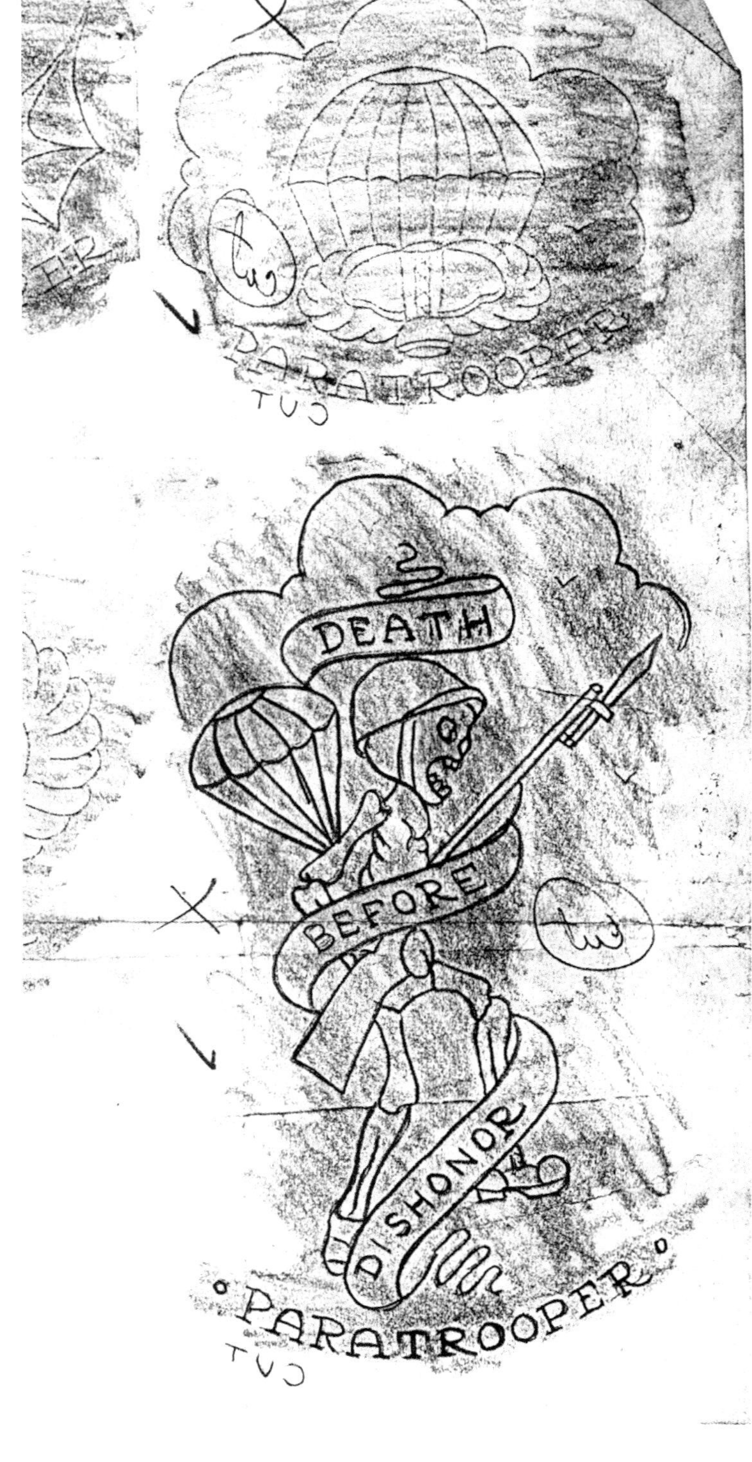

Paul Rogers Paratrooper designs via/cap coleman Charlie Barr also well done by Johnny Walker Wash. DC.

Standard Skull - Snake
Skulls Back then

standard snake Rose I did this one then seen it a hundred other styles

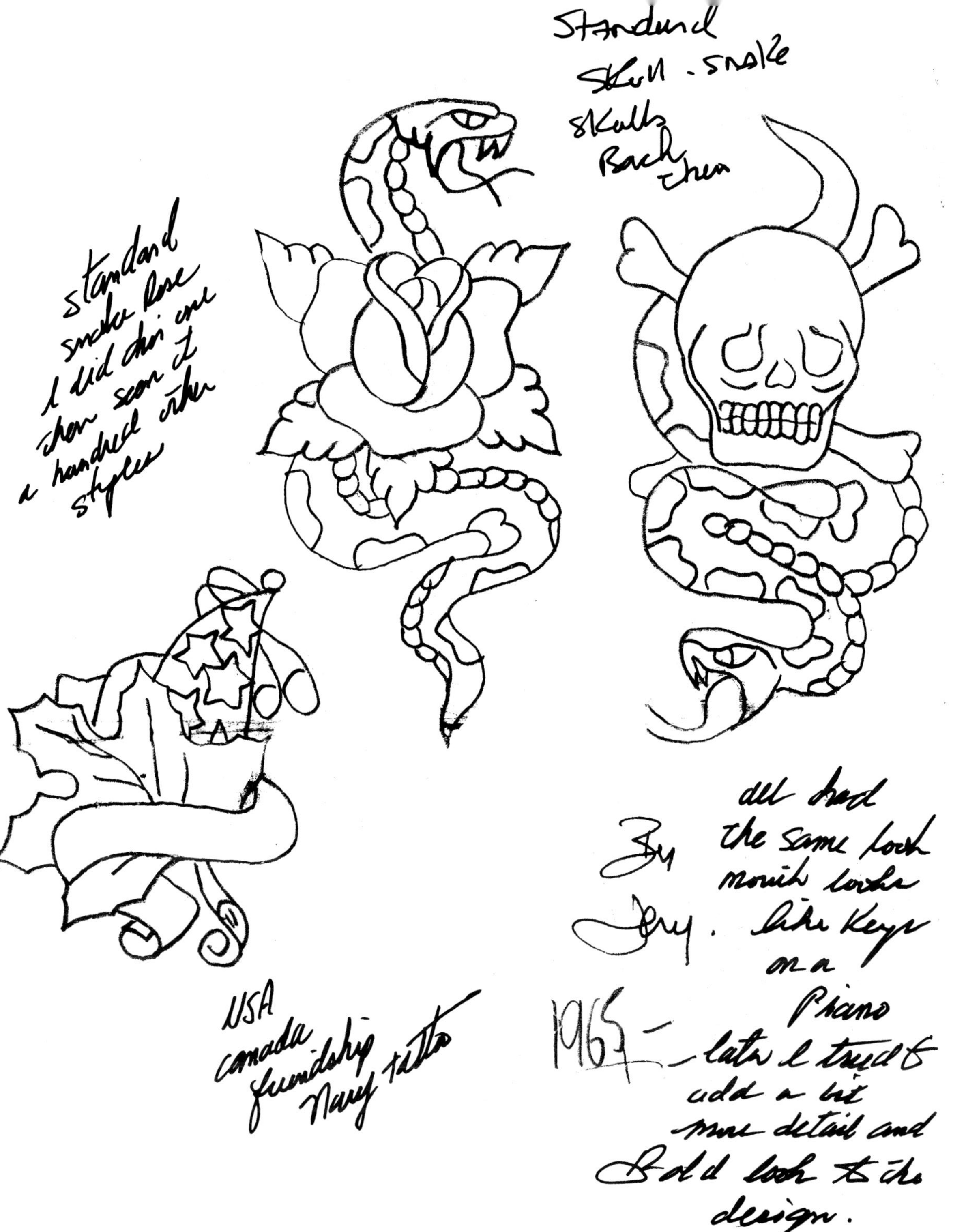

USA Canada friendship Navy tattoo

By Jerry. 1967 — all had the same look mouth looks like keys on a Piano — later I tried to add a bit more detail and Bold look to the design.

my card and longtime logo of a Charlie Barr Sailor Girl done also by Coleman and Jerry Collins

TRADITIONAL
TATTOOING
Mother
Sailor Jerry's
Since 1960
(902) 755-3911
202 Provost Street, New Glasgow, N.S.

Pin up - goes back to the 20's
a Joe Lieber Tattoo. Redone by
several artists Jerry Collins used it as
it originally was with a mandolin!
I redone it in the 80s
with her holding a heart an dagger.

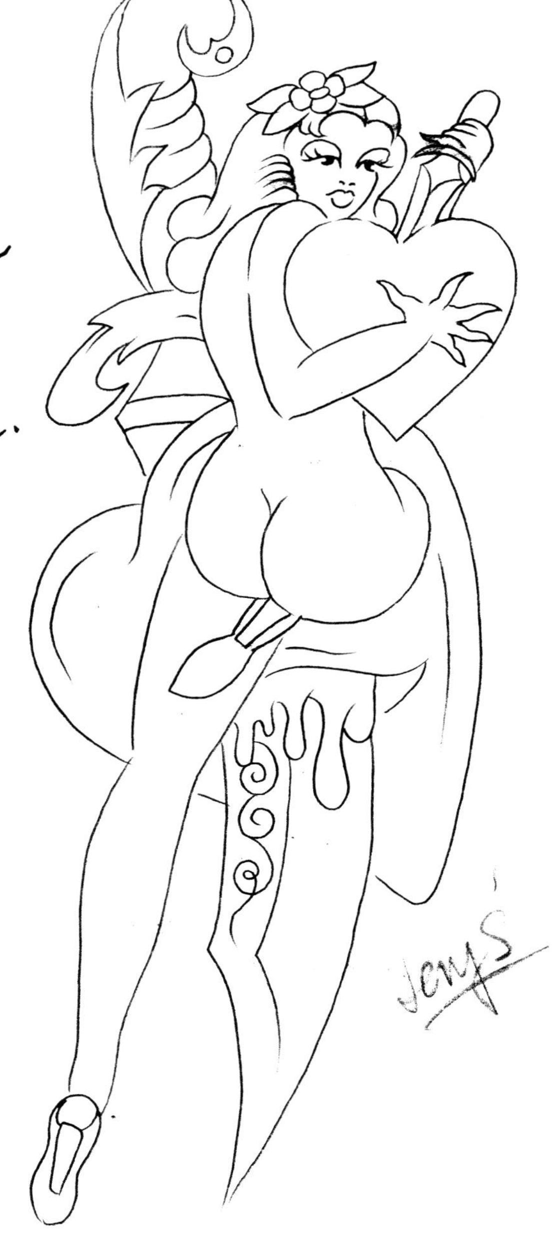

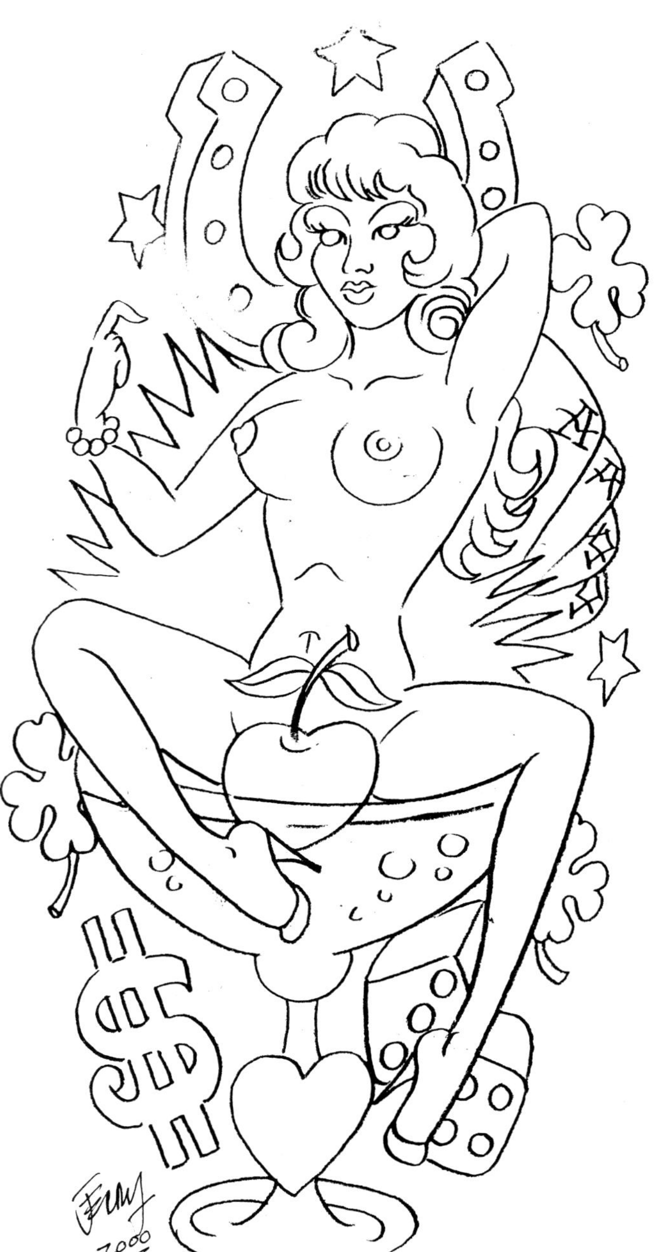

classic Mans Ruin
design re-done for the
90s!

I still rather the
older more simpler style

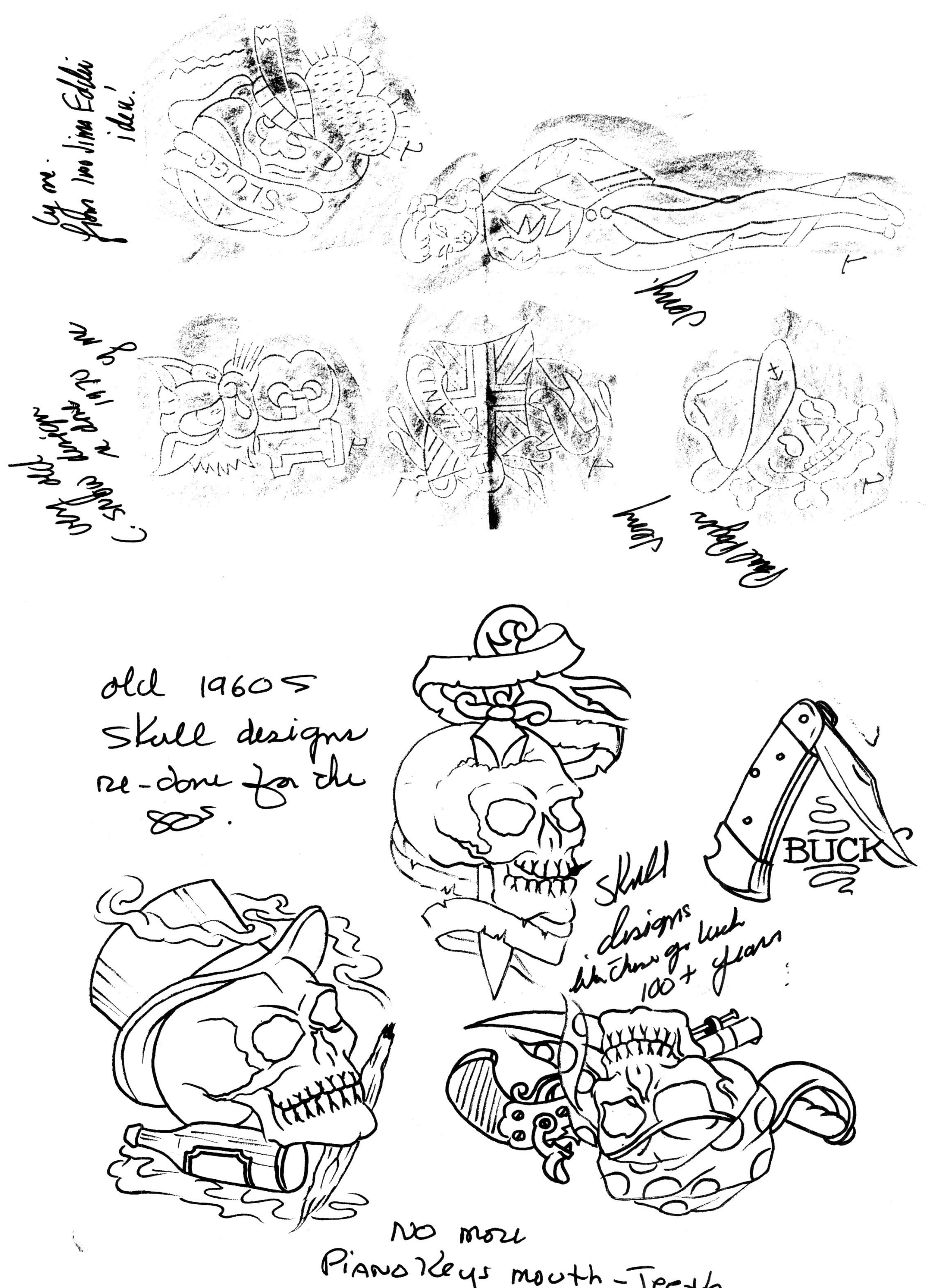

BUCK
old 1960s
Skull designs
re-done for the
80s.
Skull
designs
100+ years
NO more
PIANO Keys mouth-Teeth

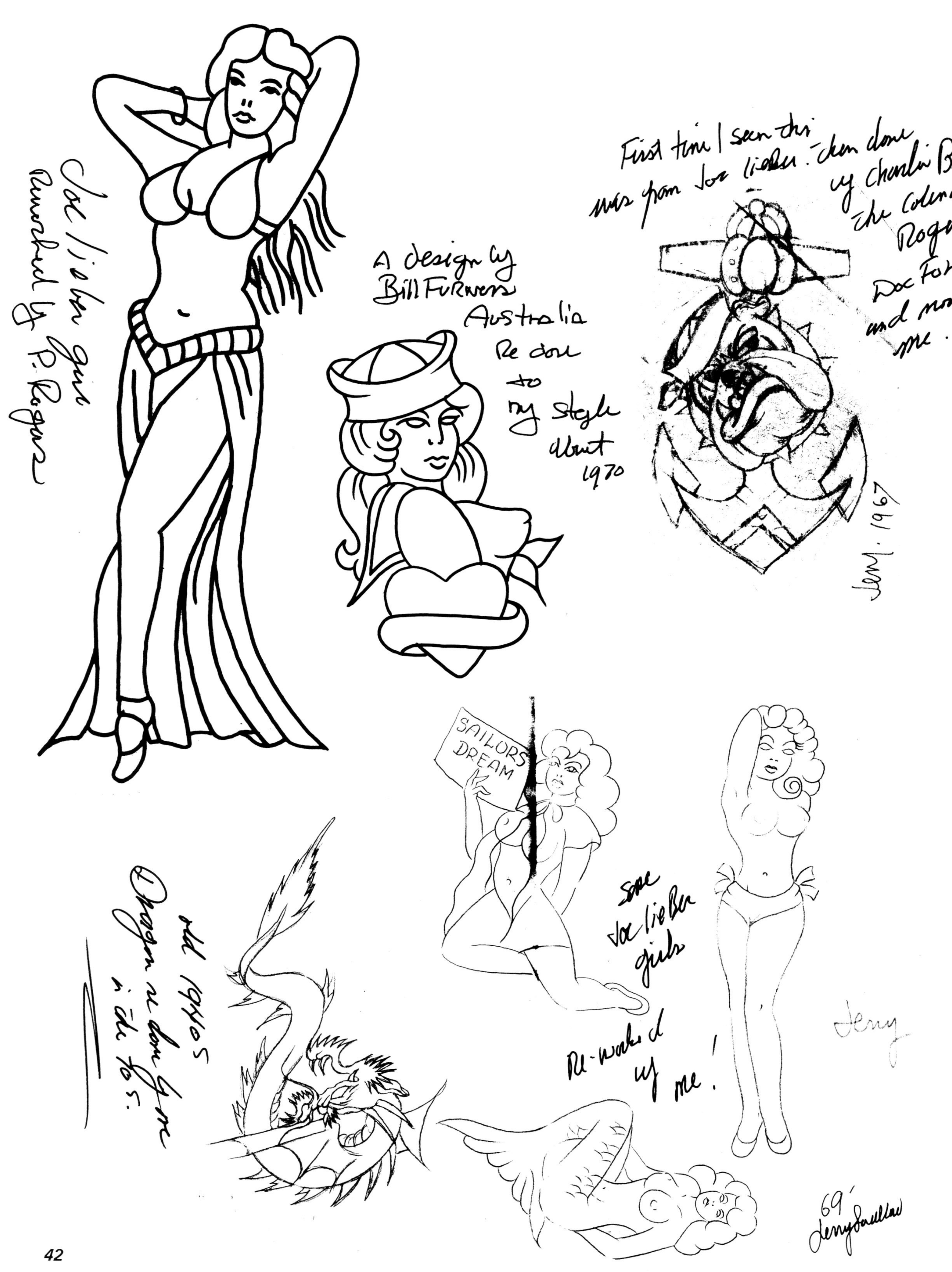
A design by
Bill Furness
Australia
Re done
to
my style
about
1970
SAILORS
DREAM
Jerry

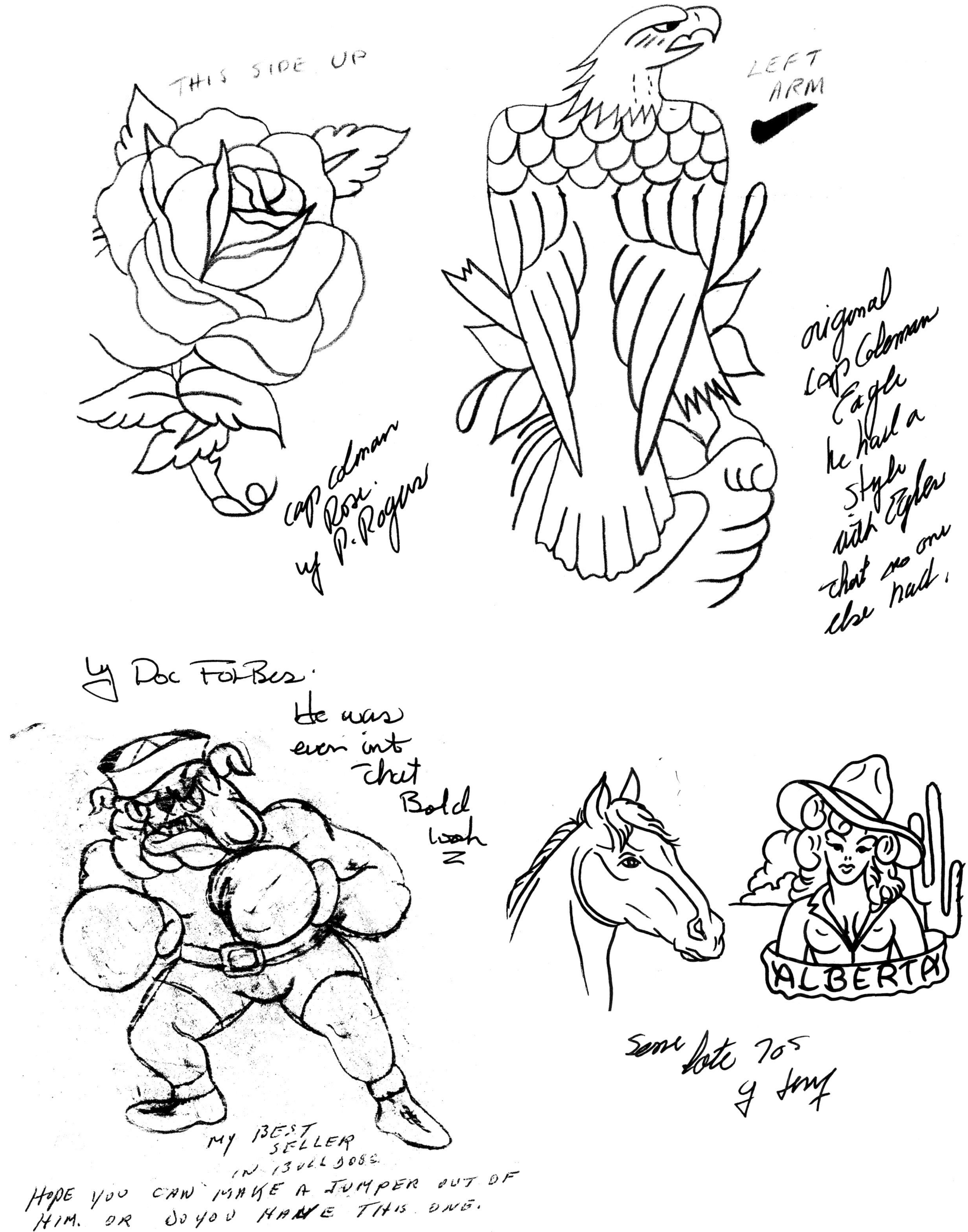
THIS SIDE UP
Cap Coleman
Rose
by P. Rogers
LEFT ARM
original
Cap Coleman
Eagle
he had a
style
with Eagles
that no one
else had.
by Doc Forbes.
He was
ever into
that
Bold
look
MY BEST
SELLER
IN BULLDOGS
HOPE YOU CAN MAKE A JUMPER OUT OF
HIM. OR DO YOU HAVE THIS ONE.
ALBERTA
Same late 70s

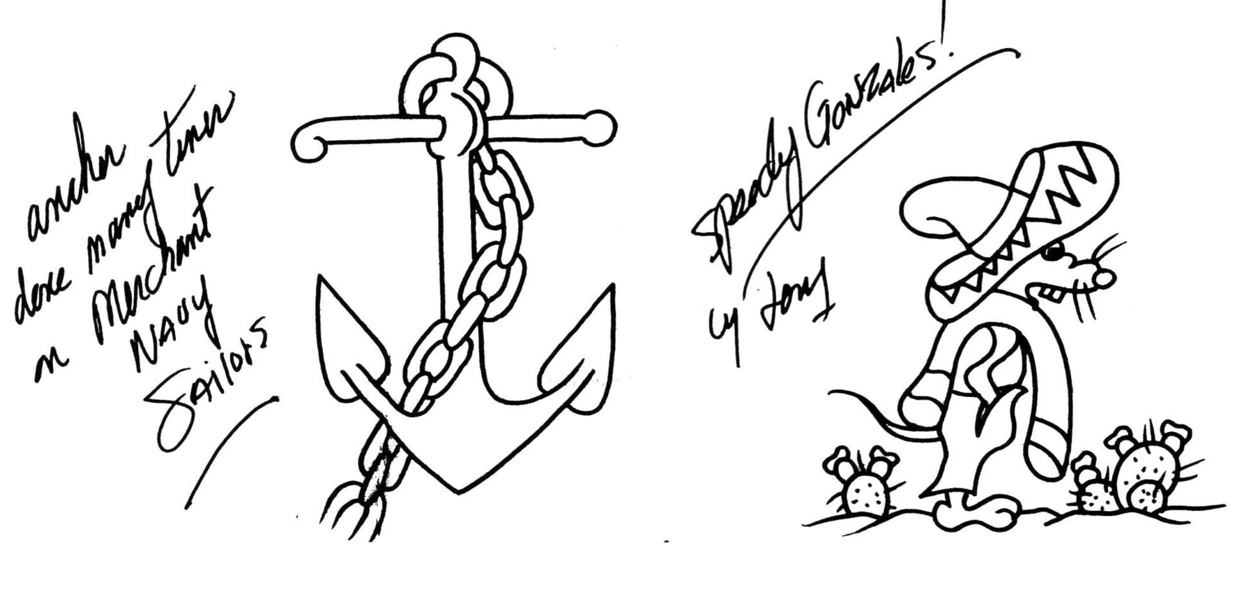

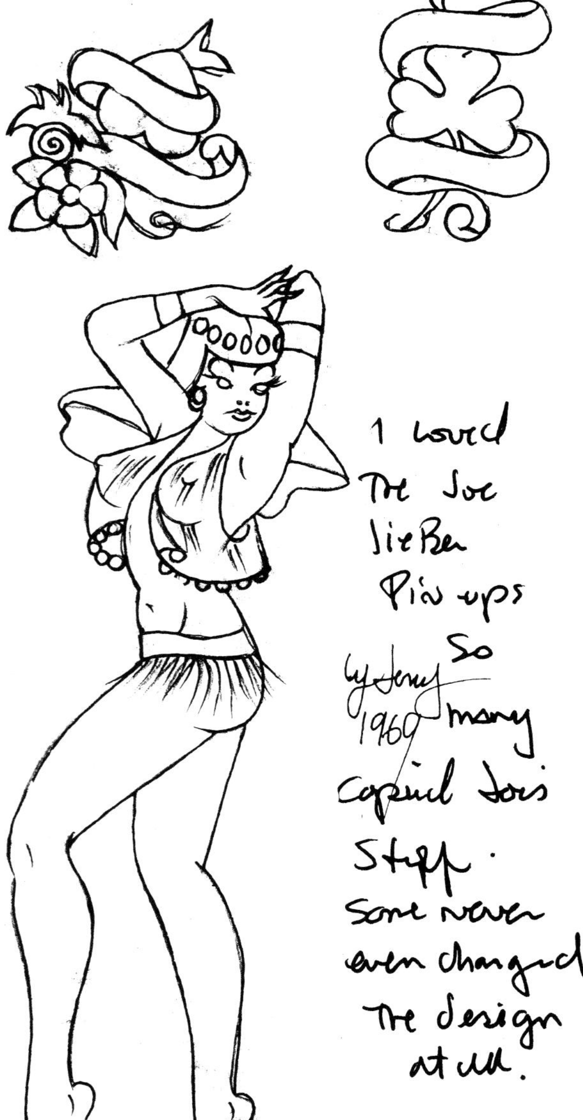

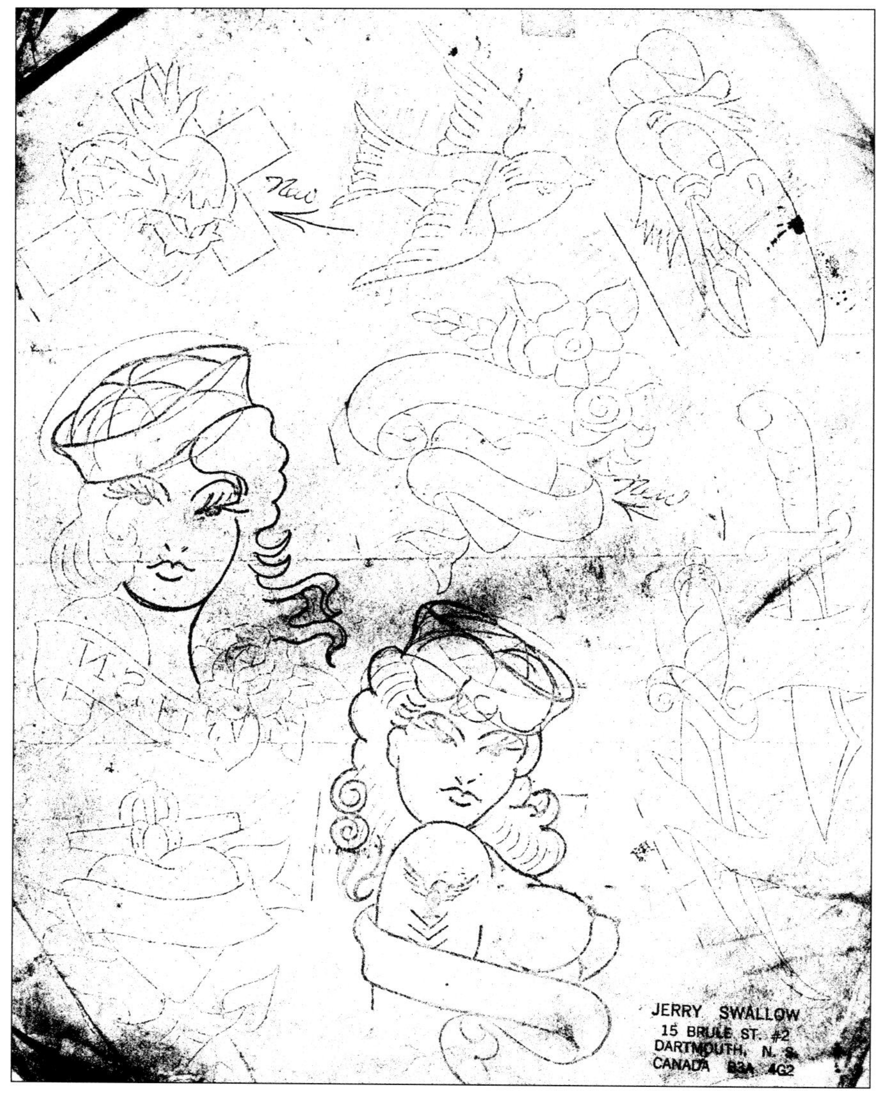

Stencil Prints 1970 - by then I had that original Cap Coleman Look. Thanks to so many who kept at it, that made Coleman one of the Best.

9/27/20

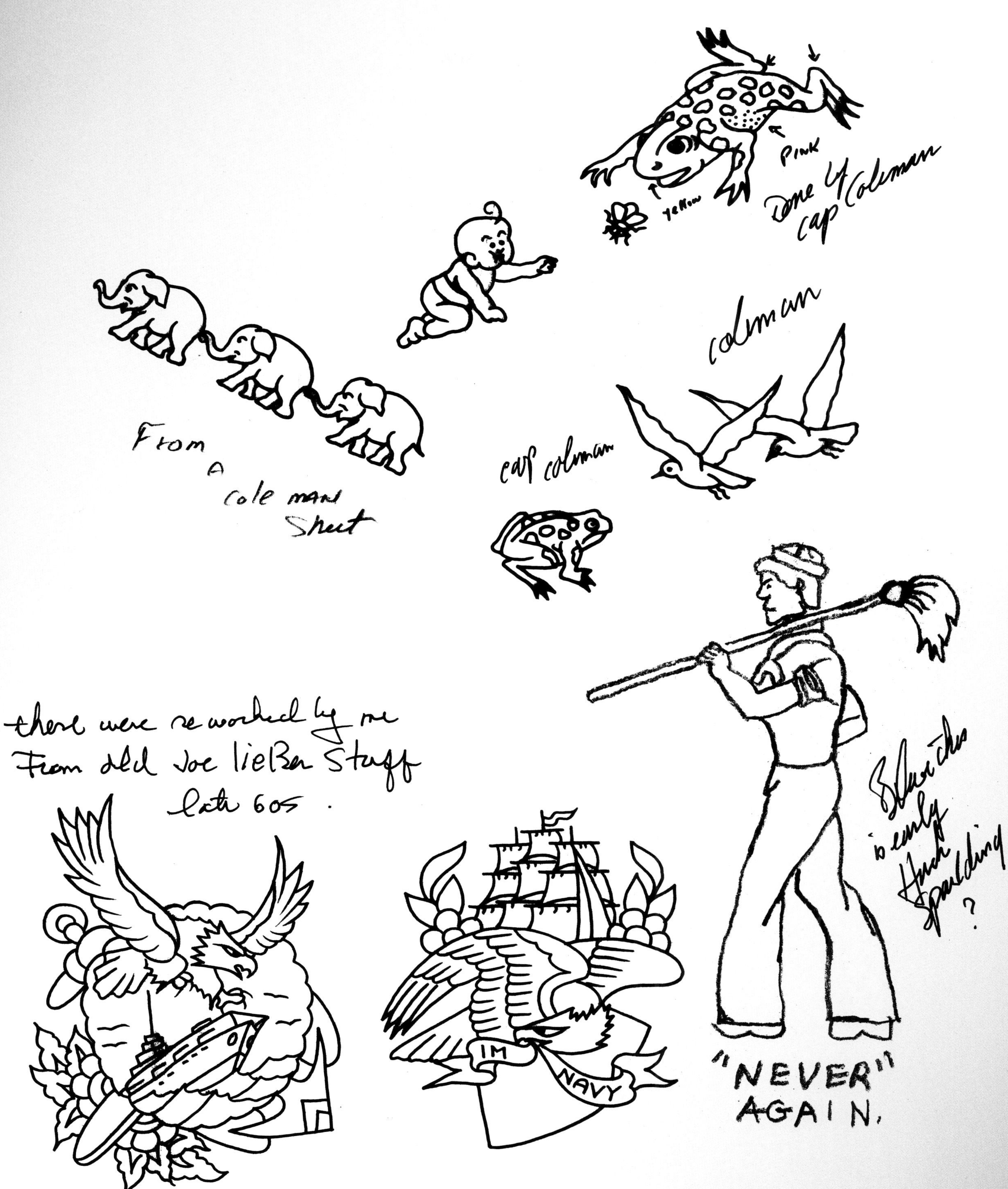
PINK
YELLOW
Done by cap Coleman
From A cole man Sheet
colman
cap colman
these were reworked by me From old Joe lieBer Stuff late 60s.
IM NAVY
"NEVER" AGAIN.

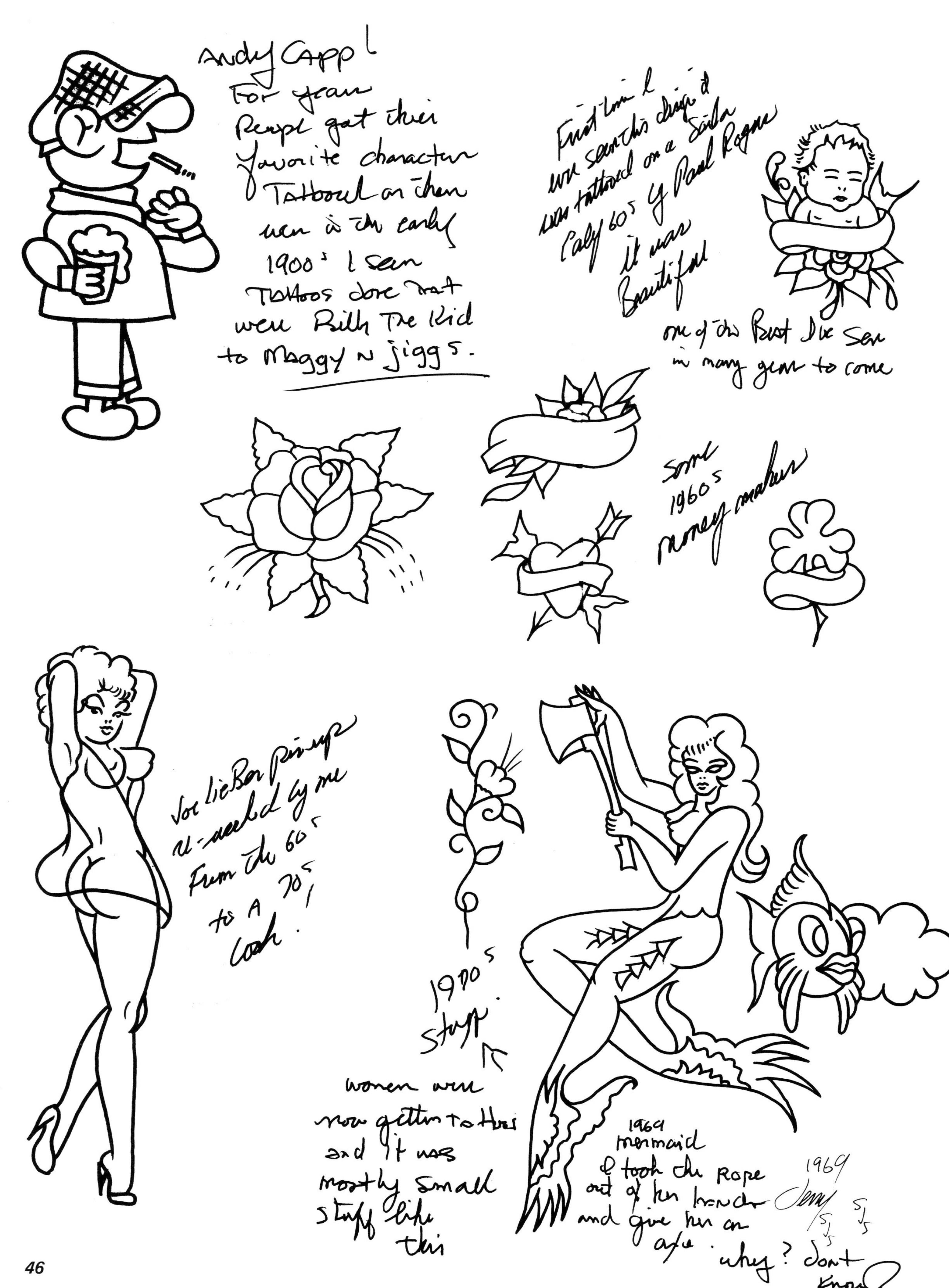
Andy Capp
For years
People got their
favorite character
Tattooed on them
even in the early
1900's I seen
Tattoos done that
were Billy The Kid
to Maggy n jiggs.
First time I
ever seen this design it
was tattooed on a Sailor
early 60's by Paul Rogers
It was
Beautiful
one of the Best I've seen
in many years to come
Some
1960's
money makers
Joe LieBer pinup
re-worked by me
From the 60's
to a 70's
look.
1900's
stuff
women were
now getting tattoos
and it was
mostly small
stuff like
this
1969
mermaid
I took the Rope
out of her hands
and give her an
axe. why? don't
know?
1969

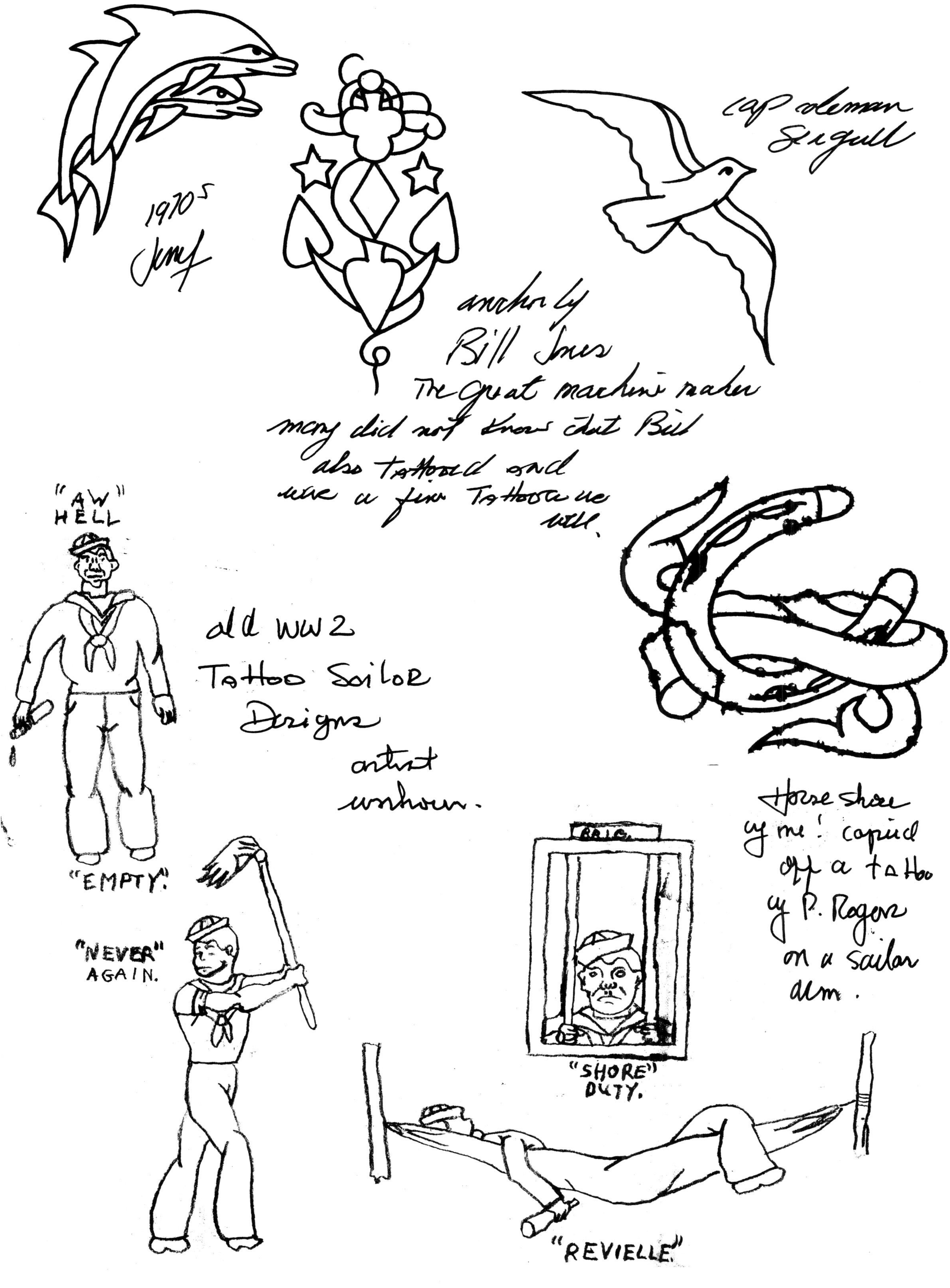
1970s
cap coleman Seagull
anchor by Bill Jones The great machine maker many did not know that Bill also tattooed and was a fine Tattooer as well.
"AW" HELL
old WW2 Tattoo Sailor Designs artist unknown.
Horse shoe by me! copied off a tattoo by P. Rogers on a sailor arm.
"EMPTY".
BRIG.
"NEVER" AGAIN.
"SHORE" DUTY.
"REVIELLE"

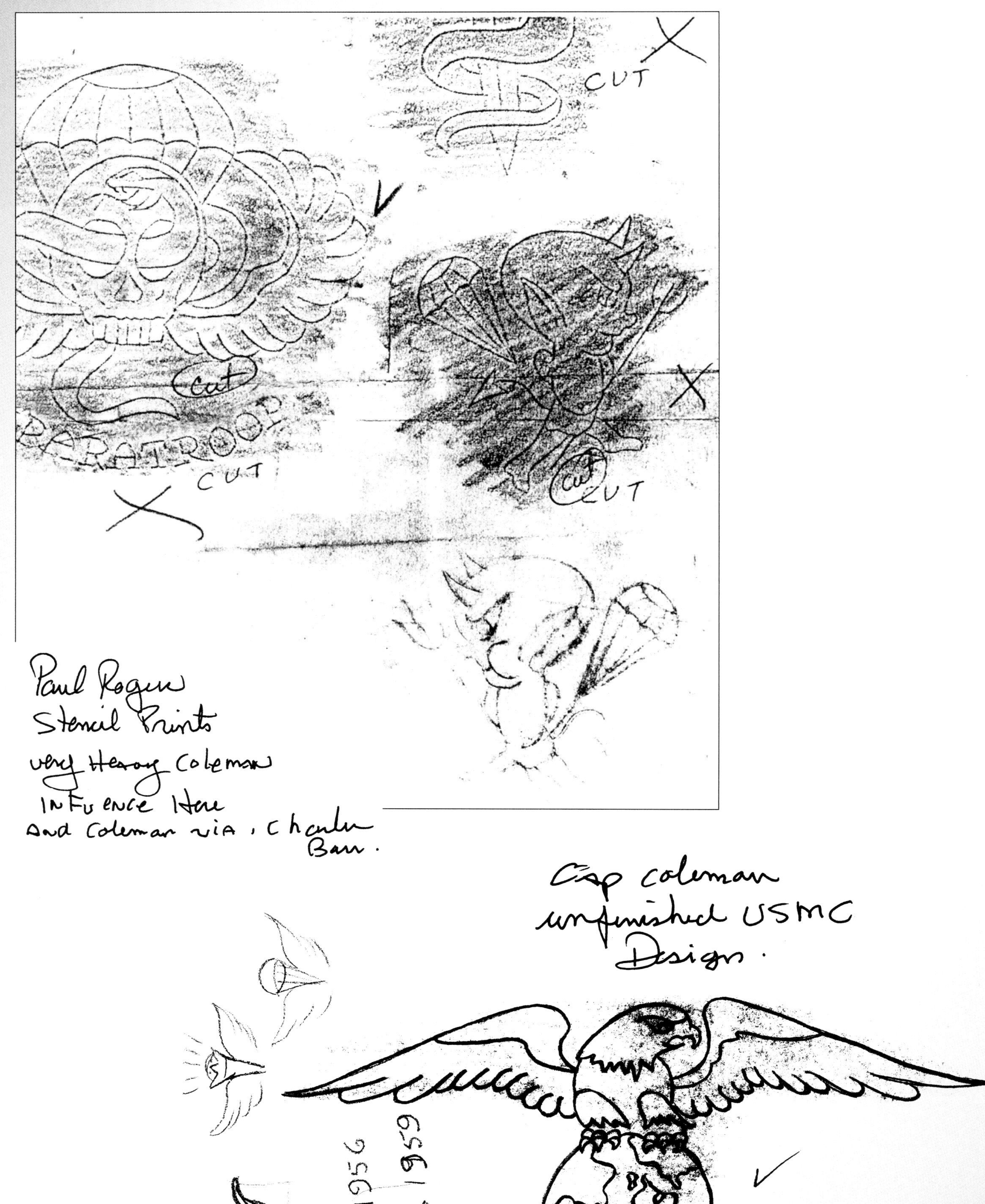
CUT
cut
PARATROOP
CUT
cut
CUT
Paul Rogers
Stencil Prints
very Heavy Coleman
InFuence Here
and Coleman via, Charlie
Barr.
Cap coleman
unfinished USMC
Designs.
1956
1959
cap coleman

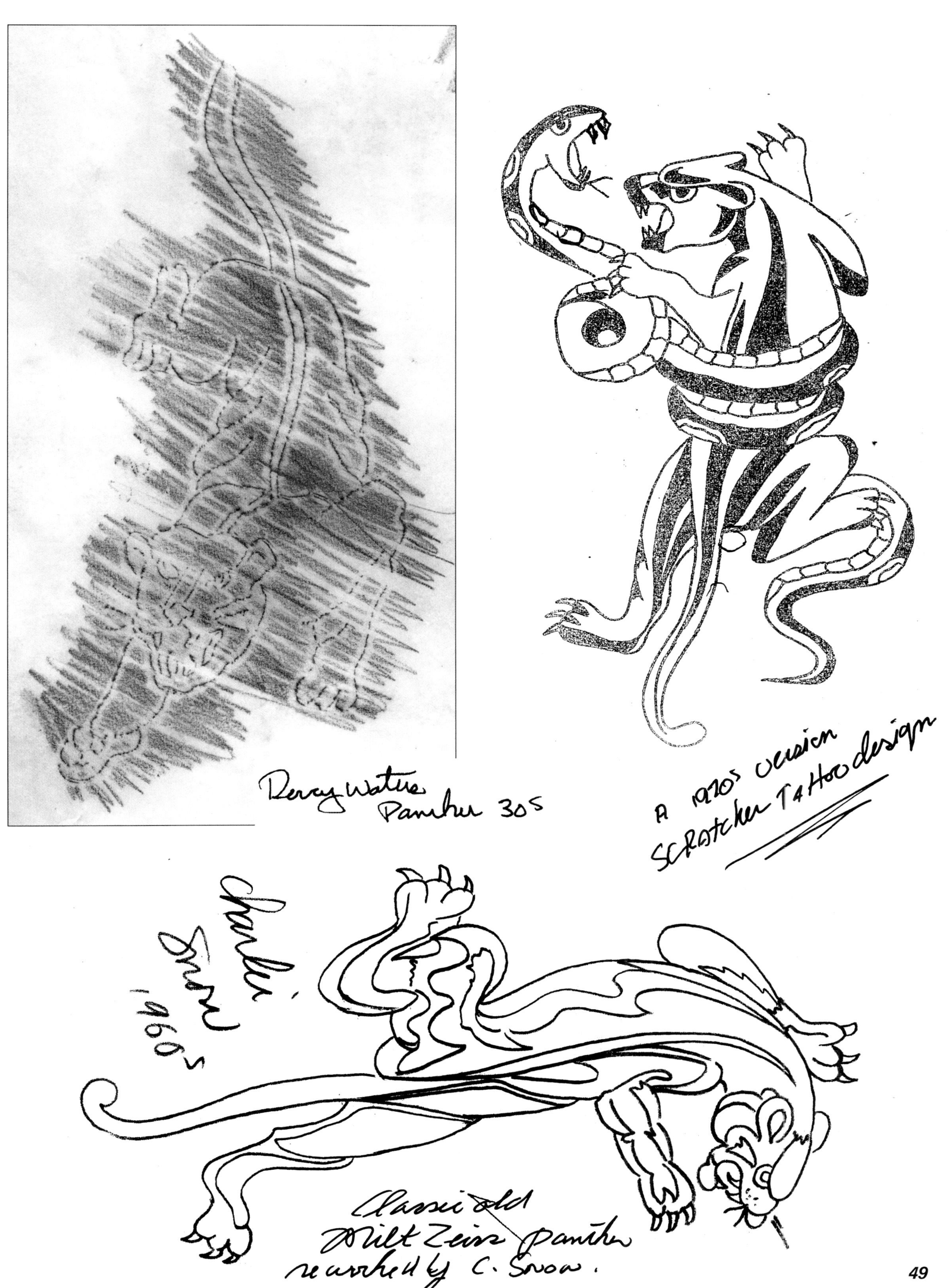
Percy Waters
Panther 30s
A 1920s version
SCRATCHER TATToo design
Charlie Snow
1960s
Classic old
Milt Zeis panther
reworked by C. Snow.

Who me?

Tattoo by Charlie Barr

when it comes right down to it the Artist responsible for the Classic Bold American Traditional Tattoo were Joe Lieber, Lew the Jew, Charlie Barr, Cap Coleman, P. Royce, H. Spaulding, John Walker!

HONOLULU

194

Joe Lieber
Pre-WW2 Design
many tattooers used this and done it in several styles

U.S.N

Charlie Barr
nice clean Bold look

Barr and Coleman worked together and Coleman learned a lot from Barr

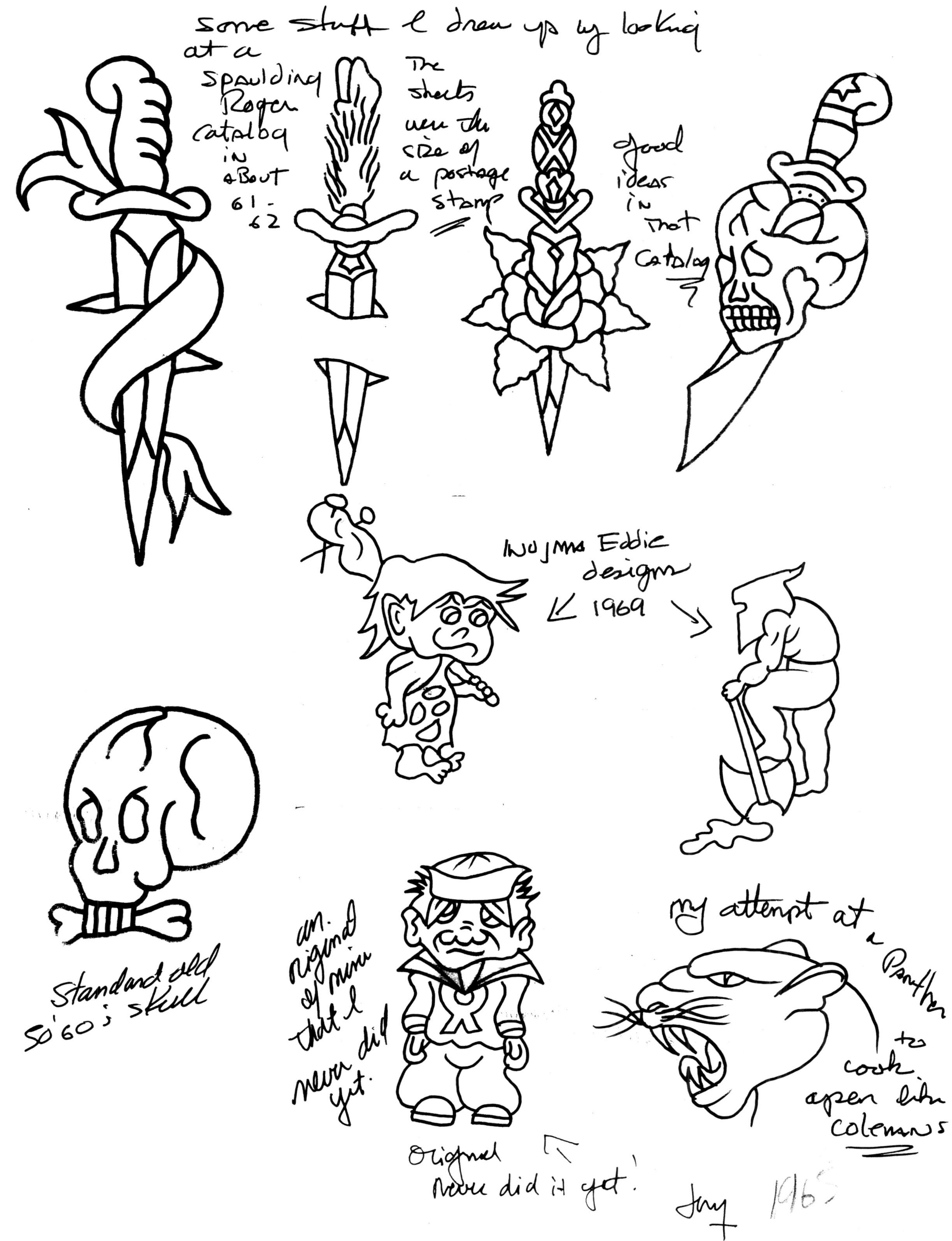

some stuff I drew up by looking at a Spaulding Rogers catalog in about 61-62
The sheets were the size of a postage stamp
good ideas in that catalog
Iwo Jima Eddie designs
1969
Standard old 50's 60's skull
an original of mine that I never did yet.
my attempt at a Panther to cook open like Colemans
Original never did it yet!
Jerry 1965

I drew this off of one of Charlie Swans sheets with an ink pen

one of my first designs 1960 Jerry Swallow

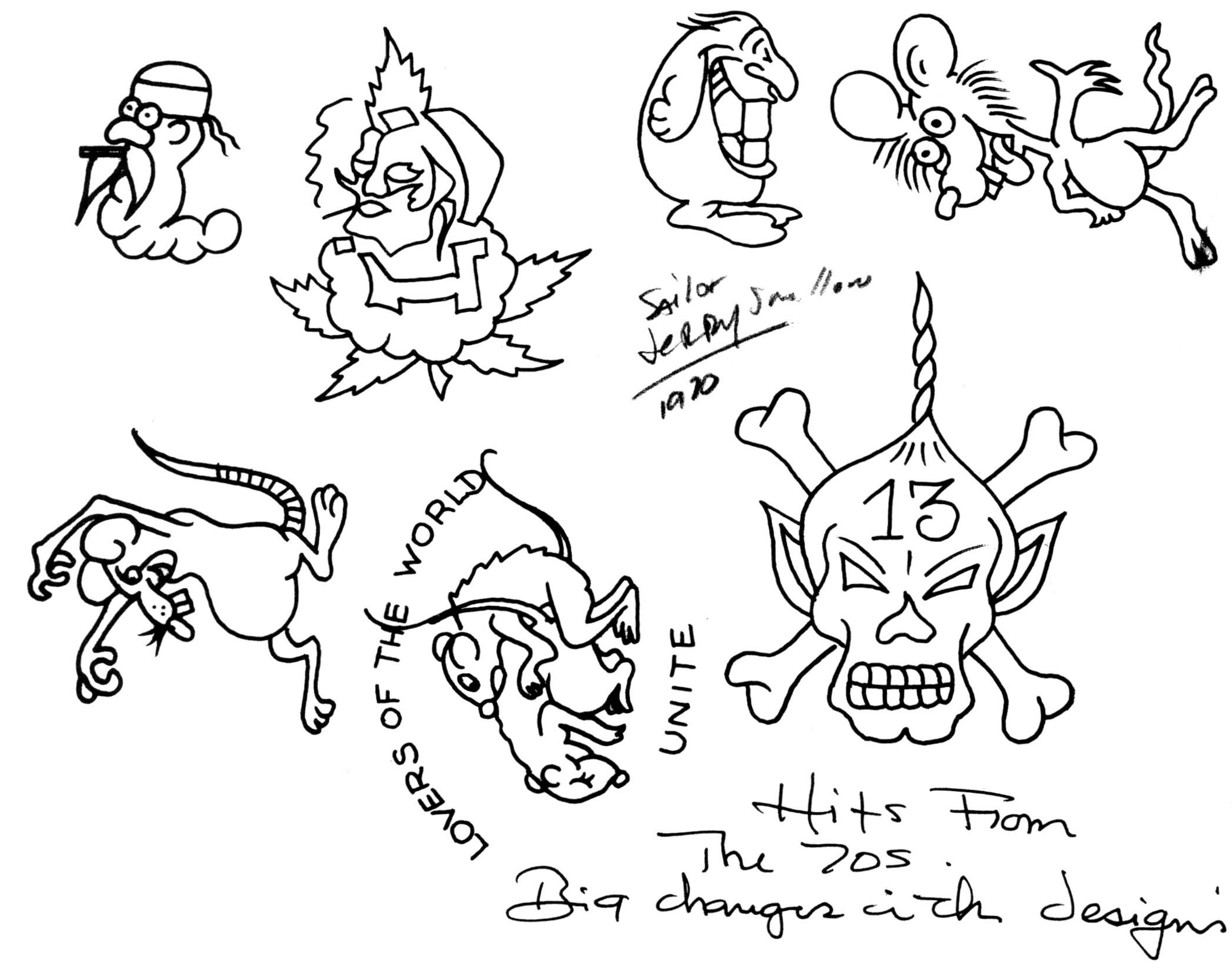

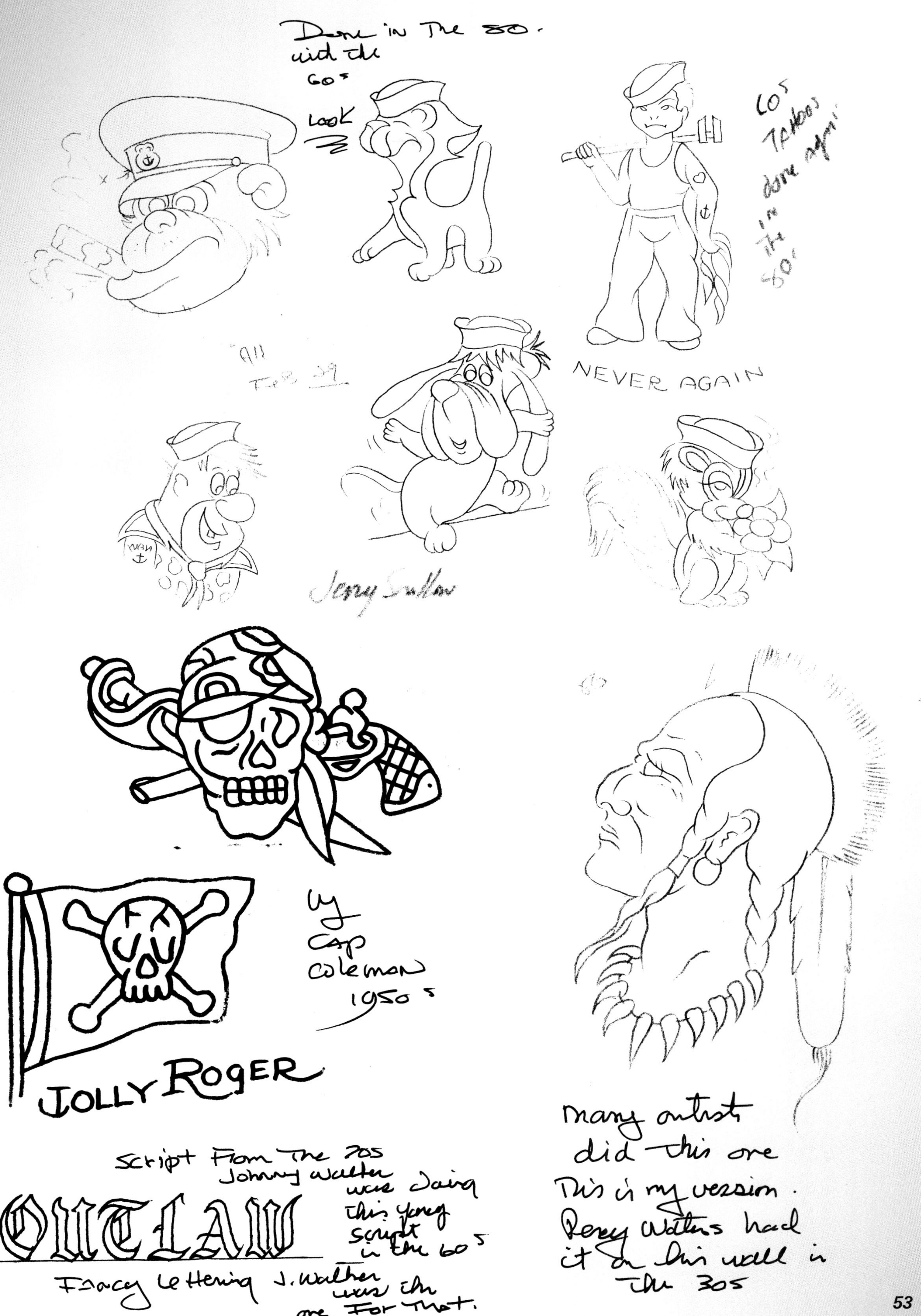
Done in The 80.
with the
60s
look
LOS
TATTOOS
done again
in
the
80s
NEVER AGAIN
JOLLY ROGER
by
Cap
Coleman
1950s
OUTLAW
Script From The 70s
Johnny Walker
was doing
this fancy
script
in the 60s
Fancy lettering J. Walker
was the
one For That.
Many artists
did this one
This is my version.
Percy Waters had
it on his wall in
The 30s

Another P. Rogers Rose

all cap coleman style.

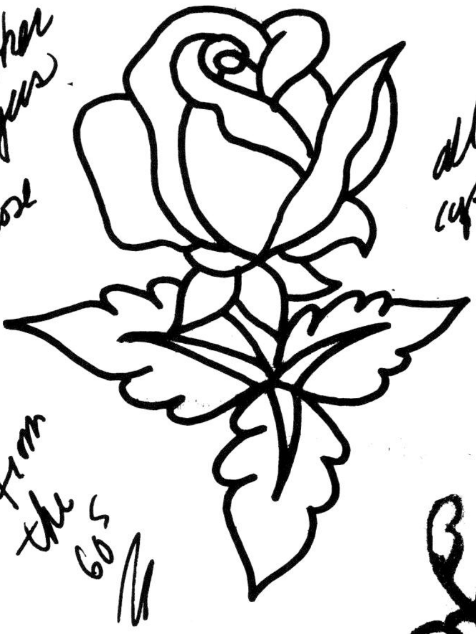

From the 60s

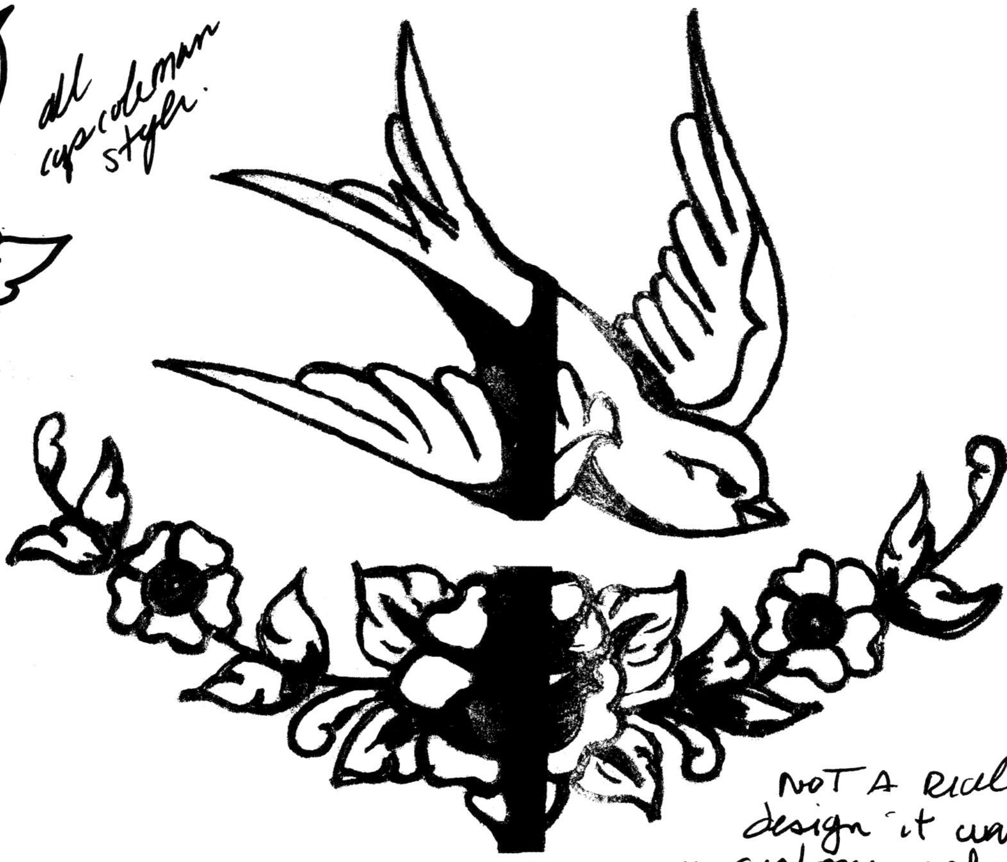

NOT A REAL OLD design it was one a customer asked me to do one exact if it was done in early 60s

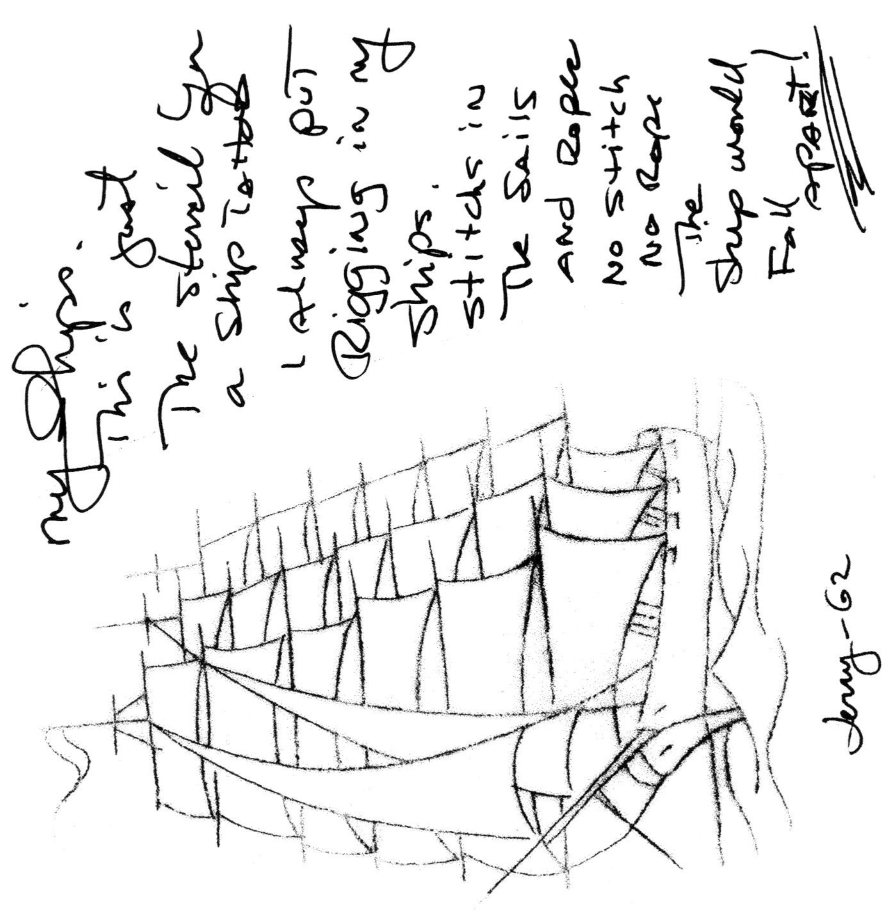

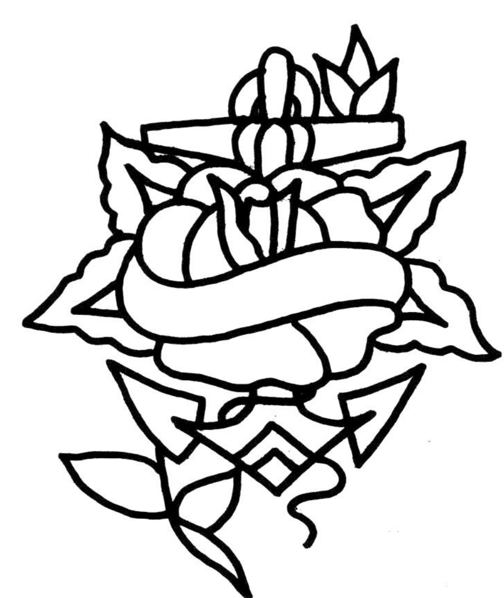

SAW This Tattoo ON A SAILORS ARM IN 62 63 Done by P. Rogers it was so Bold and Stood out great. I Just had to do my StuFF This way it took a lot of work But did it.

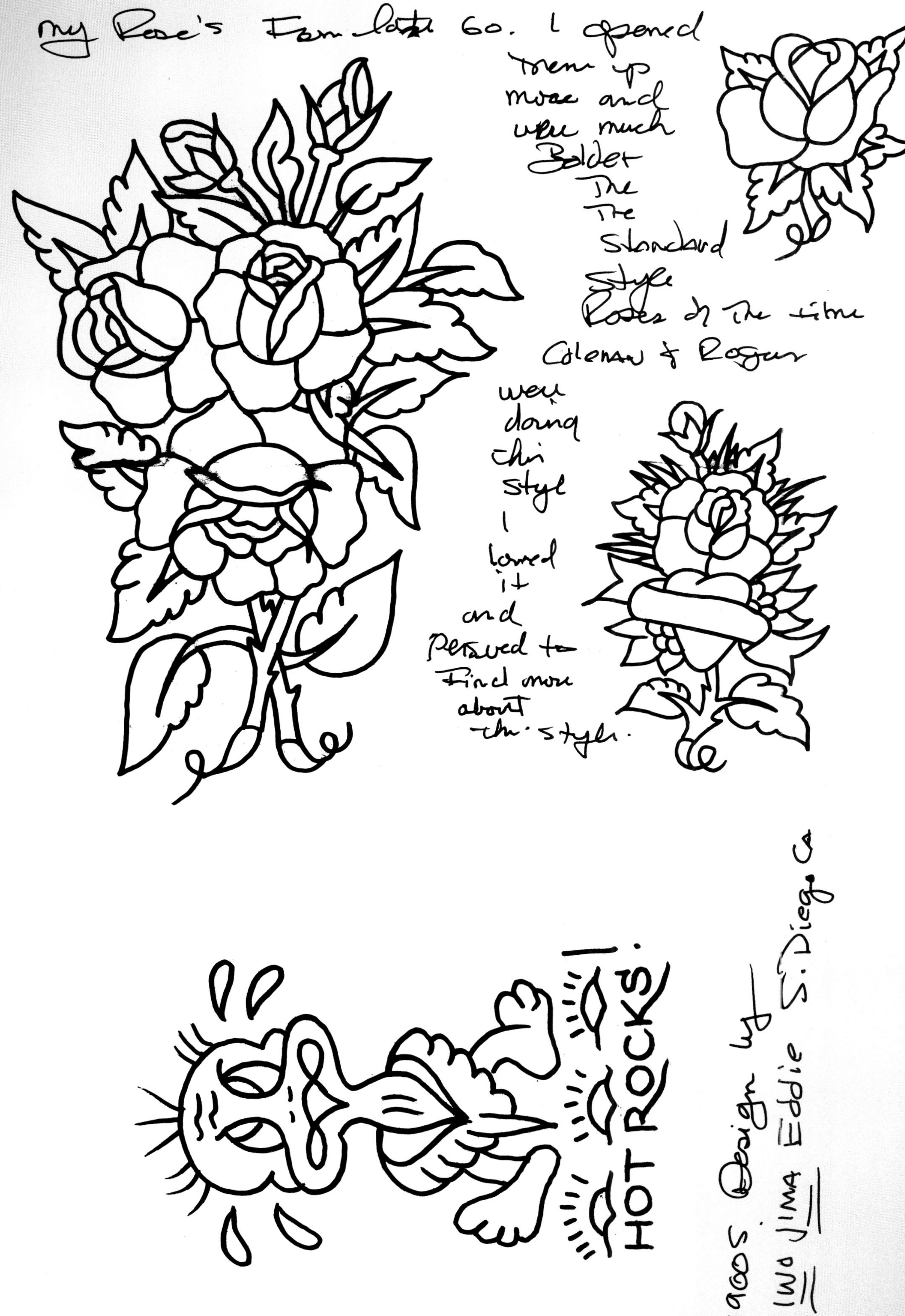
my Rose's Fam late 60. I opened
them up
more and
were much
Bolder
The
The
Standard
Style
Roses of the time
Coleman & Rogers
were
doing
this
style
I
loved
it
and
persued to
Find more
about
this style.
HOT ROCKS!
1960s Design by
Iwo Jima Eddie S. Diego Ca

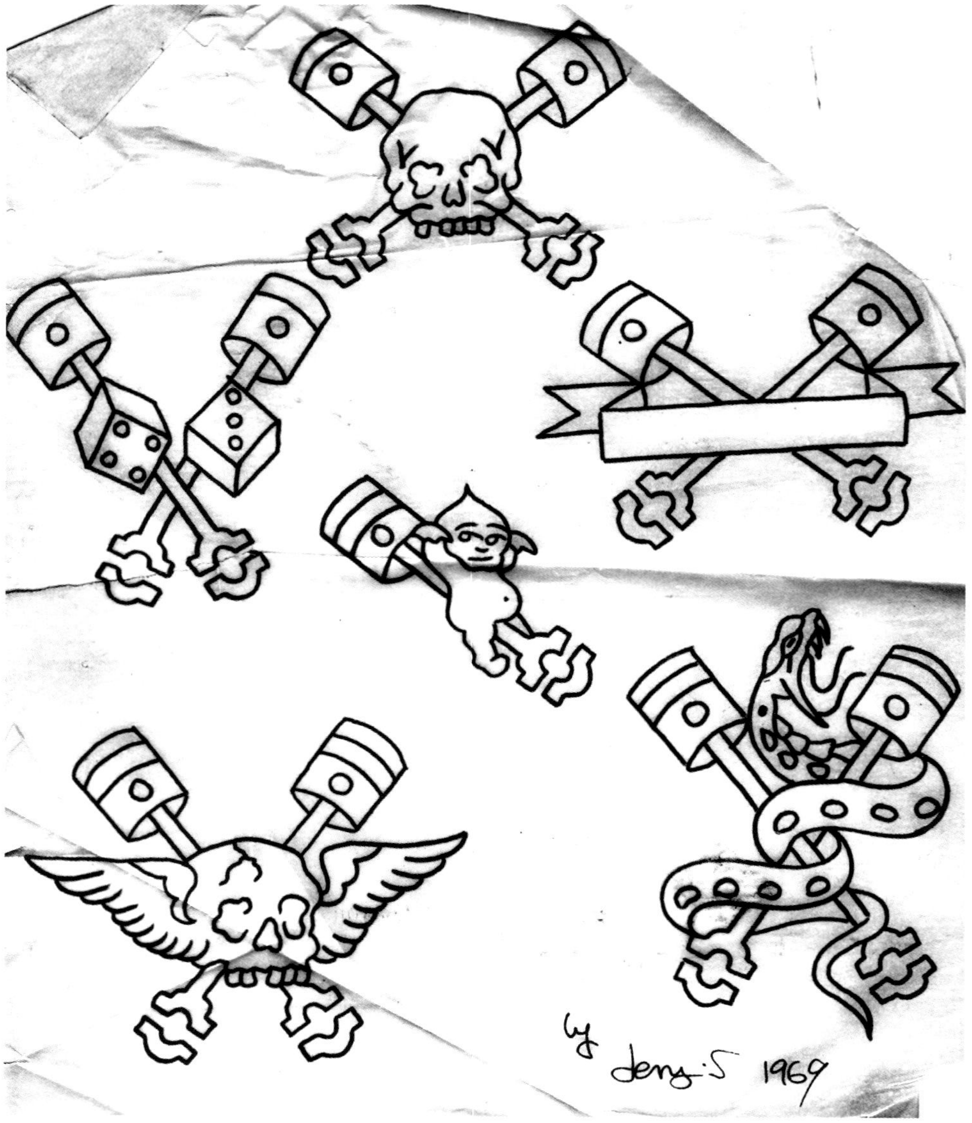

by Jerry S 1969

This stuff was "considered new" in 69 Charlie Snow hated changes and Hated this sheet.

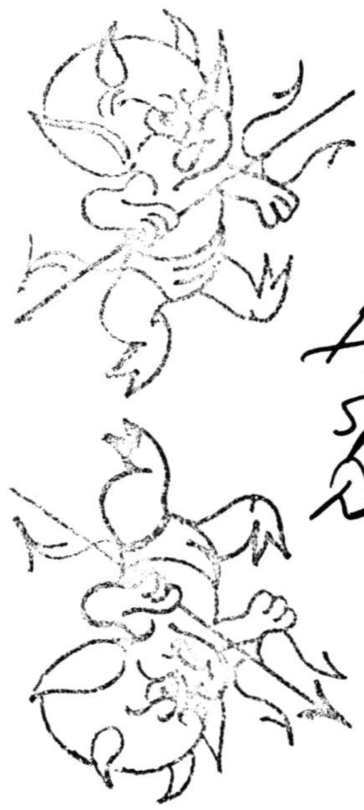

Huck Spaulding Devils

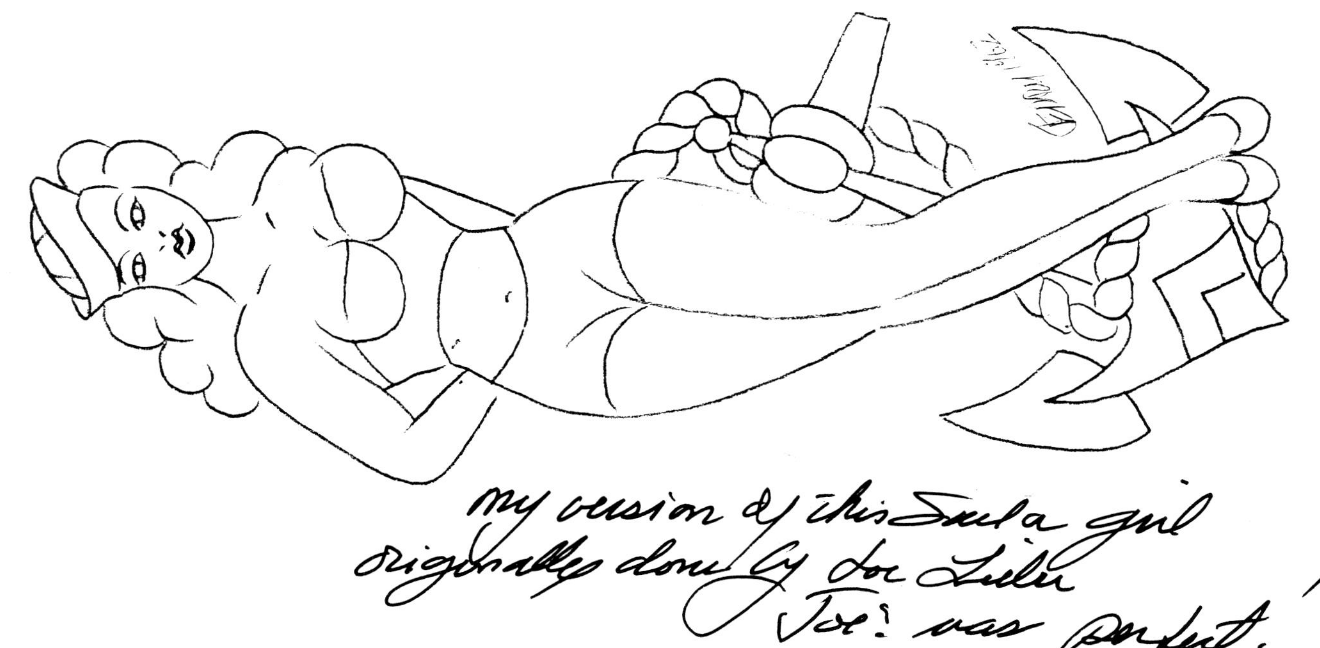

my version of this Hula girl originally done by Joe Lieber Joe! was perfect!

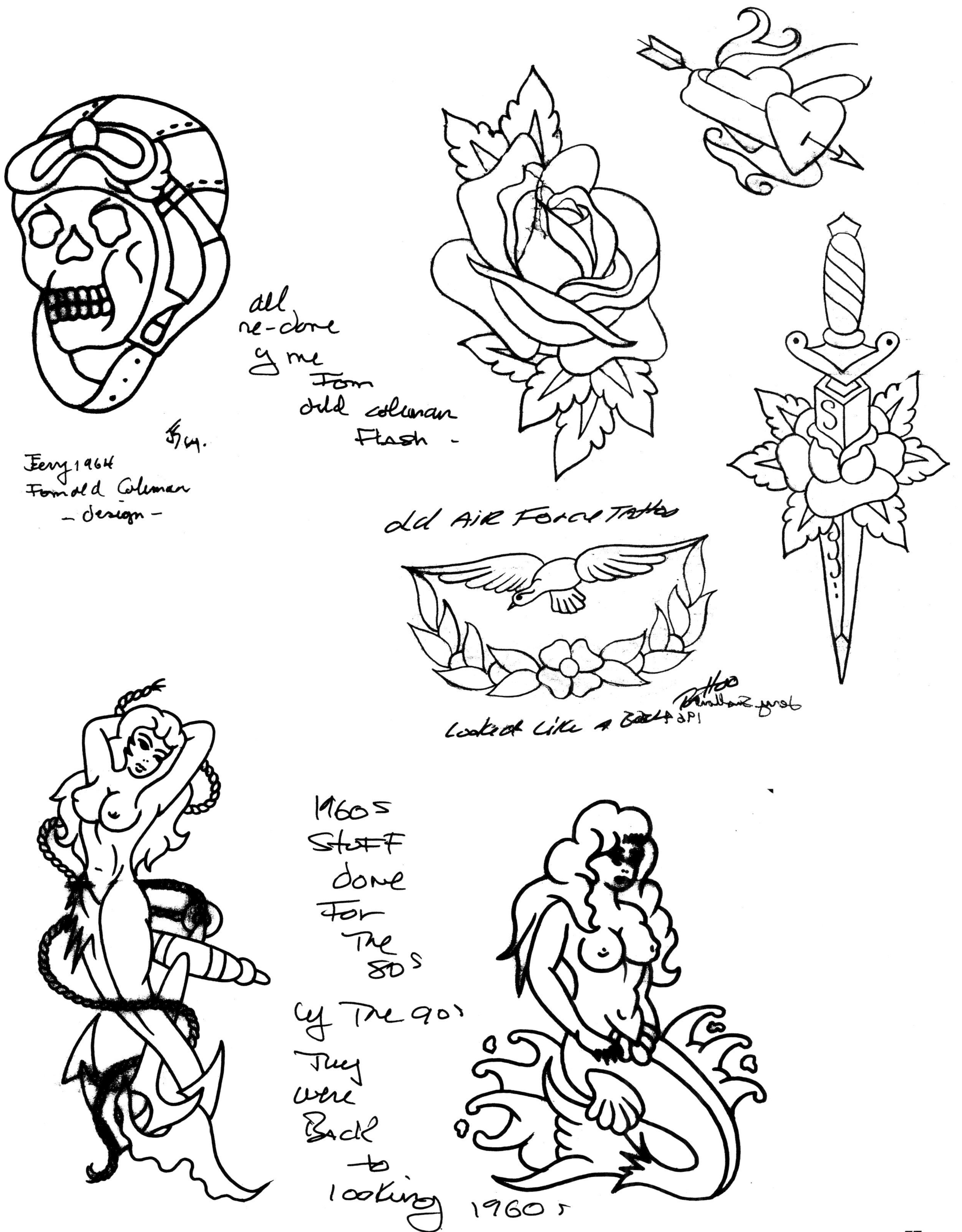

all re-done by me from old coleman Flash -
Jerry 1964 From old Coleman - design -
old Air Force Tattoo
1960s Stuff done for The 80s & The 90s They were Back to looking 1960s

all old stuff from Snow
liberty Baldwin Forbes
that I took and rebuilt
to look clean and
Bold easy to
line and could
tell what it
was from across the street.

Jerry Swallow
60's

LAST PORT

A SAILOR'S GRAVE

one of
Pauls
Paratrooper
designs
this is
a first
rough
drawing
he
cleaned
it up
later

1960S
P Rogers

I used
to draw my
stuff 3 or
4 times for I got
that & when
I was happy with it

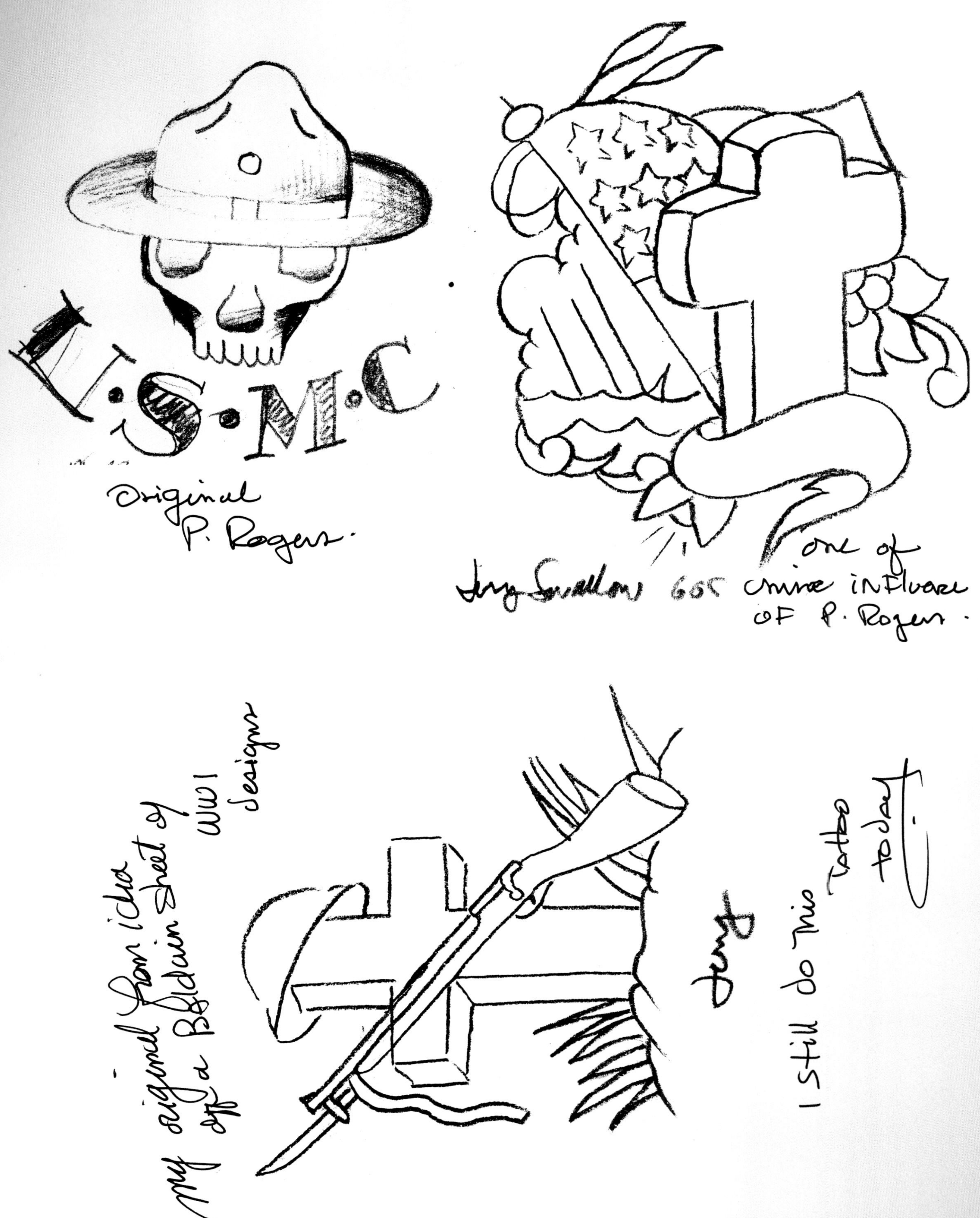
U.S.M.C
Original
P. Rogers.
one of
Jerry Swallow 60s cruise influence
of P. Rogers.
My original from idea
off a Baldwin sheet of
WW1
designs
Jerry
I still do this tattoo
today.

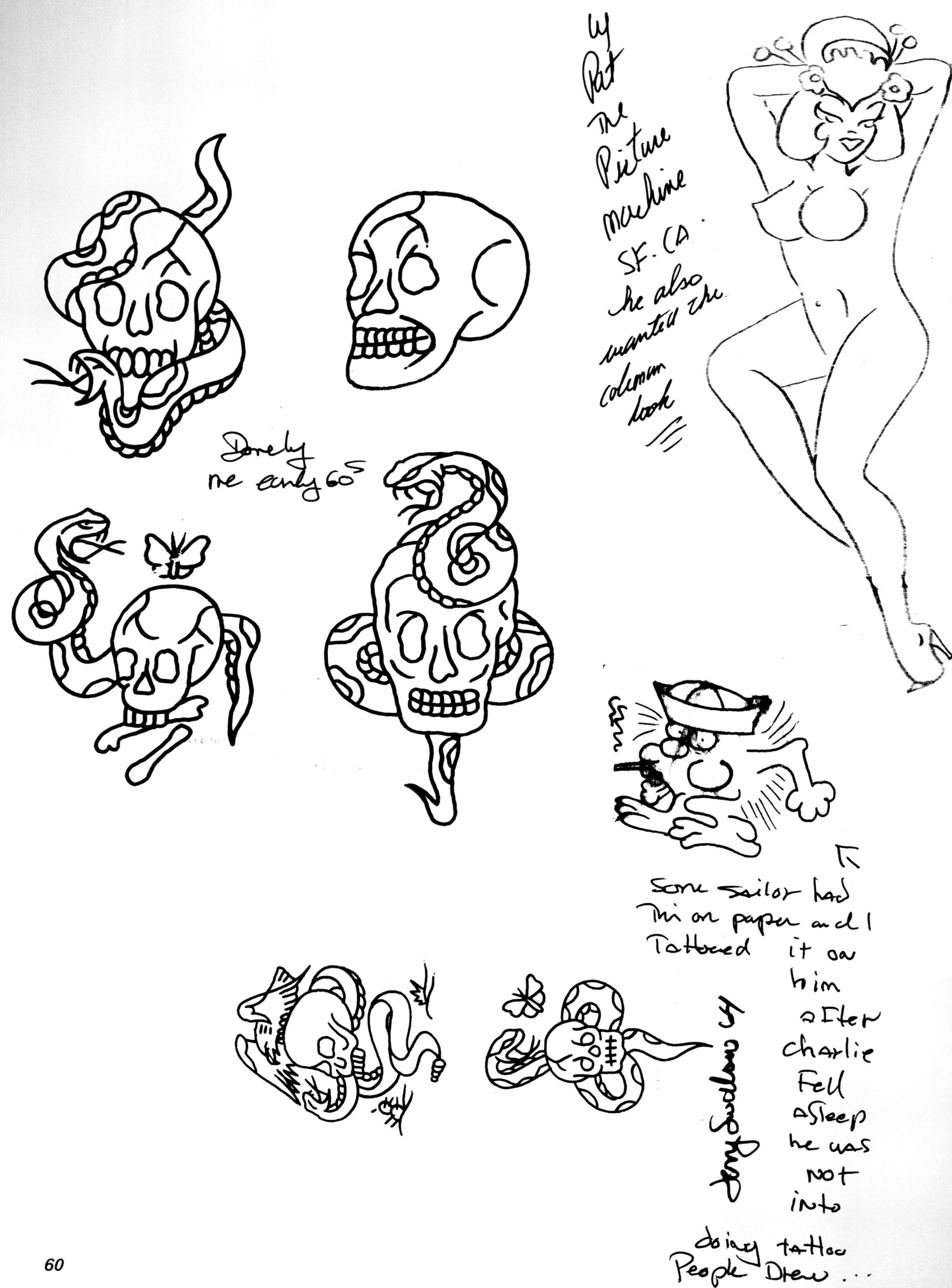
by Pat
the Picture machine
SF. CA.
he also wanted the coleman look
Done by me early 60s
Some sailor had this on paper and I Tattooed it on him after charlie Fell asleep he was not into doing tattoo People Drew . . .

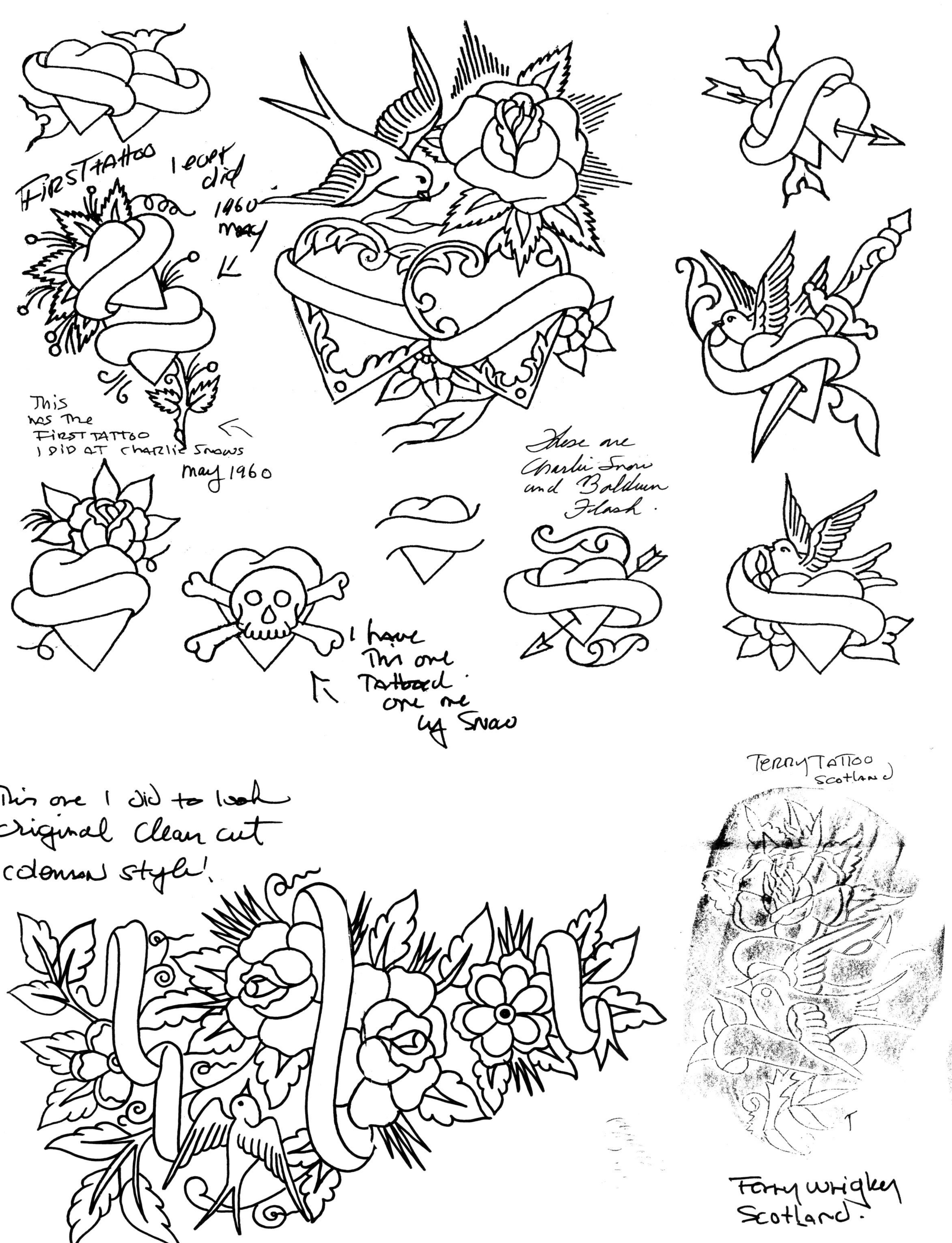
FIRST TATTOO I ever did 1960 May
This was the FIRST TATTOO I DID AT Charlie Snows May 1960
These are Charlie Snow and Baldwin Flash.
I have this one Tattooed on me by Snow
This one I did to look original clean cut coleman style!
TERRY TATTOO Scotland
Terry Wrigley Scotland.

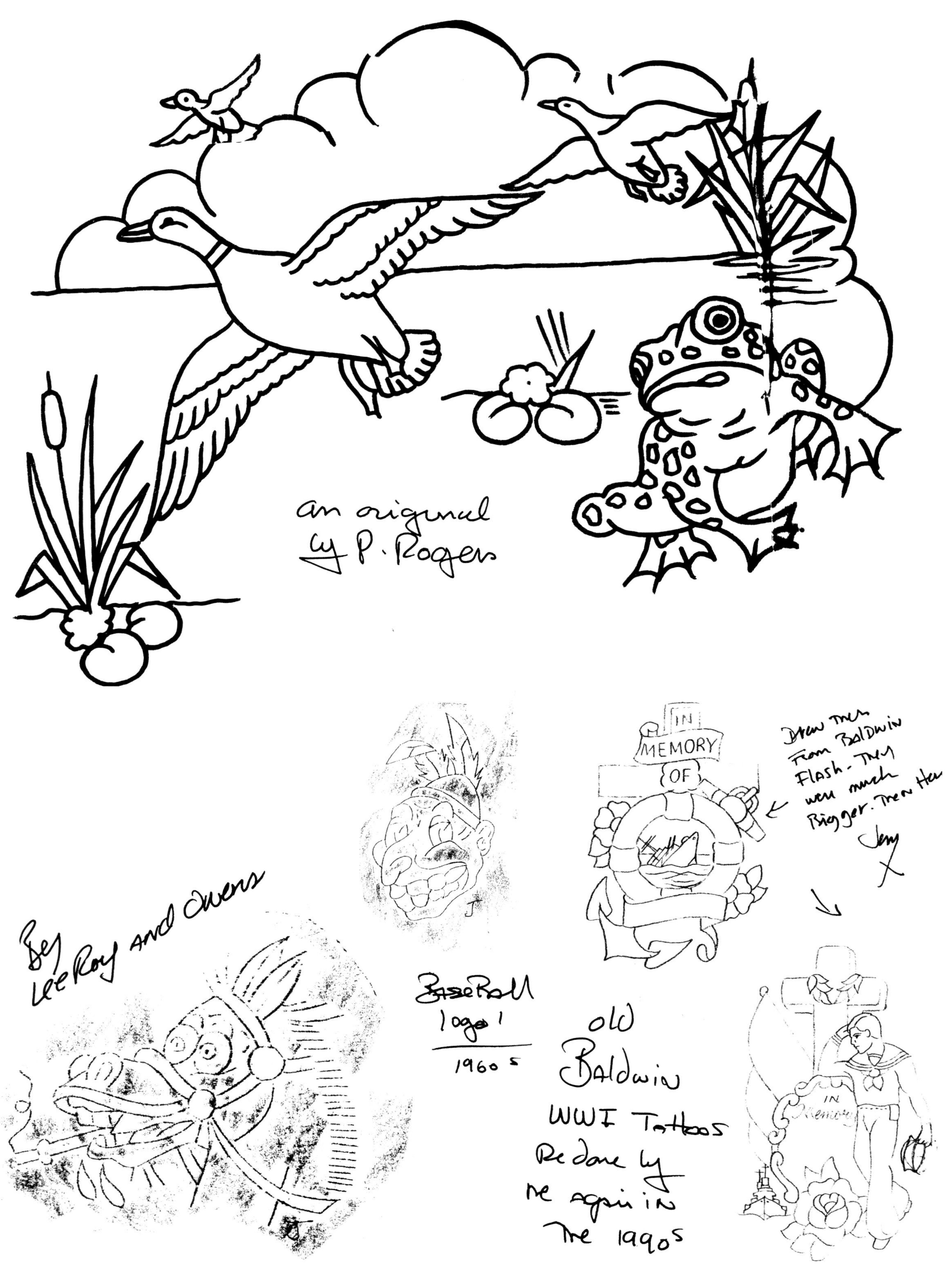
an original
by P. Rogers
IN
MEMORY
OF
Drew these
From Baldwin
Flash. They
were much
Bigger. Then these
Jerry
X
By
LeeRoy and Owens
BaseBall
logo!
1960s
old
Baldwin
WWI Tattoos
Redone by
me again in
the 1990s
IN
Memory

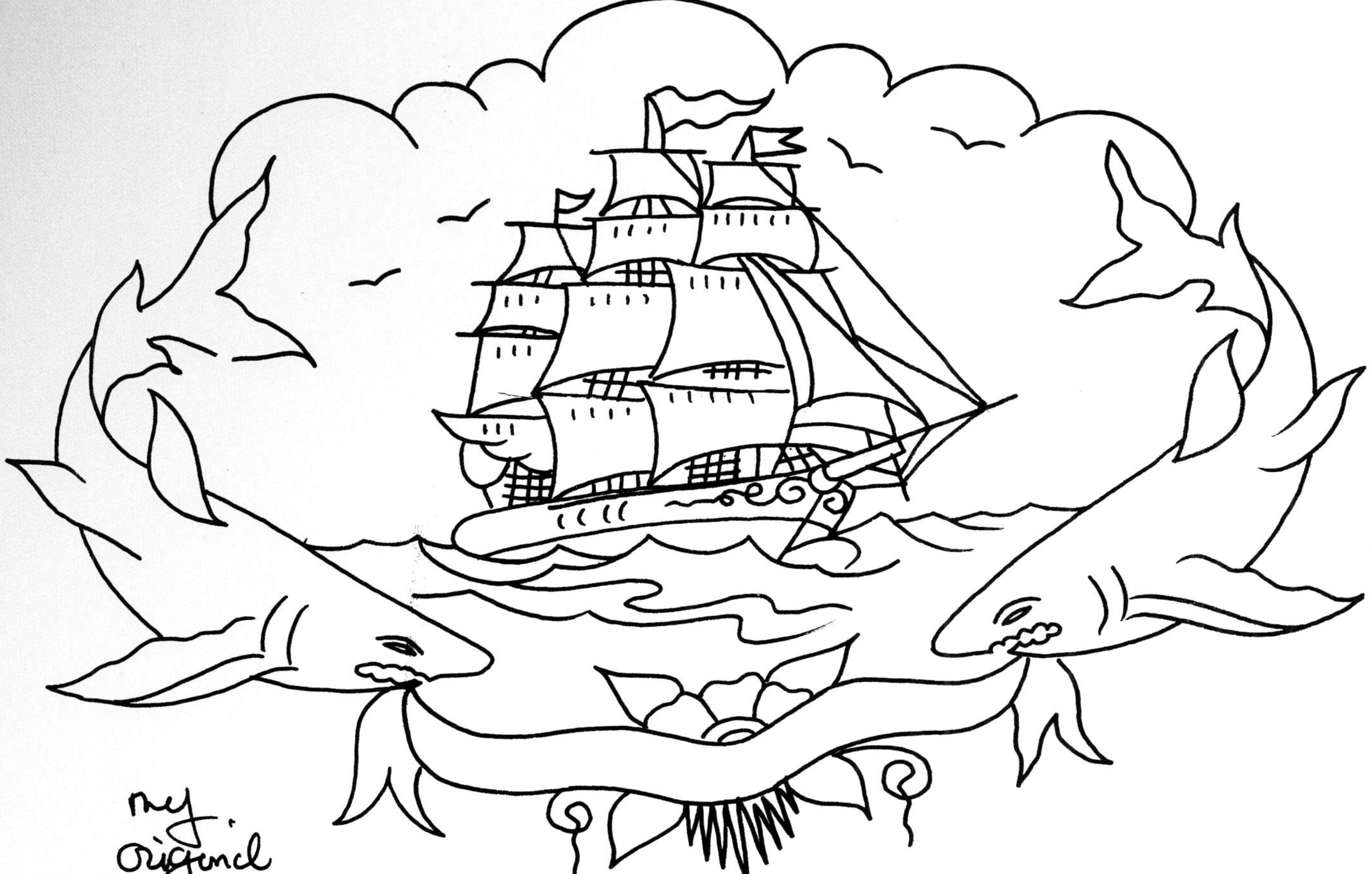

my original
a got the idea From a Joe Lieber desing
and went n done my own thing to it,
and done it with Flags and Eagle as well.

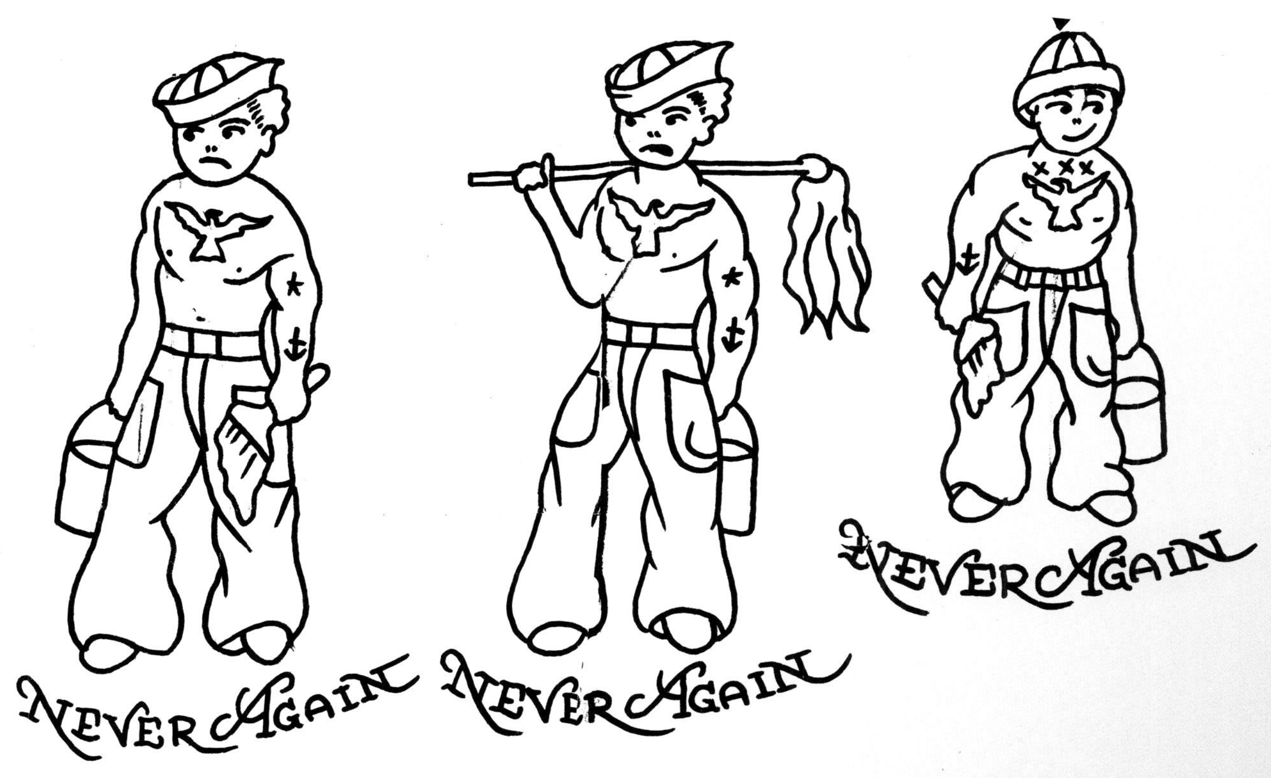

were Charlie Barrs design at First
done again by Hank Spaulding and several others
These are my versions · 1969

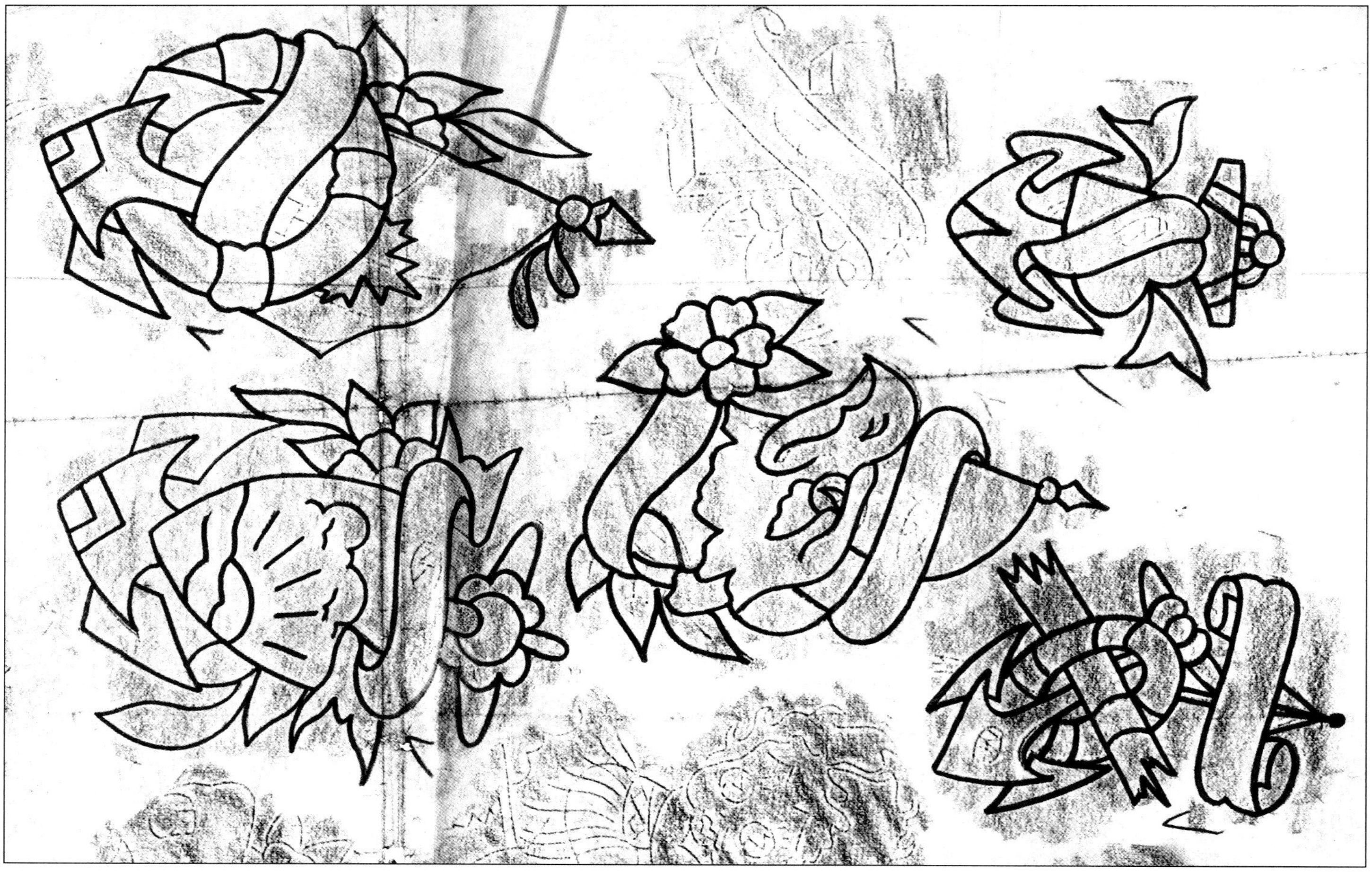

Sailor Jerry Collins Stencil prints
I went over them to change the look.
These were First done Joe Lieber and C Barr

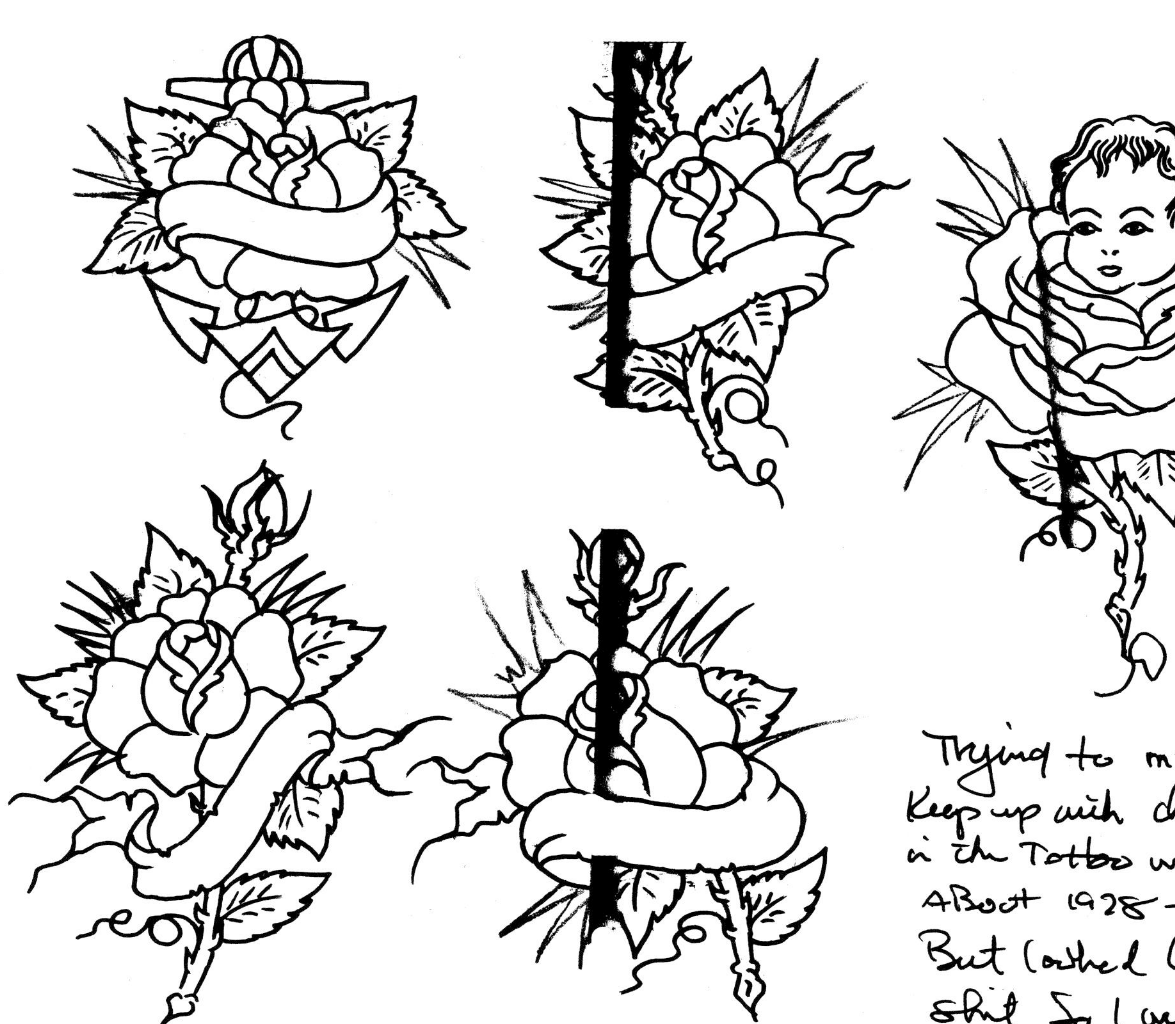

Trying to modernize
Keep up with changes
in the Tattoo world.
About 1928 —
But looked like
shit So I went
back to 60s look!

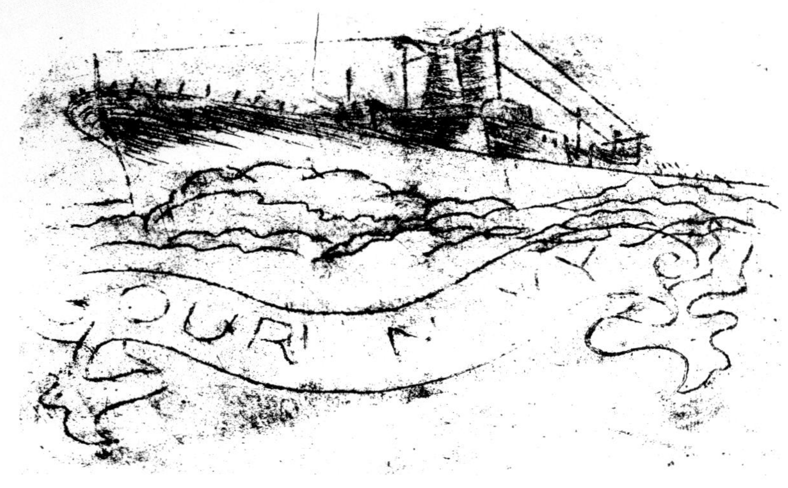

original by
Doc Forbes

Charlie Barr
and
Cap Colman

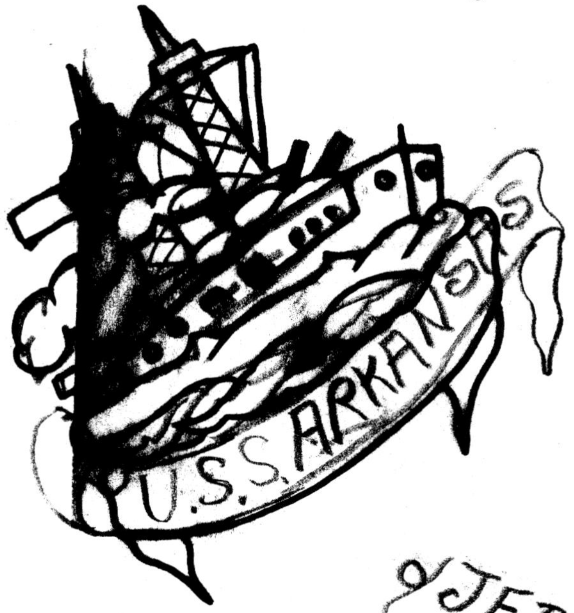

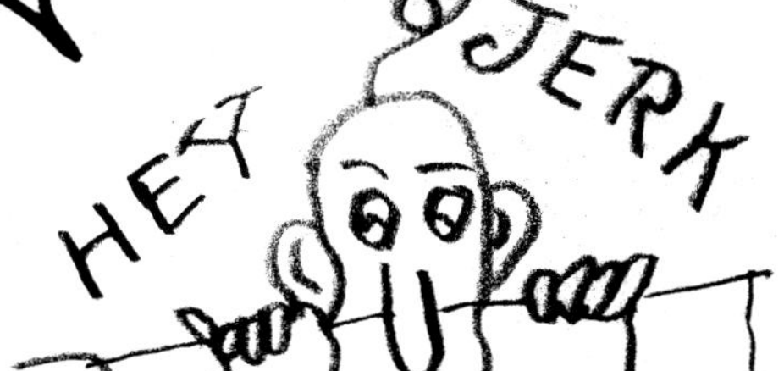

U.S.S. ARKANSAS

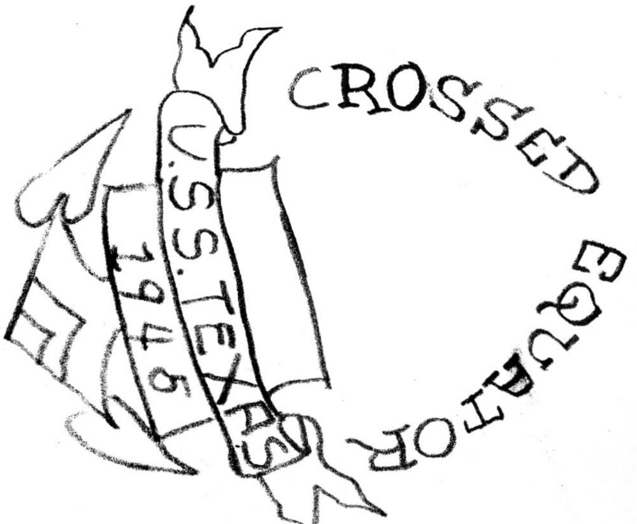

CROSSED EQUATOR

U.S.S. TEXAS
1945

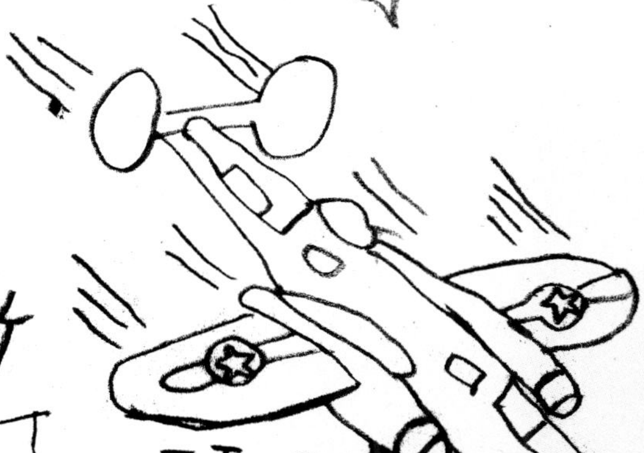

HEY JERK

U.S.A.

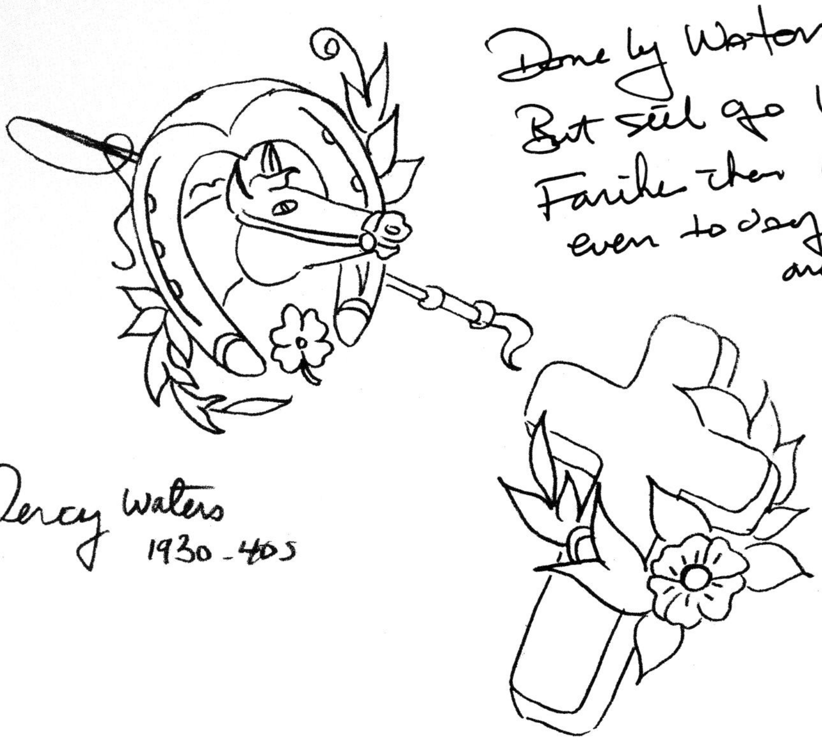

Done by Waters!
But still go back
Farther than him..
even to day there
are Tattooed
by same
artists.

Percy Waters
1930-40s

Charlie Barr
design.

by
Cap Coleman

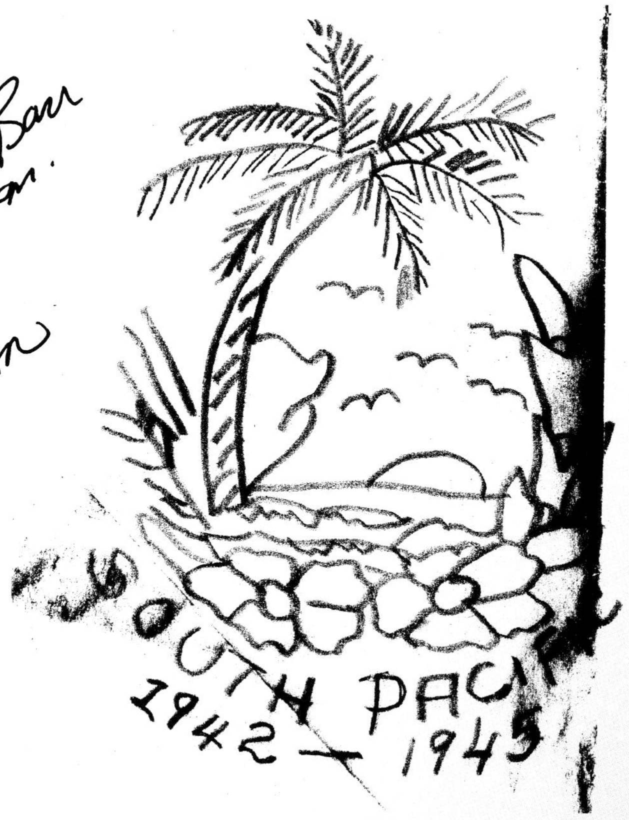

SOUTH PAC
1942 - 1945

originally done by Joe Lieber and re done several ways by several

SWEETNESS

Eddy 2007

Tattooed over the years Jerry Collins Coleman Spaulding - Rogers etc.

A Huck Spaulding very early on in his career

Practise makes Perfect! Huck was one of The Best!

Pirate girl from a stencil of the 1930s.

Small Jerry Swallow 1970

Charlie Barr design. Redone by.

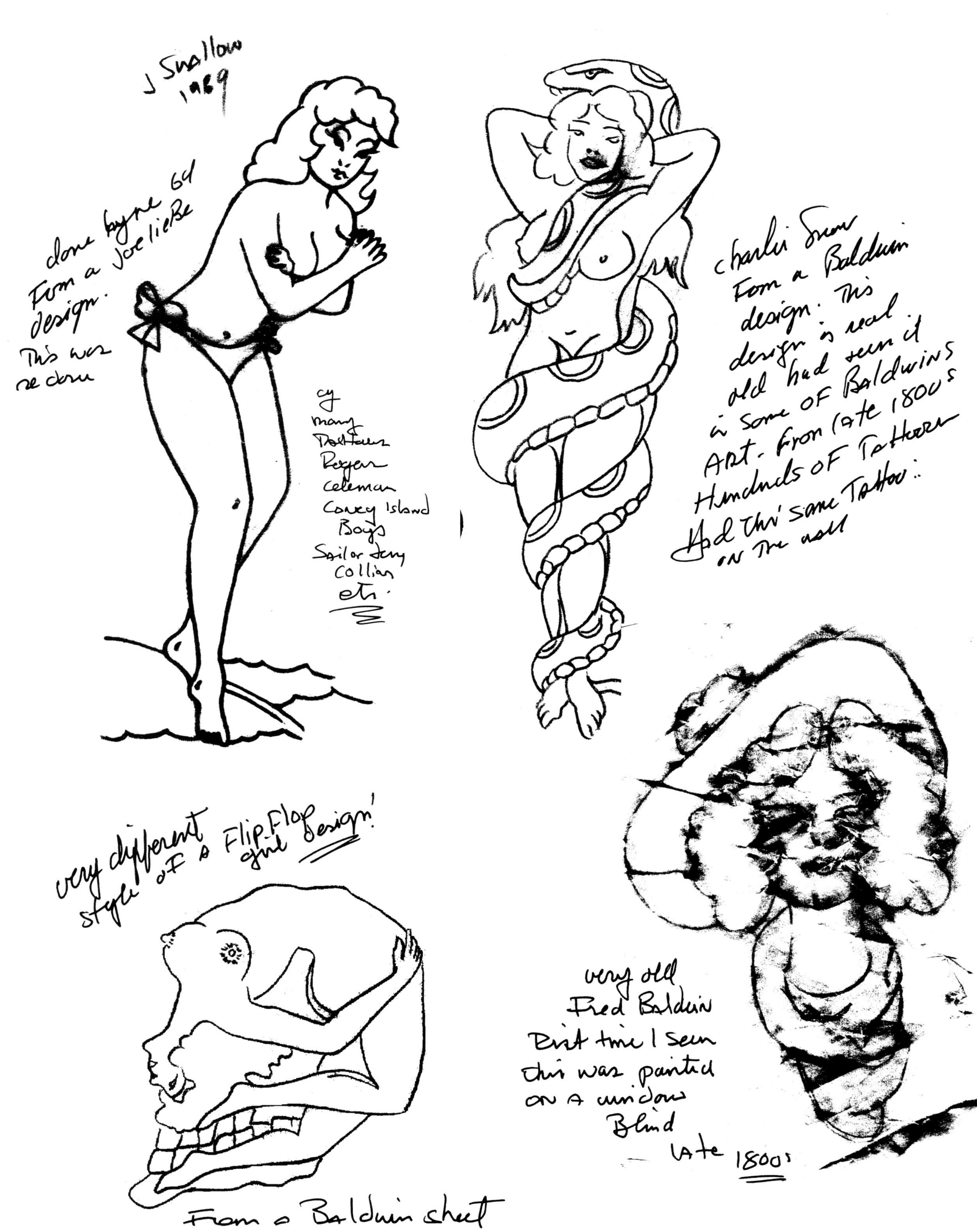
J Swallow 1969
done by me 64 From a Joe lieBe design. This was re done
cy many Dot Fowers Rogers Coleman Coney Island Boys Sailor Jerry Collins etc.
Charlie Snow From a Baldwin design. This design is real old had seen it in some of Baldwins Art. From late 1800's Hundreds of Tattoos Had this same Tattoo on the wall
very different style of a Flip Flop girl design!
From a Baldwin sheet -1914-
very old Fred Baldwin First time I seen this was painted on a window Blind late 1800's

Eagle anchor Flag design This is a Ted Liberty 50s style. But I seen this drawing like, in The few and many other Sailor Jerry Collins P. Rogers. Coleman et Owen Jensen and Wagner as well as Bill Jones done a nice version of this

TED LIBERTY

if you see new school tattoos like this They look more realistic But where would we be done on! if The old times were

when I first started in 1960 The finest Tattoos I ever saw were done by Cap Coleman and Paul Rogers and I wanted to Tattoo like That

1969

One of them 1964 Drawn off a Baldwin sheet from 1900 Later I seen This done by 50 + other Tattooers. Joe Lieber done The Best version

One of my designs in about 64 Trying to catch on to That Rogers Coleman look

Terry

Gene spent a few months with me in about 71' I helped him with his tattooing a lot He got discouraged in the late 70s. and quit!

1970 Designs by Gene Hall who studied under LeRoy And Jensen in Long Beach Gene was 50+ yrs old when he started out never got to far He was a nice person many used him!

Gene ~~Dean~~ Pretty Nice Tattoo designs

Ted Tattooed in Boston Then in Halifax with Mr. Snow He went to B.C Canada and worked years There Know as Capt' Ted

1950's Ted Liberty unique for Ted.

Ted Liberty

Original Doc Forbes Famous Canadian Tattooer learned the art from Prof. Fred Baldwin who taught Charlie Snow who taught me.

Doc was friends with Huck Spaulding Indian design you can see

Forbes

Forbes

1960's The Spaulding - Coleman look too.

old navy designs by Spaulding Rogers
Early 1960s

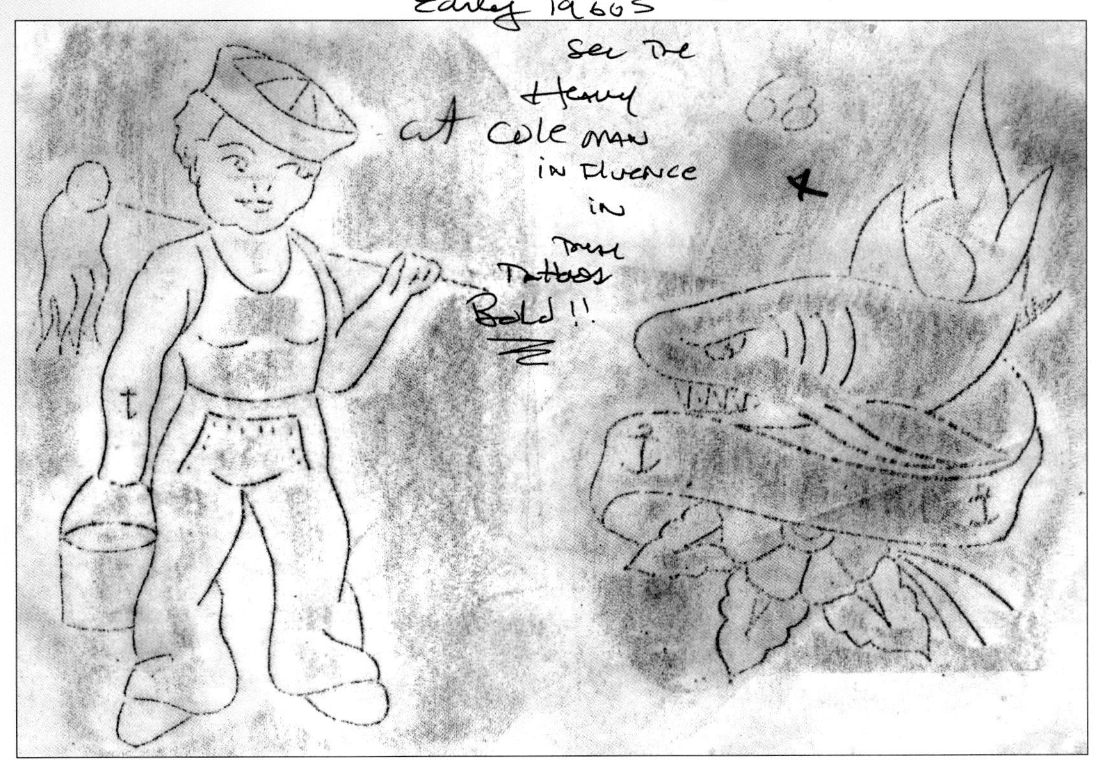

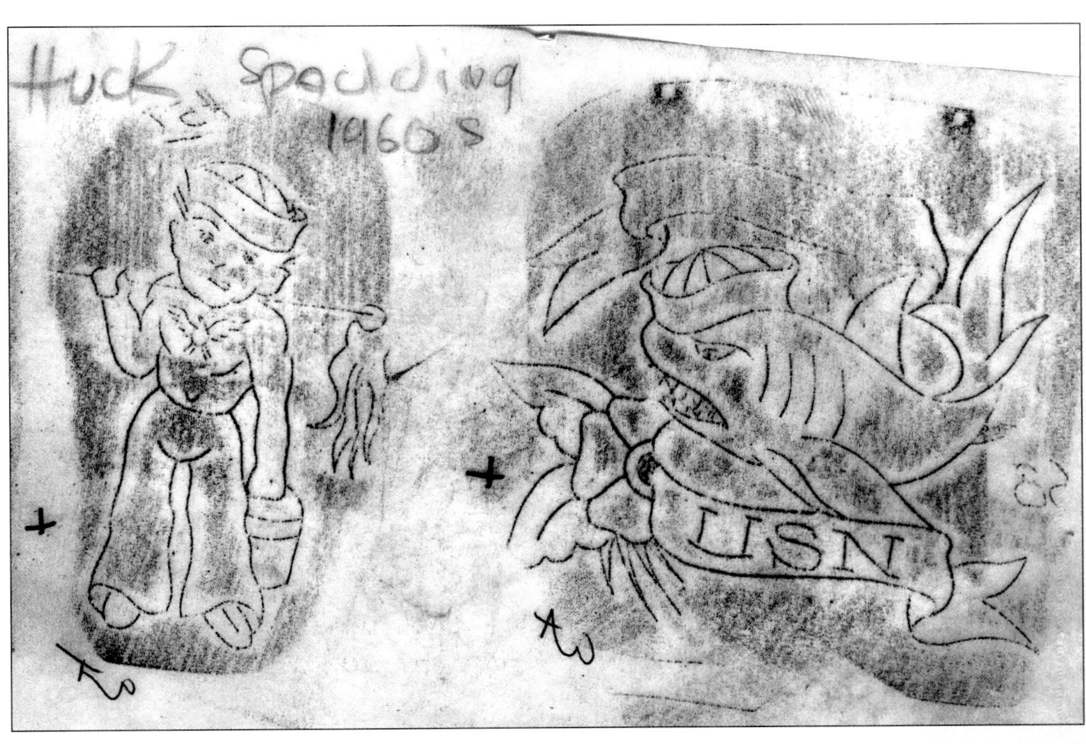

Huck Spaulding via Cap Coleman

Huck Spaulding original

Tattoo designs by Ted Liberty of Boston's Liberty Brothers

Ted worked w/ charlie Snow off n on in 1950.s These daggers go Back to The 20s even today Dagger design are done Pretty much The Same look.

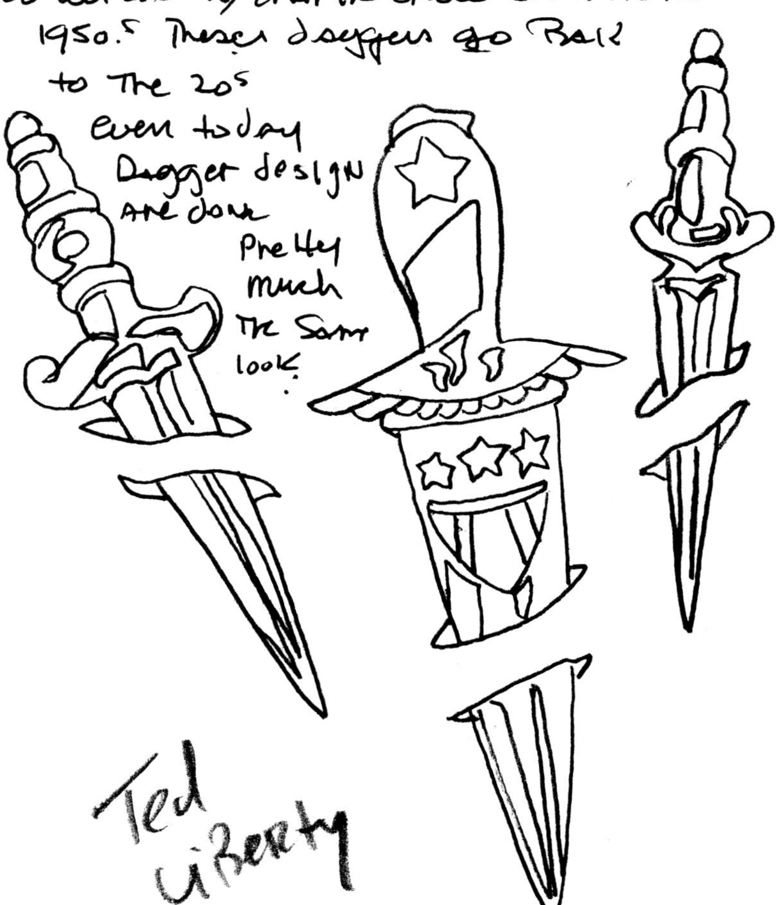

Sailor girl a classic Tatto! Done by Every Tattoo artist ever n doubt!! The original artist of this classic tattoo was Brooklyn Joe Lieber not 3y very well known tattooer of the past it was first done by Lieber and that like 1920s But every one who ve done this made it look pretty much The same This one was done by Paul Rogers! I done it to my own version as well but it still looked like it why change a perfect thing

Panther Head by Cap Coleman He had about The Best style of The time.

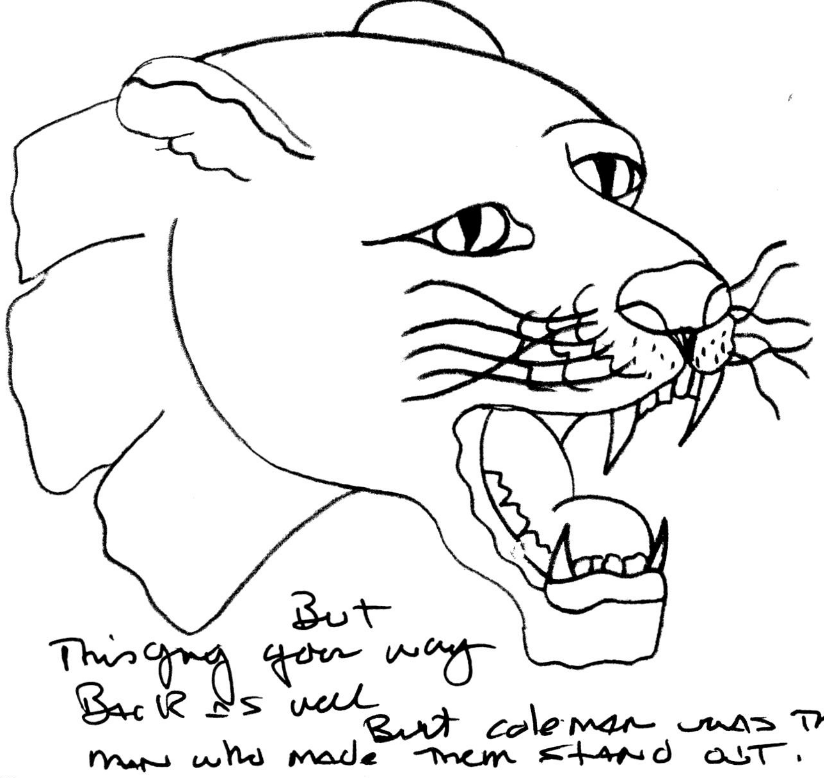

But This one goes way Back as well But coleman was The man who made them stand out.

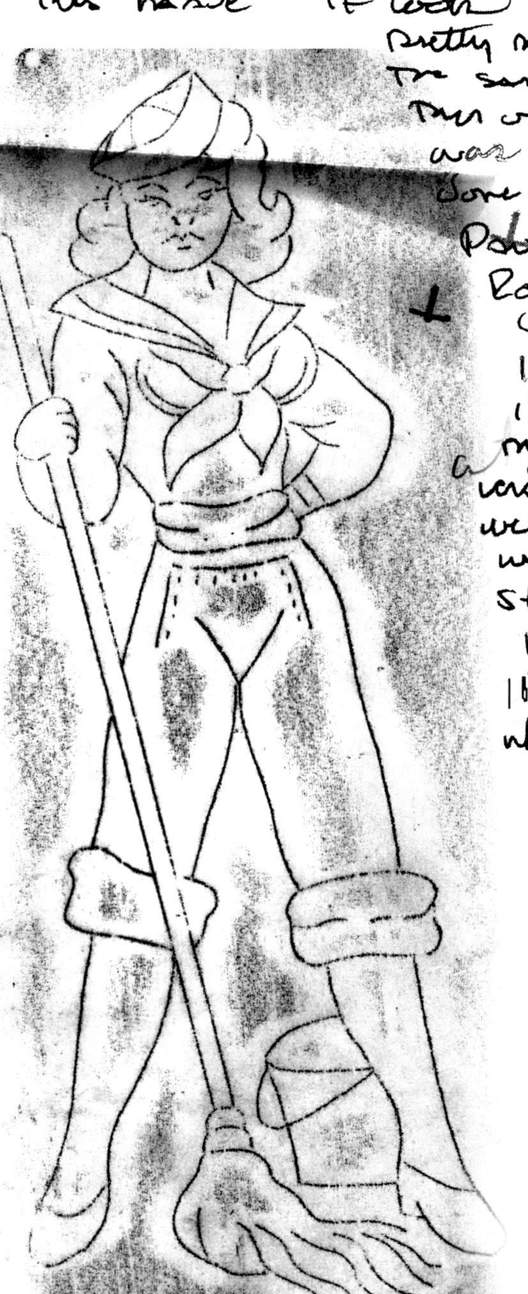

Hock Spaulding Devil

This one with a NAZI Helmet on!

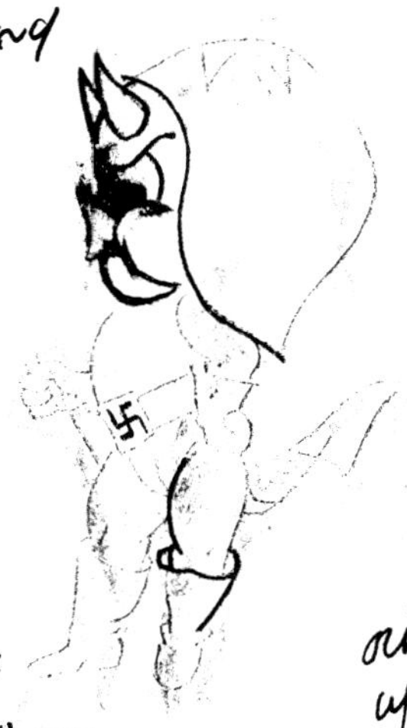

Hot Stuff was a popular Tattoo Done with every kind of occupation in mind From Sailor Devil to Police Devil.

original by Hank Spaulding 1960s

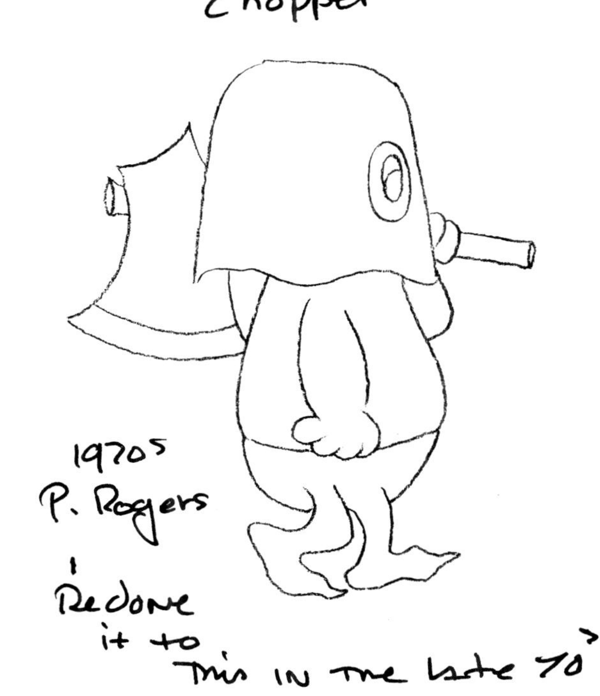

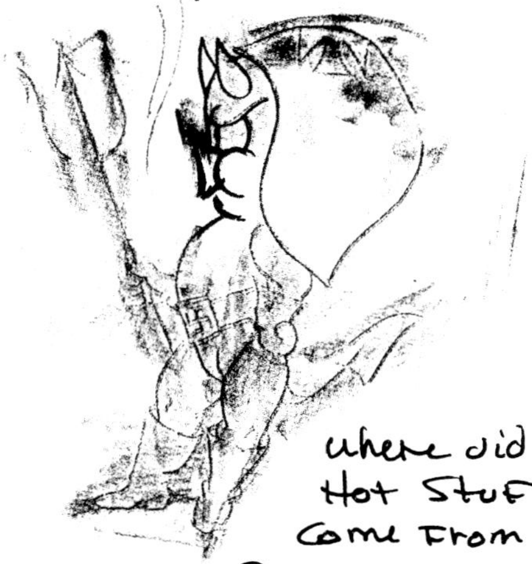

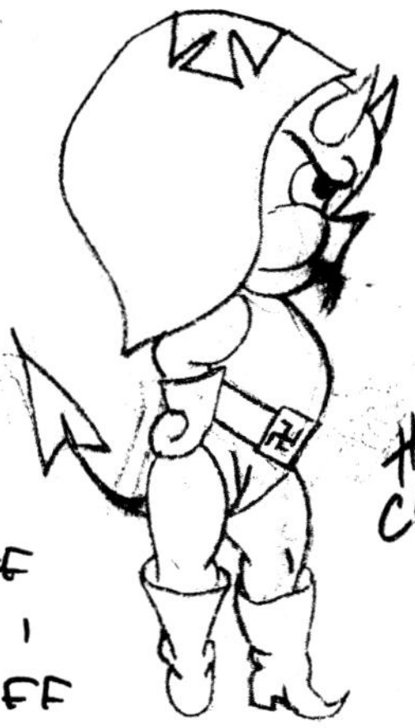

CUT

where did Hot Stuff come from, I seen Hot Stuff years ago done by Percy Waters in the 30s I dont know if He is that old ?.

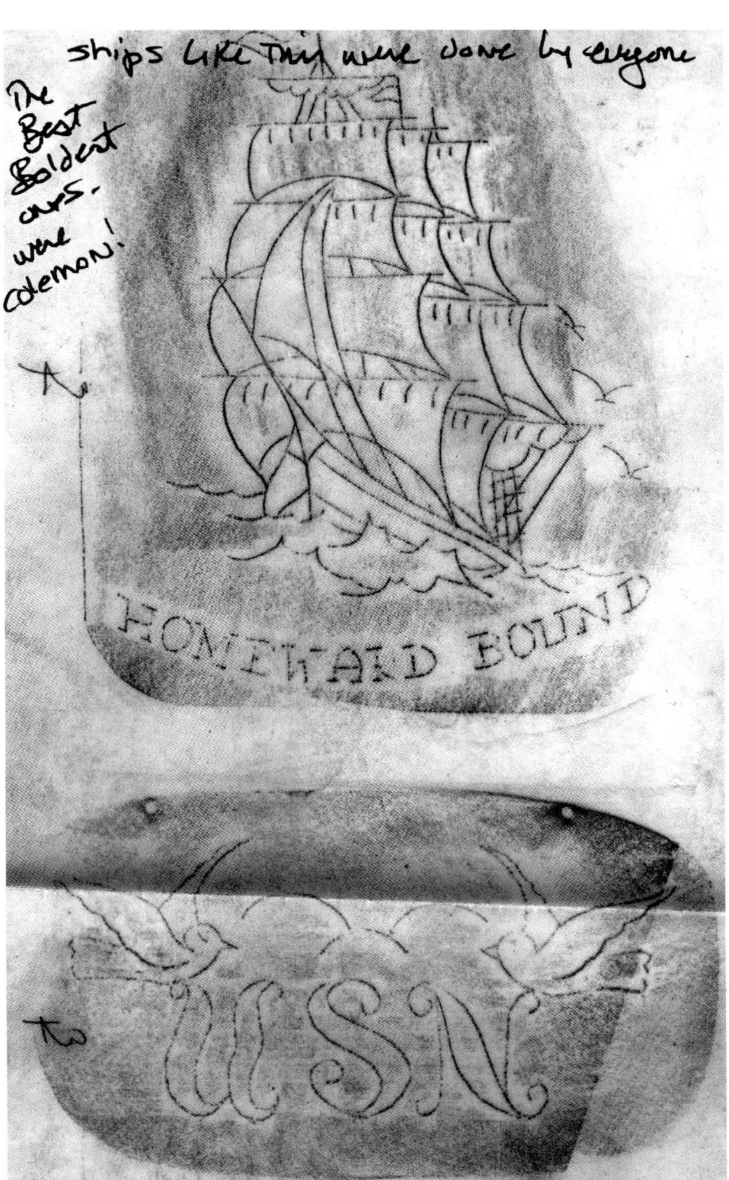

Re-done by everyone even my self. great style....

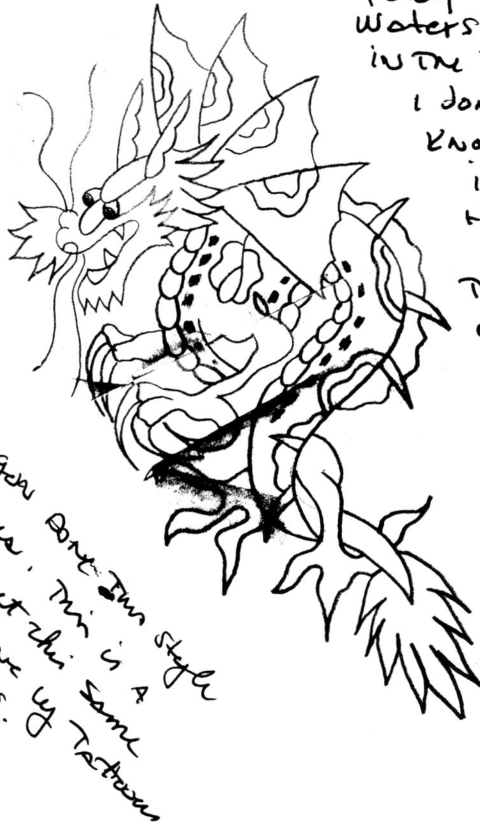

Classic old Dragon Done this style for 50 60 years. This is a Paul Rogers, But this same style was done by Tattooers in the 1920s.

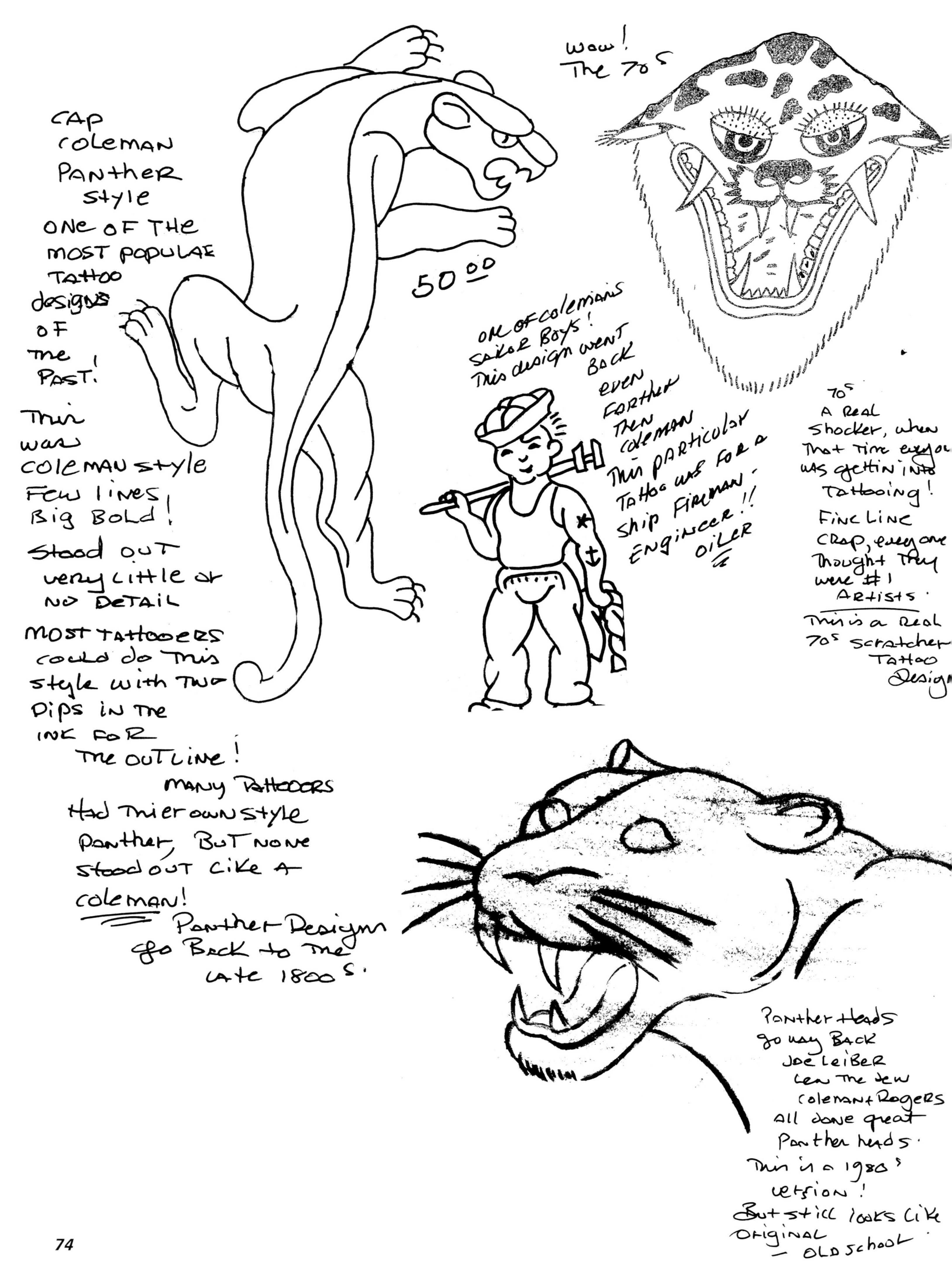

CAP COLEMAN PANTHER STYLE ONE OF THE MOST POPULAR TATTOO designs OF THE PAST!
This was COLEMAN style Few lines, Big Bold! Stood OUT very Little or NO DETAIL
MOST TATTOOERS could do This style with Two Dips in The ink FOR The OUTLINE!
MANY TATTOOERS Had Thier own style panther, But none stood out like A coleman!
Panther Designs go Back to The Late 1800s.
50.00
Wow! The 70s
One of colemans Sailor Boys! This design went Back even Farther Then coleman
This particular Tattoo was for a ship Fireman - Engineer!! Oiler
70s A Real Shocker, when That Time everyone was gettin into Tattooing!
Fine Line Crap, everyone Thought They were #1 Artists.
This is a Real 70s scratcher Tattoo Design
Panther Heads go way Back Joe Leiber Len The Jew coleman + Rogers All done great Panther heads.
This is a 1980s version! But still looks like original - OLD School

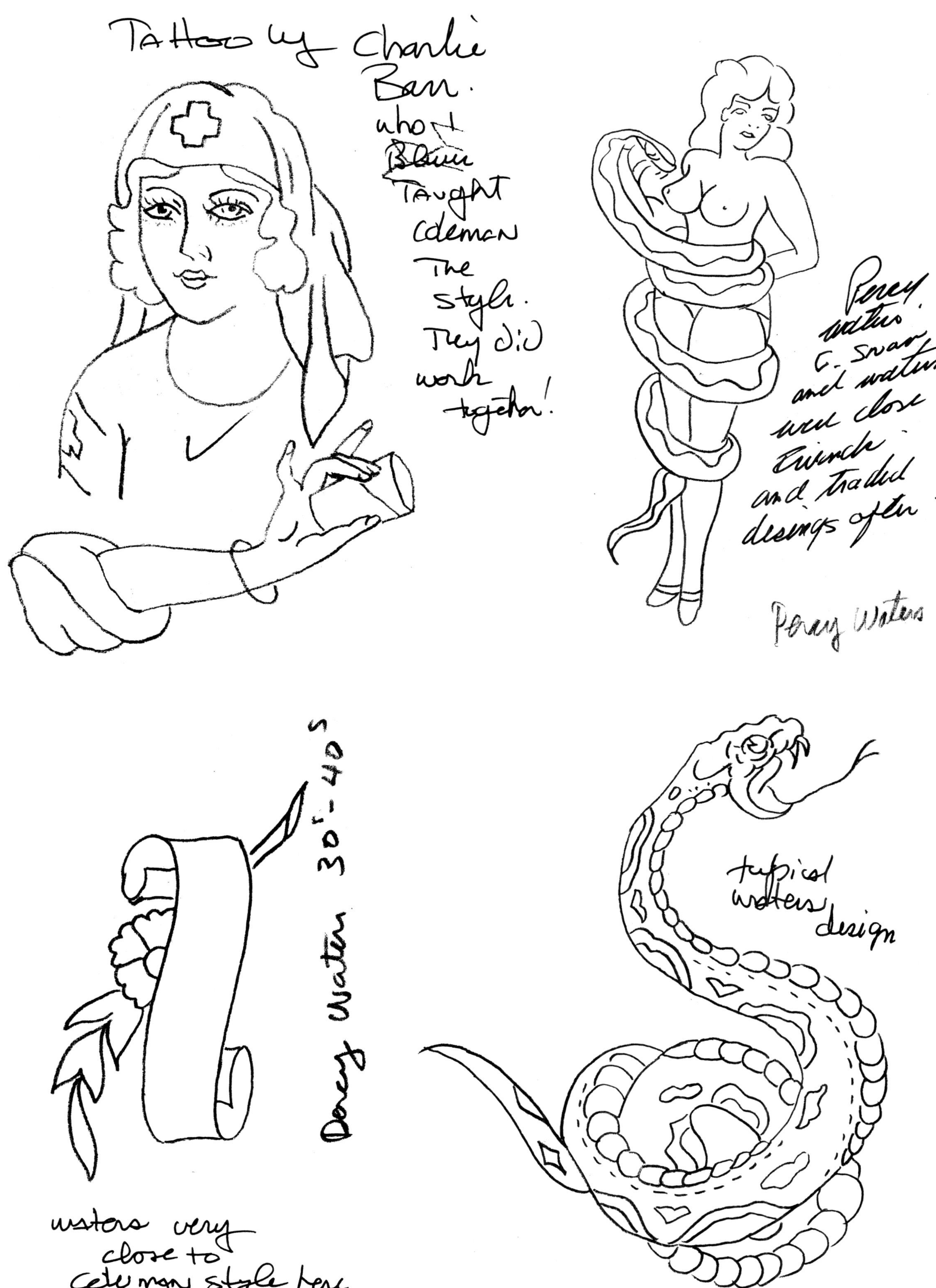
Tattoo by Charlie Barr. who Blum taught coleman the style. They did work together!
Percy. waters. G. Swan and waters were close friends and traded desings often
Percy Waters
Dorey Water 30's-40's
typical waters design
waters very close to coleman style here

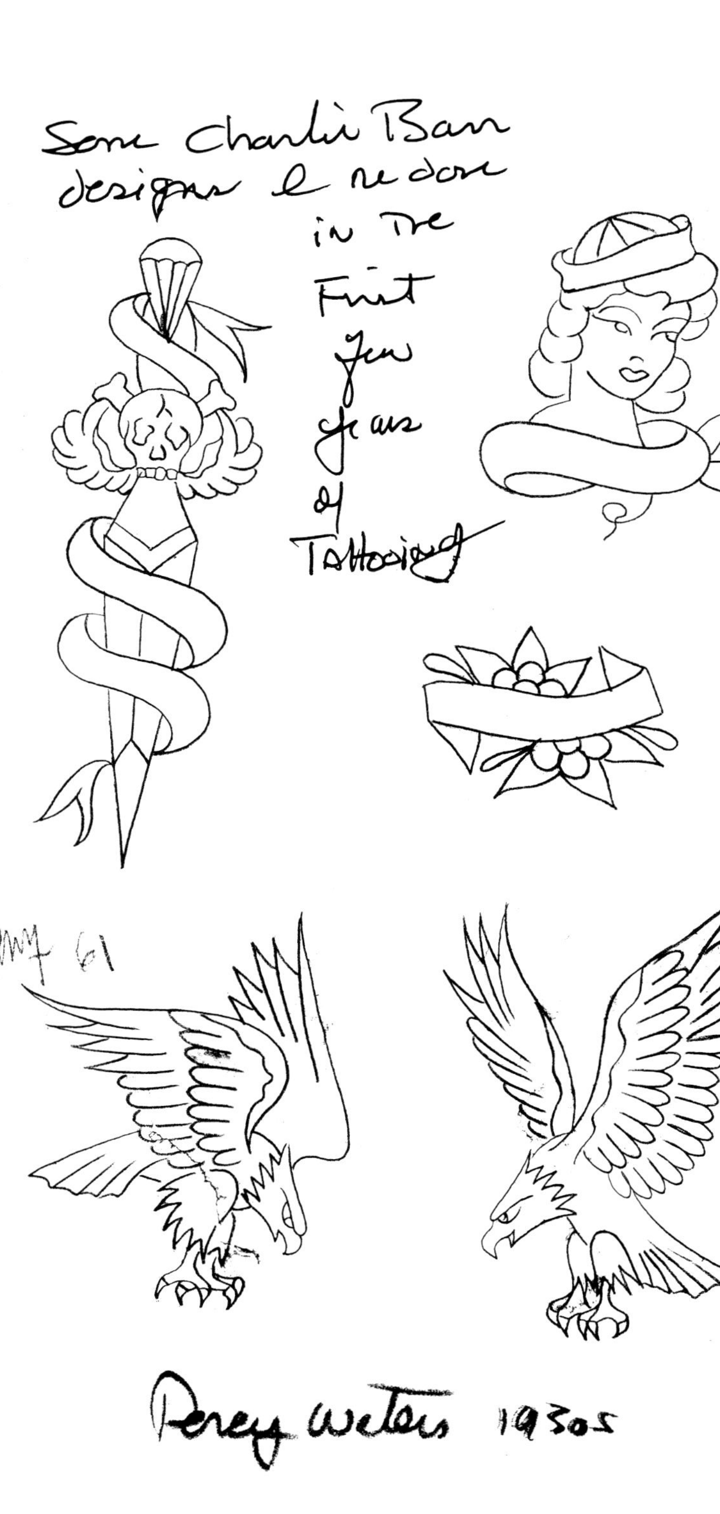

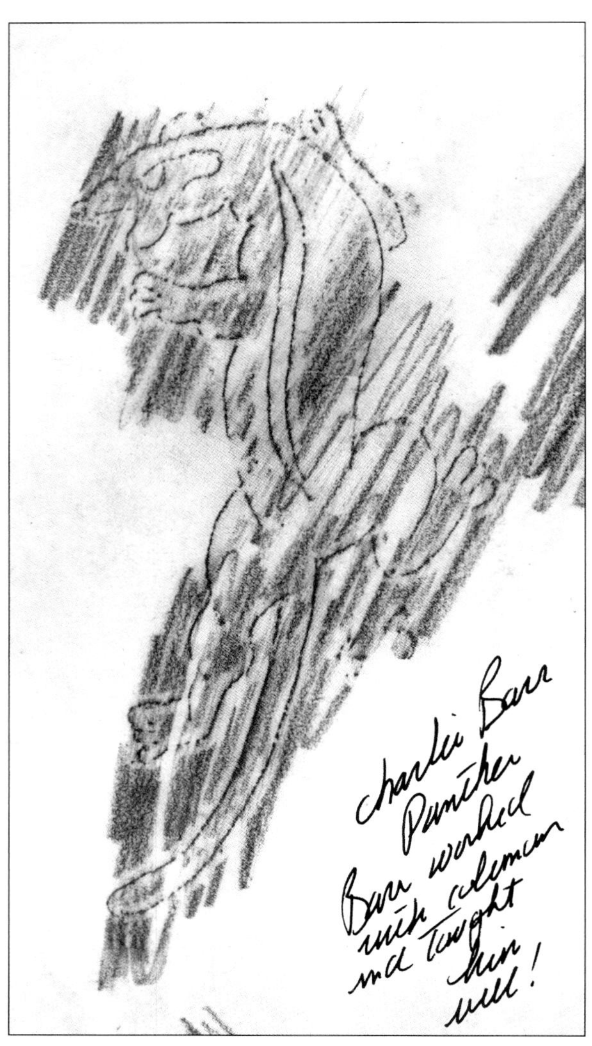

common design even
in the 30s. Coleman Rogers
done a great one
of
them
as
well

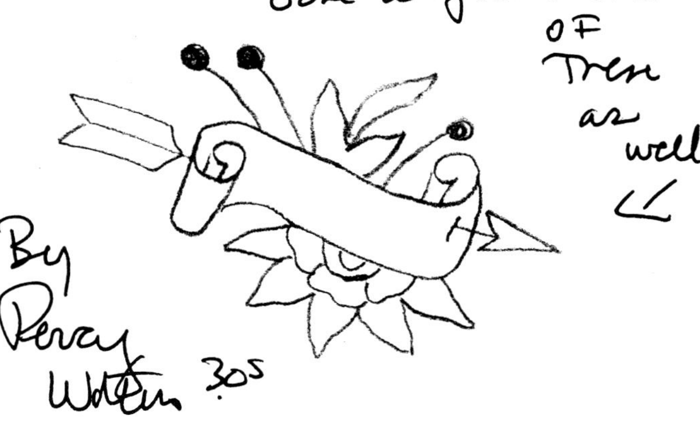

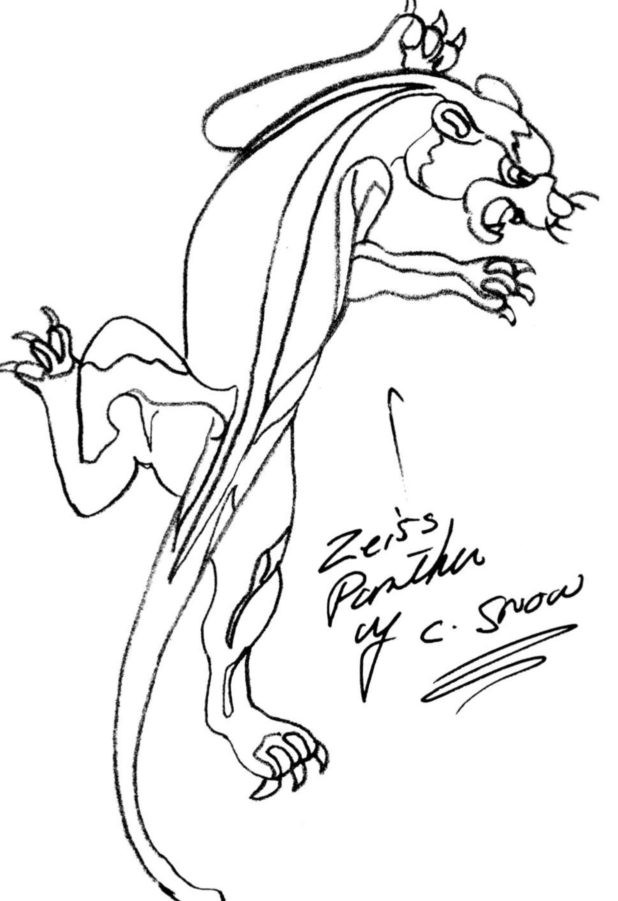

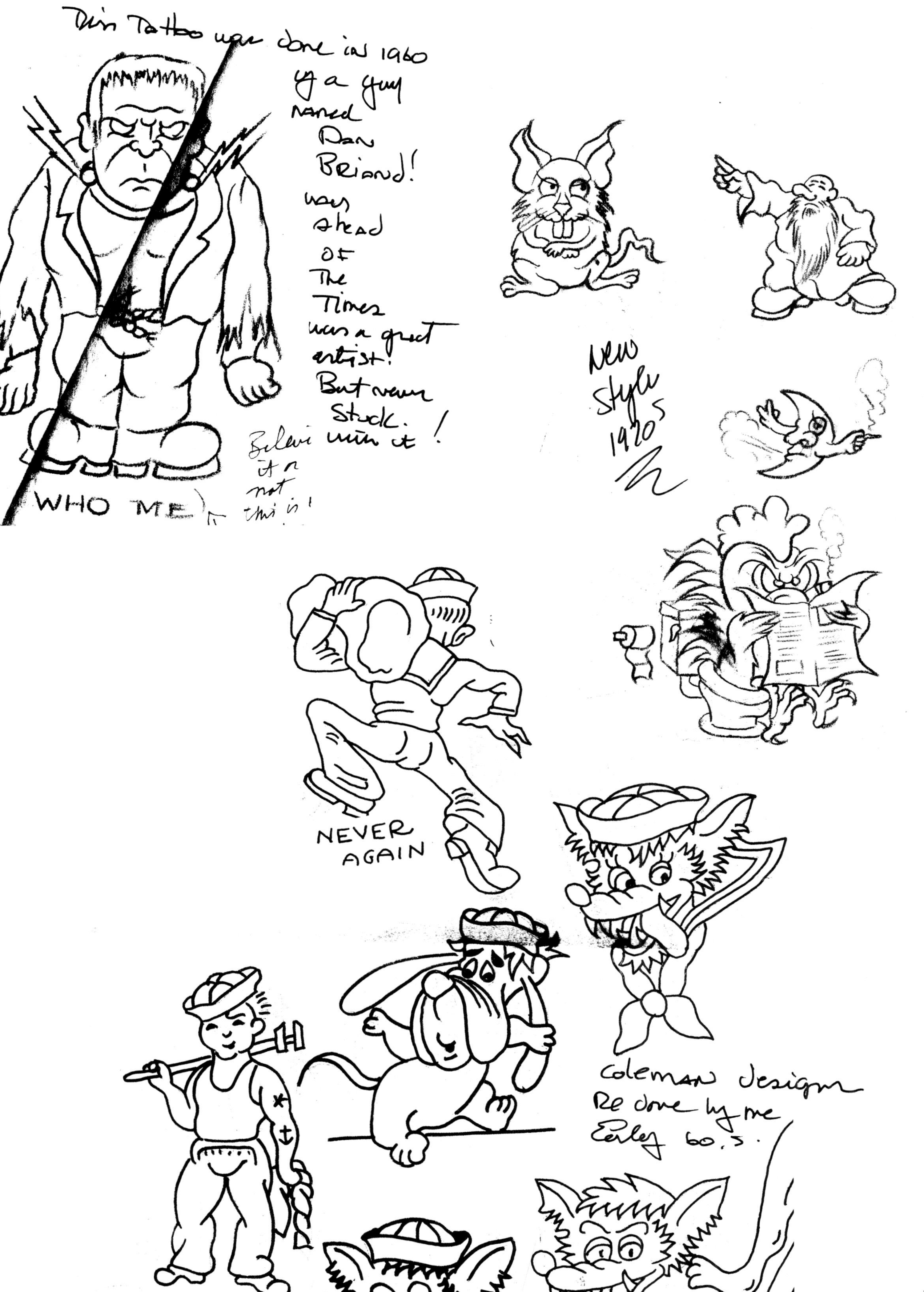
This Tattoo was done in 1960 by a guy named Dan Briand! was ahead of the Times was a great artist! But never stuck with it!
Believe it or not this is!
WHO ME
New Style 1920's
NEVER AGAIN
Coleman Designs Re done by me Early 60's.

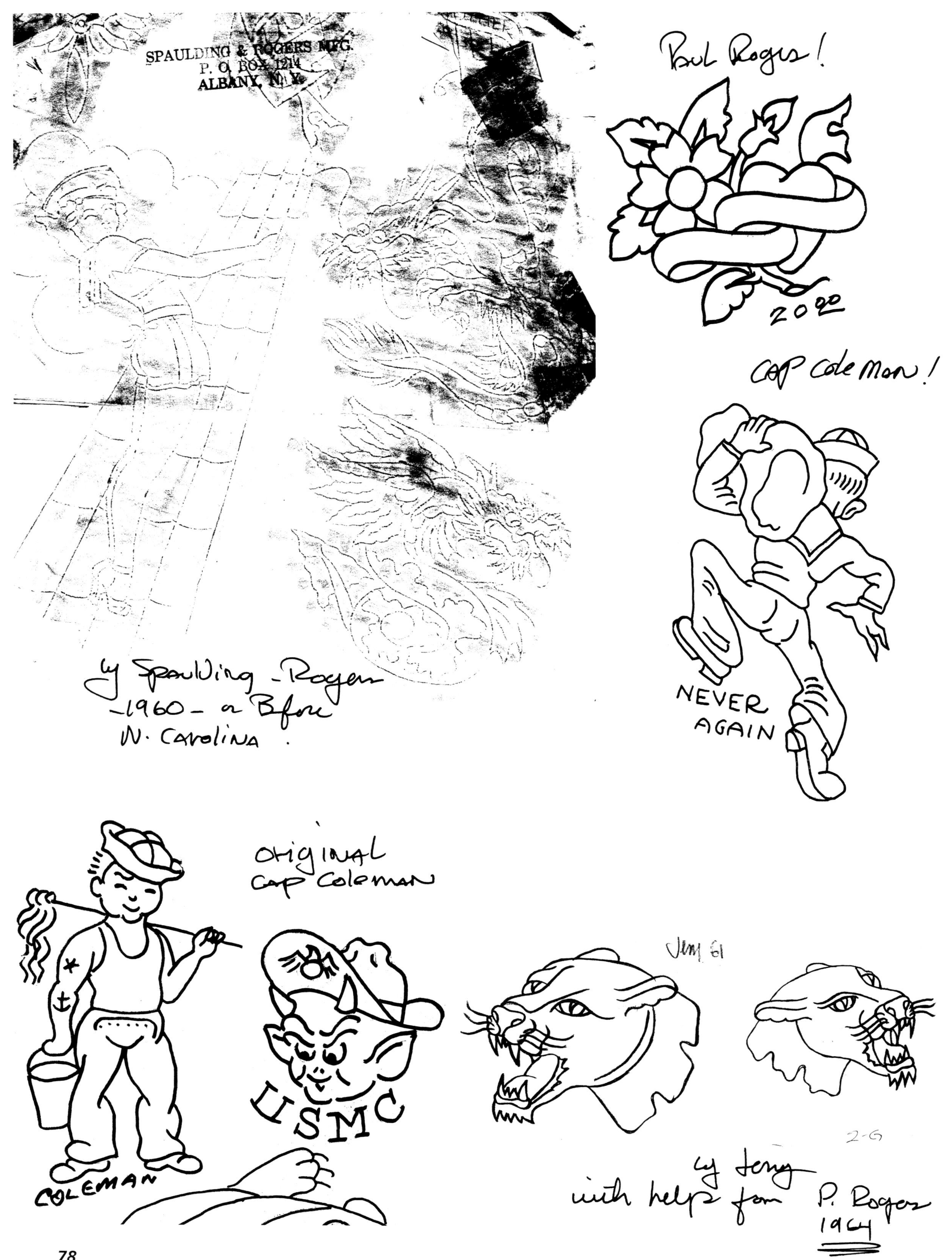
SPAULDING & ROGERS MFG.
P. O. BOX 1214
ALBANY, N. Y.
Paul Rogers!
2000
Cap Coleman!
NEVER
AGAIN
by Spaulding - Rogers
-1960- or Before
N. Carolina
original
Cap Coleman
USMC
COLEMAN
by Jerry
with helps from P. Rogers
1964

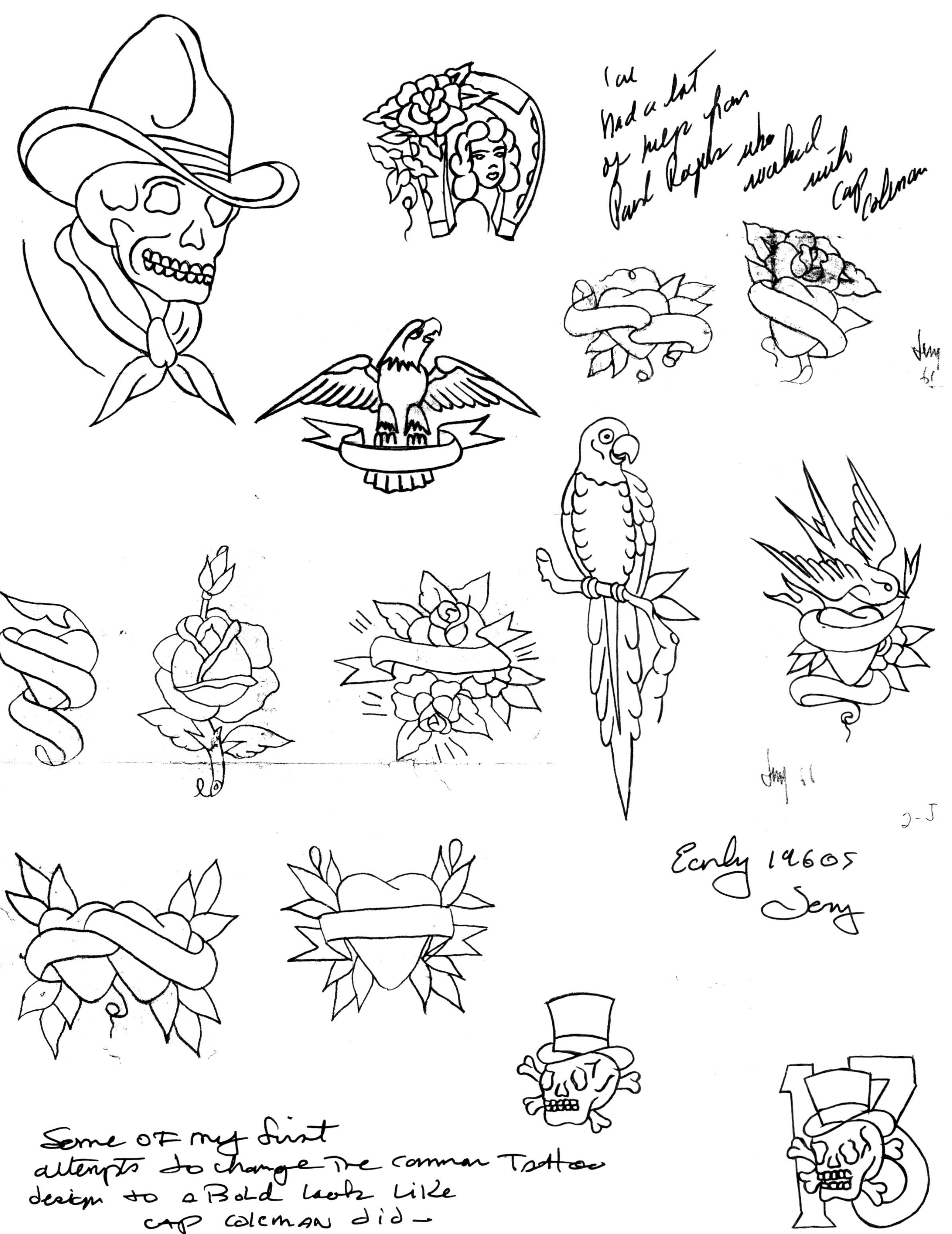
I've had a lot of help from Paul Rogers who worked with Cap Coleman
Early 1960s Jerry
Some of my first attempts to change the common Tattoo design to a Bold look like Cap Coleman did –

Designs by Les Skuse England Even then the Joe Lieber-coleman look was strong!

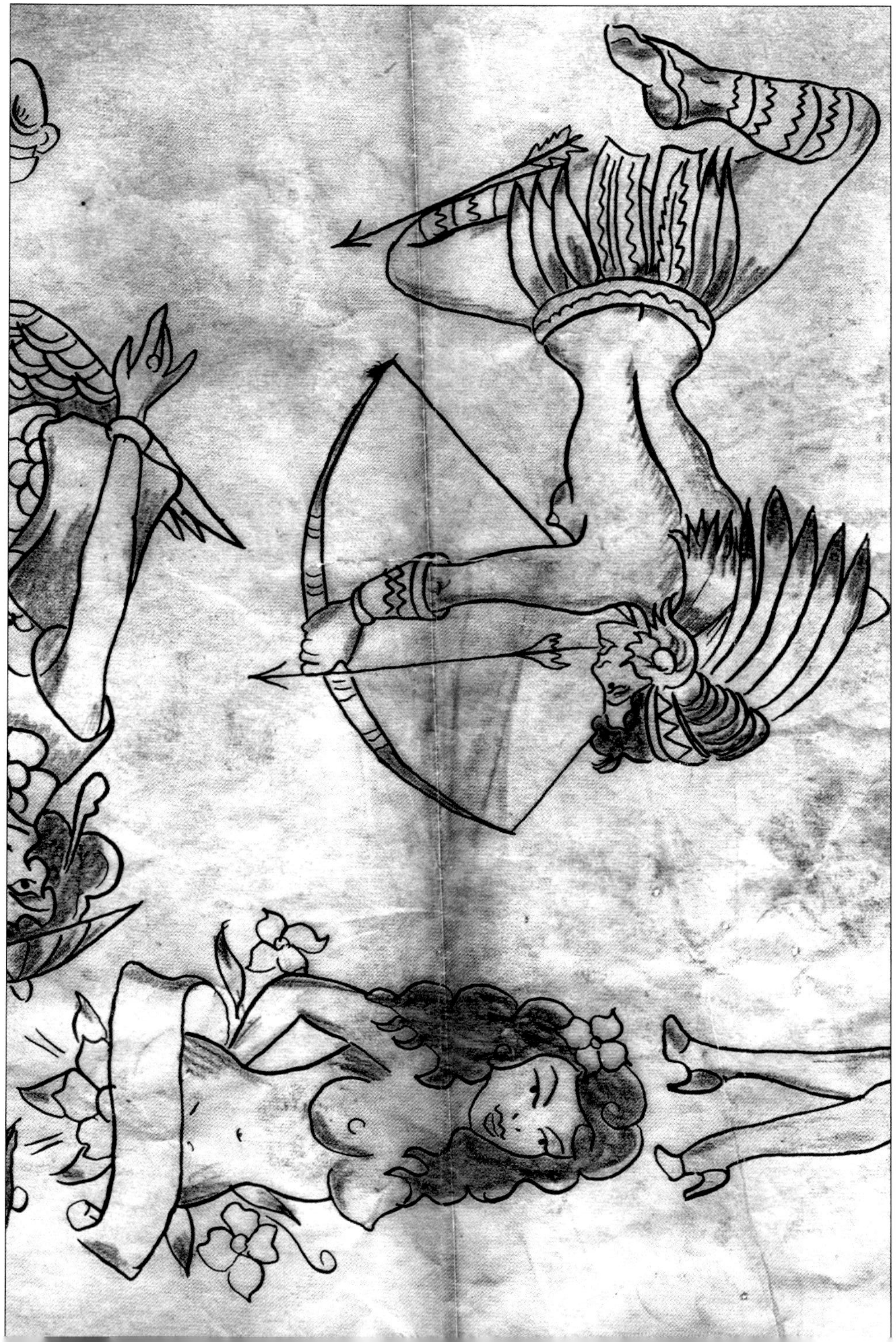

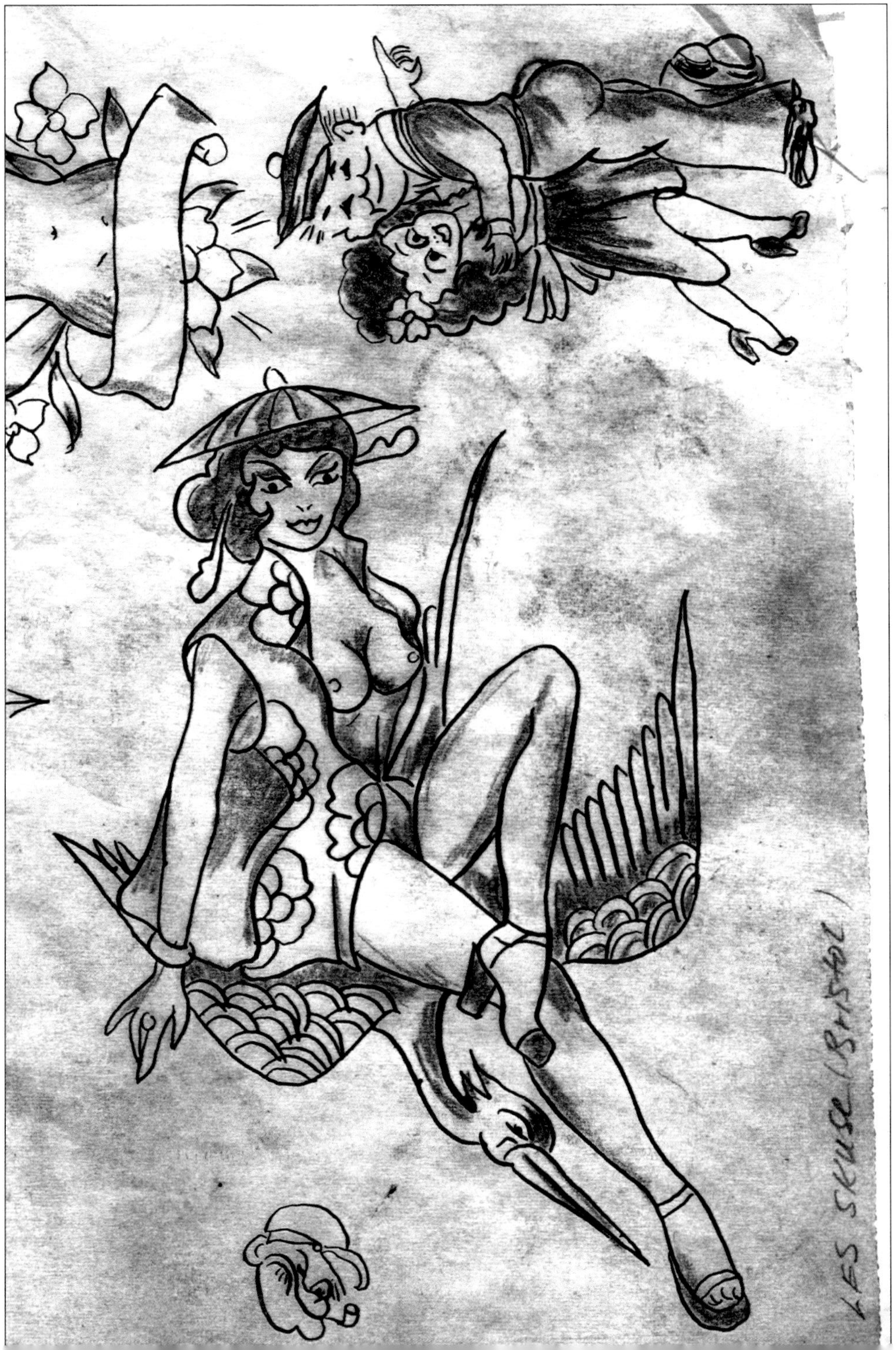

LES SKUSE (BRISTOL)

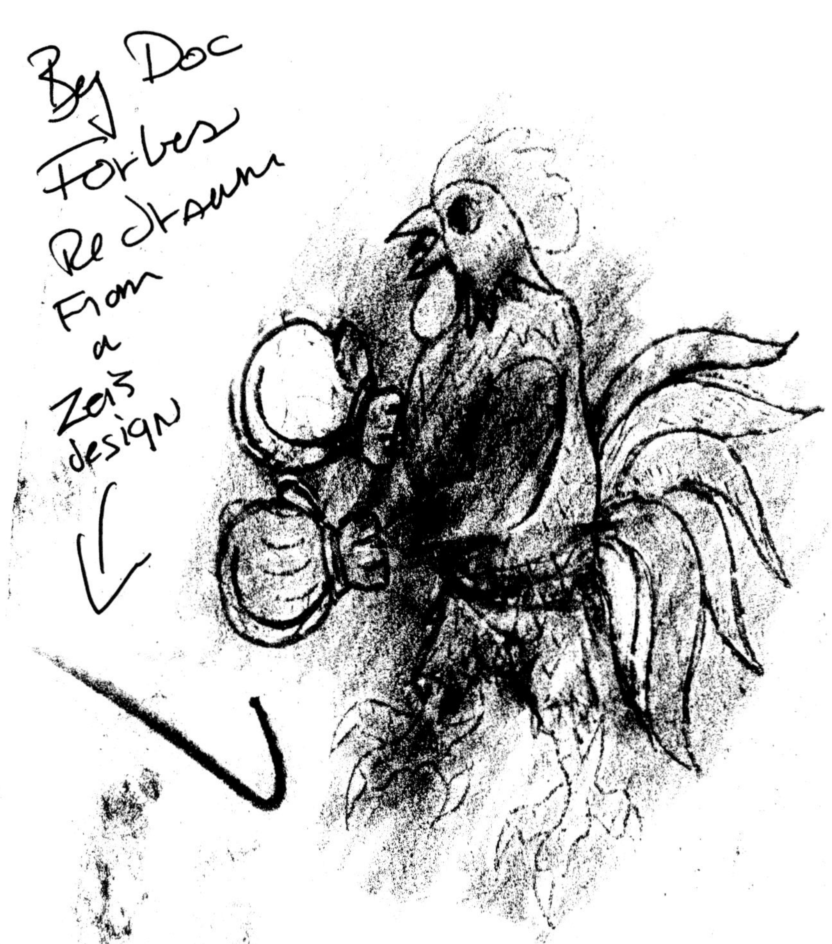

REDRAWN FROM A ZEIS IF THESE ARE NOT RIGHT HUCK LET ME KNOW.

By Huck Spaulding

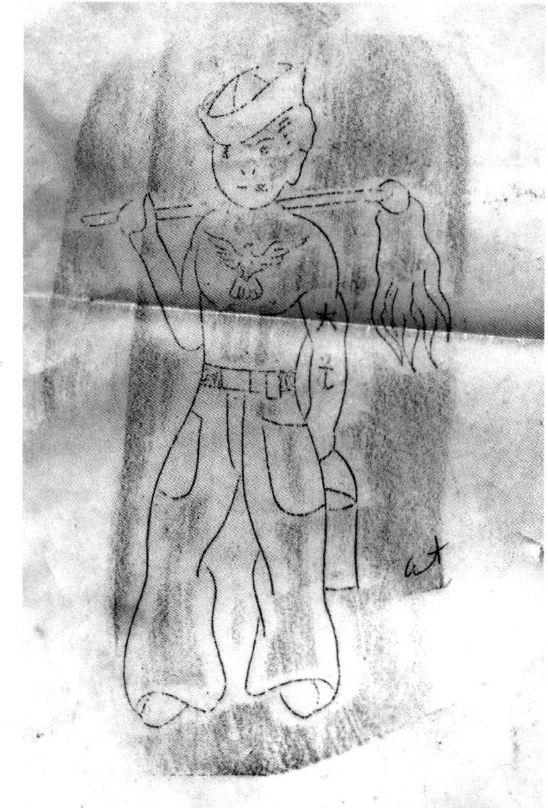

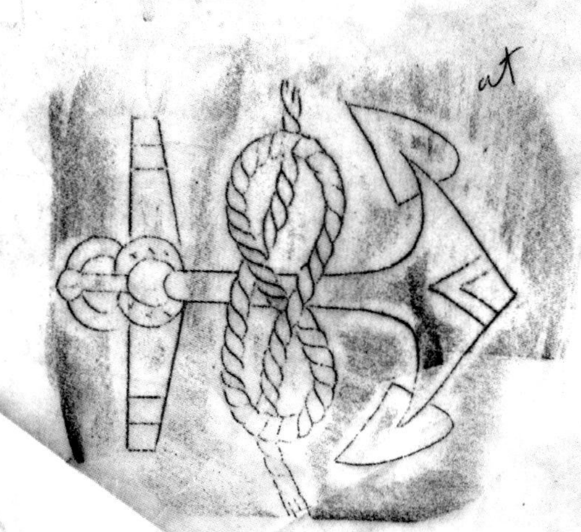

Huck a Fine Tattoo Artist who had That great coleman touch!

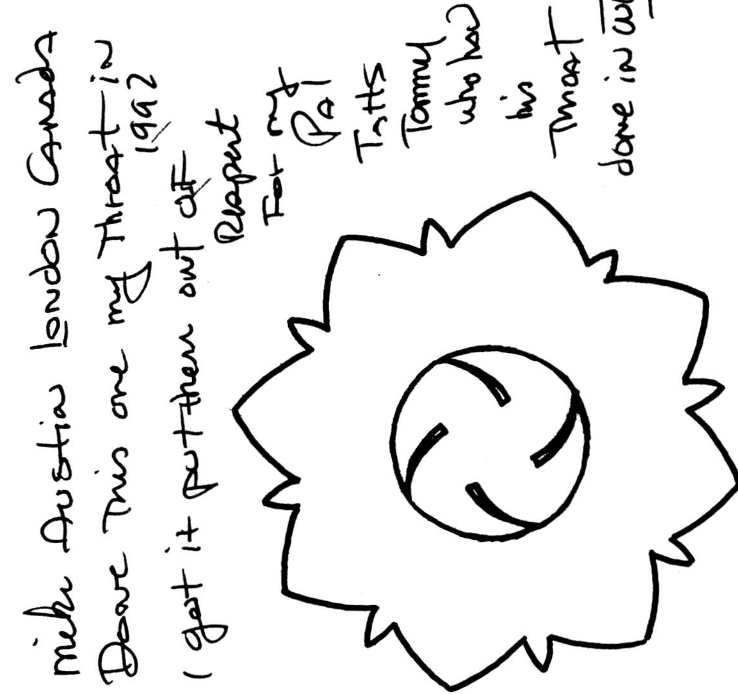

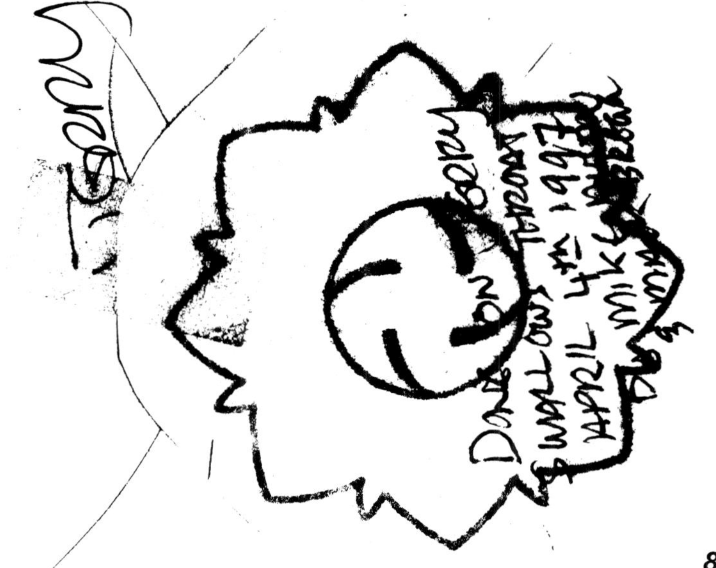

These were done by "Joe lieBer" Originals... now you see these in tattoo Books done by another popular Tattooer who never really done these. They were NOT even changed any just copied... I Redone em my self But changed them'

Tattoos by J. lieBer well before the time of Some world Famous Tattooer takes credit for it. Joe lieBer was the MAN! who done this Style!

you can see BJC IN The Stencil

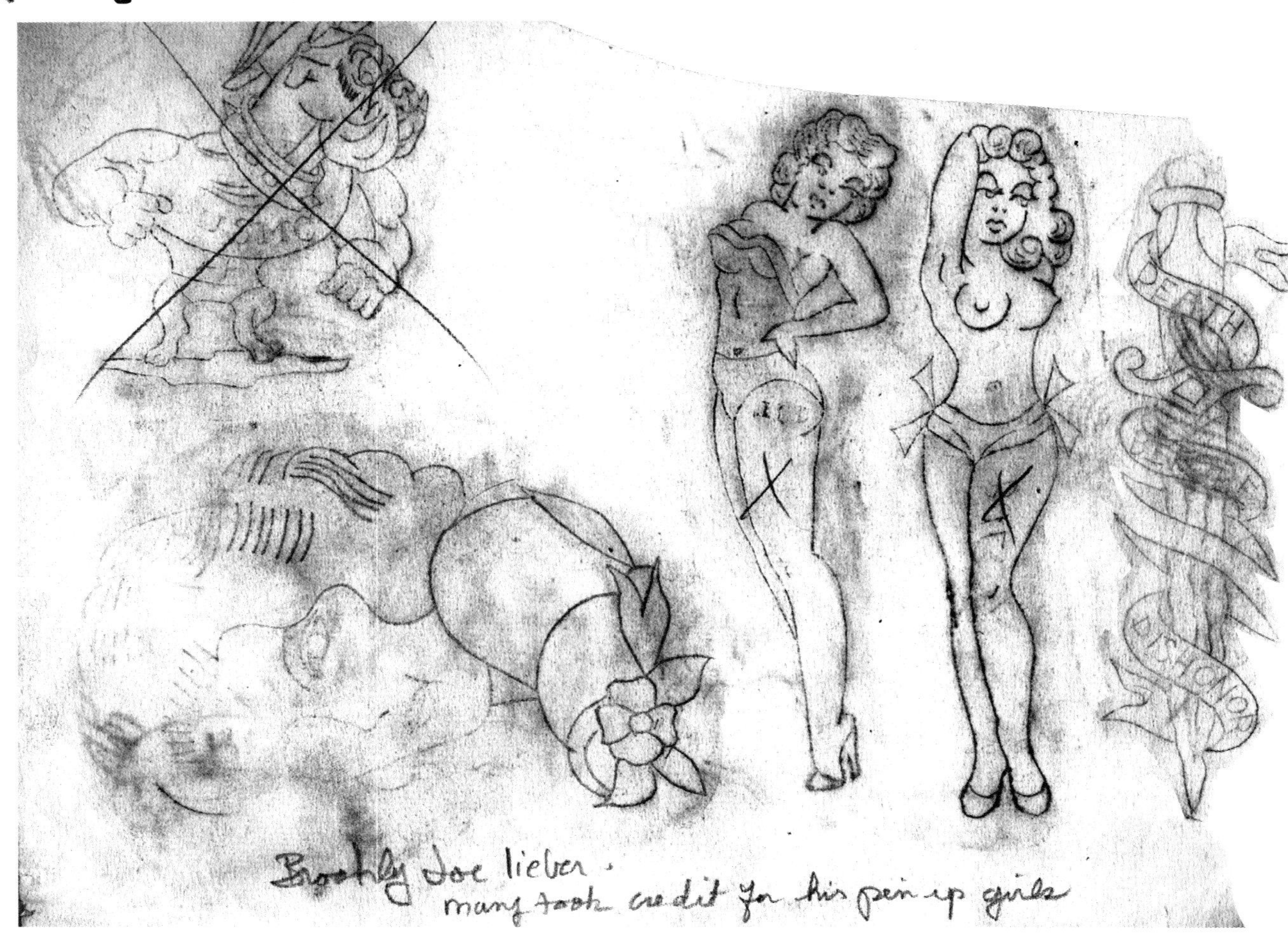

Some OF The Best designs you can get is Take a design you see N Like Redo it to you own style, it's not Stealing it Borrowing and giving it Back, most time looking Better.

Jonny

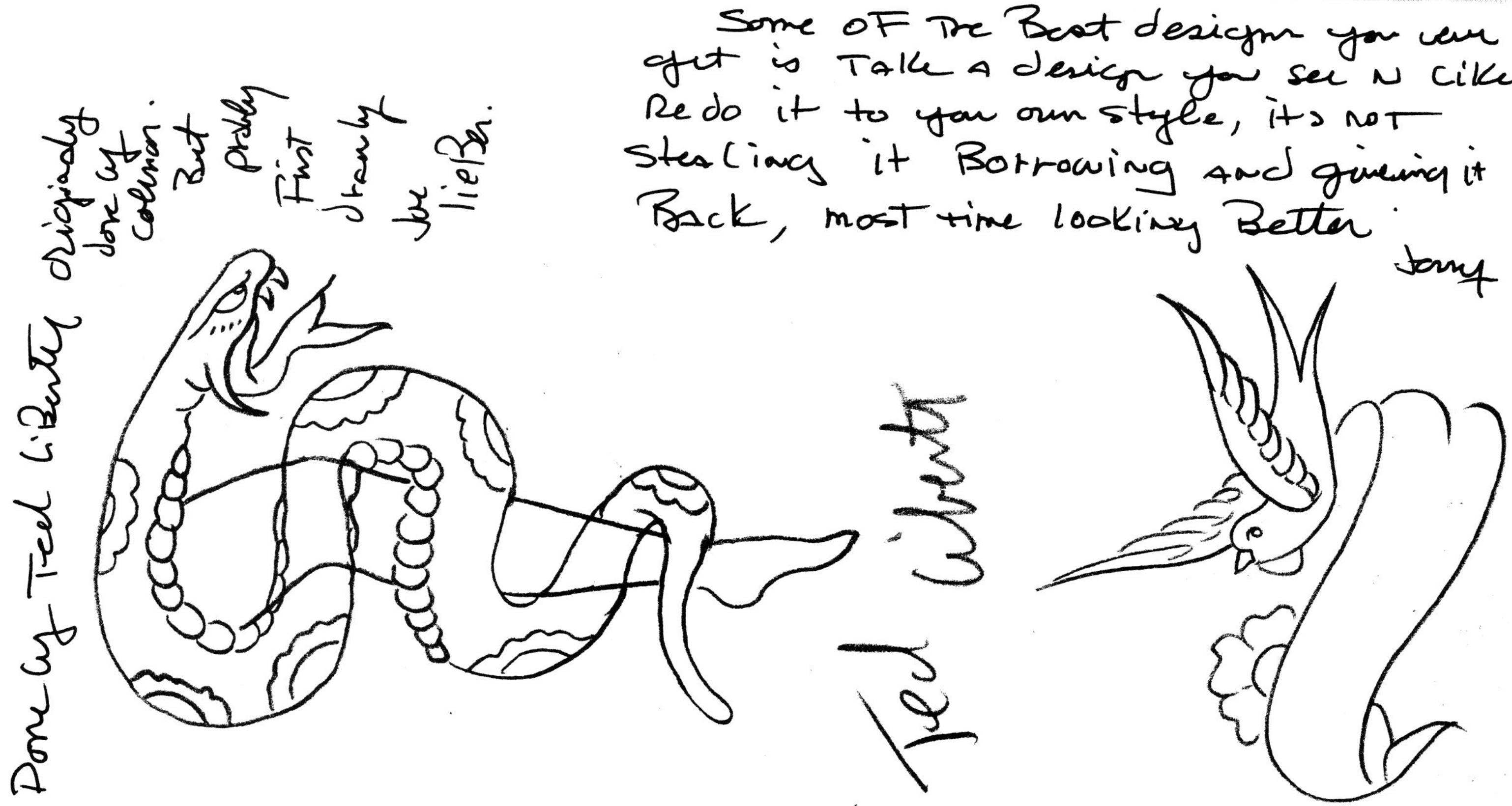

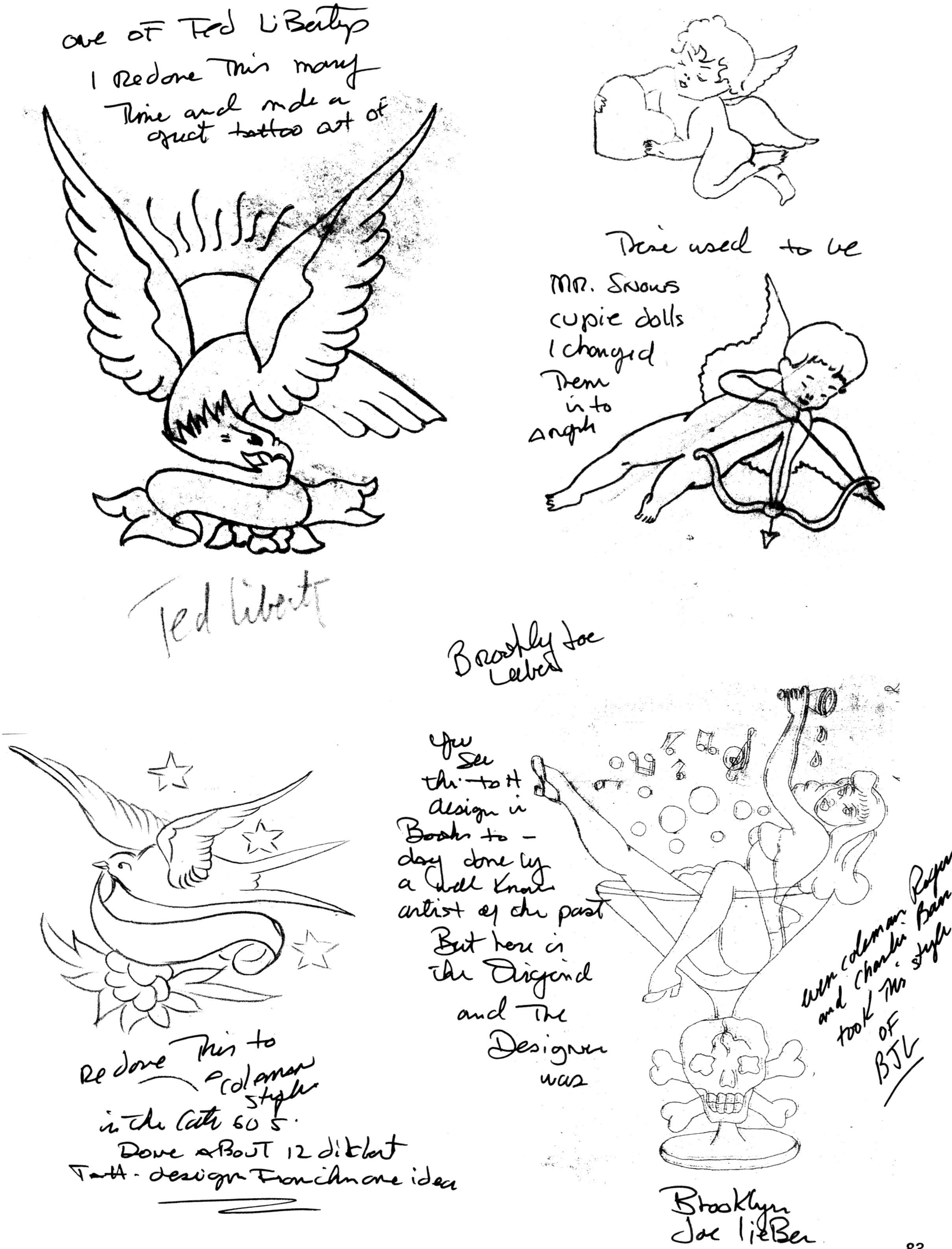
one of Ted LiBertys
I Redone This many
Time and made a
great tattoo art of
Ted liberty
These used to be
MR. Snows
cupie dolls
I changed
Them
in to
angels
Brooklyn Joe
Lieber
You
See
this tatt
design in
Books to-
day done by
a well known
artist of the past
But here is
The Original
and The
Designer
was
Brooklyn
Joe lieBer
Wm coleman Rogers
and Charlie Barr
took this style
OF
BJL
Redone This to
a coleman
style
in the late 60 s.
Done aBouT 12 different
Tatt-design from the one idea

TED LiBerty and Family Business card!

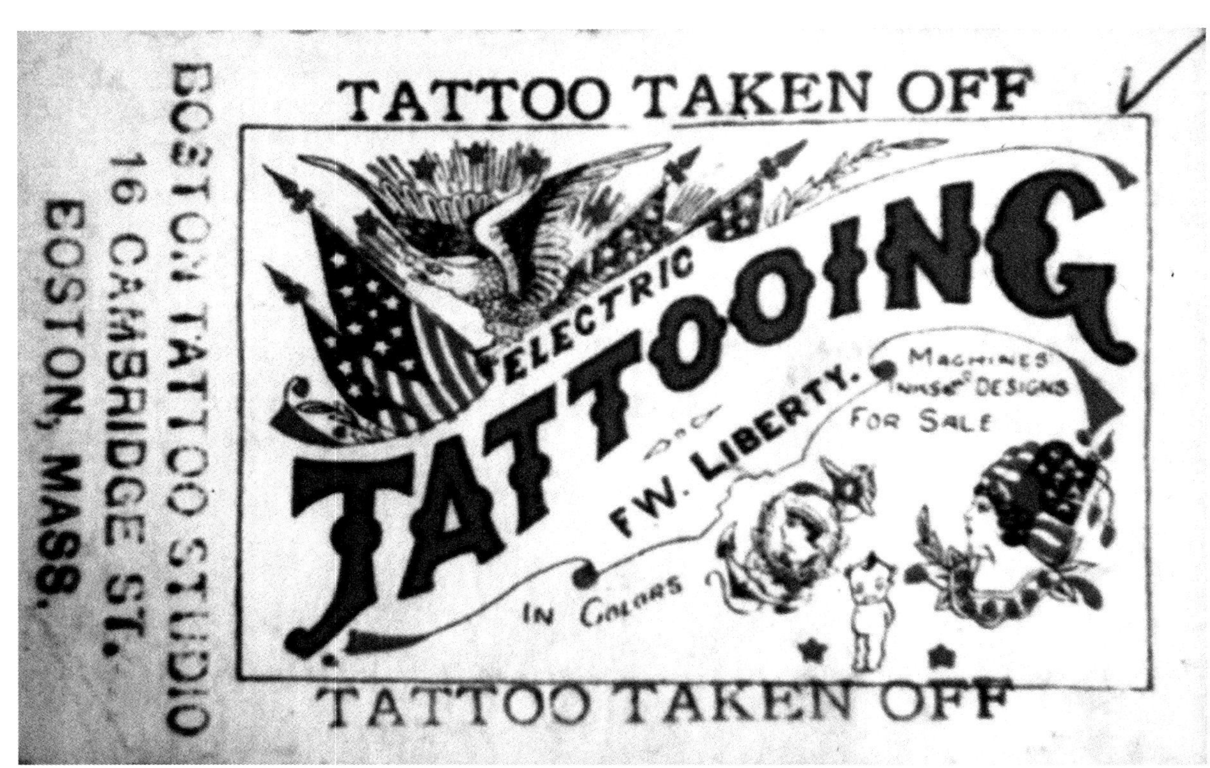

Ted Liberty Rose

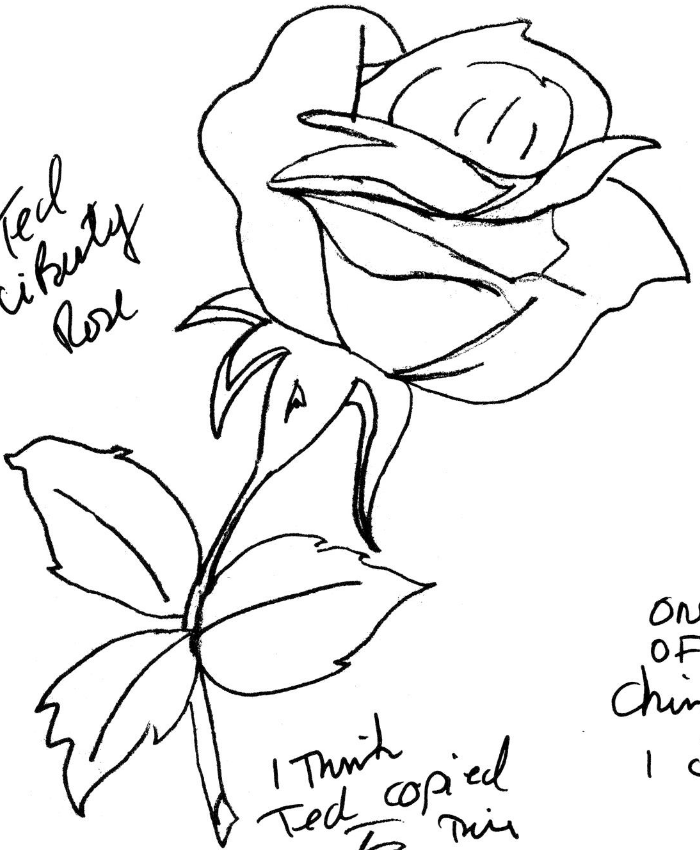

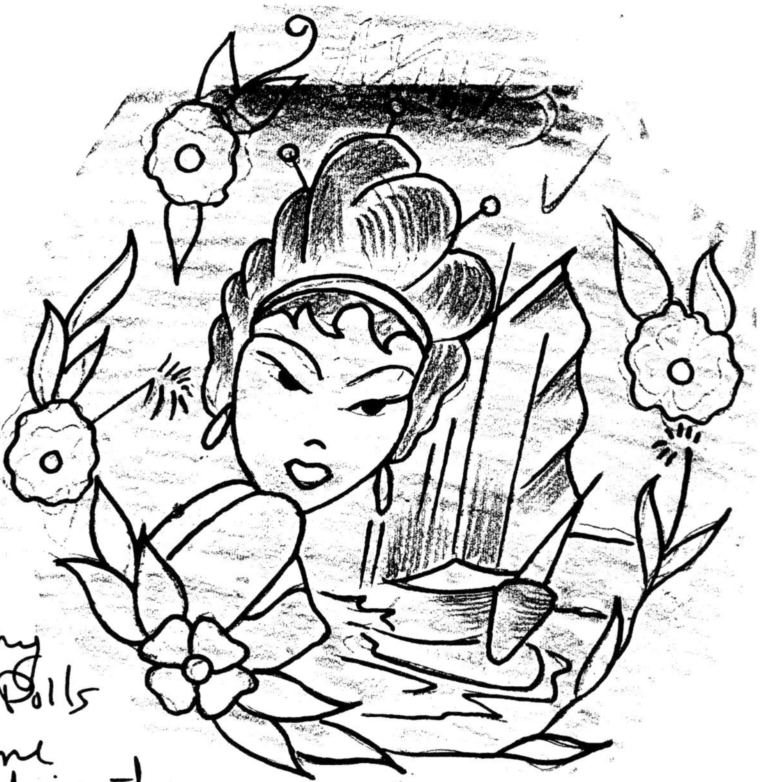

I Think Ted copied this OFF of a Tea Box!

One OF my China Dolls I done this with Roses - egles and Birds all around it so many different ways.

CLASSIC Al Newcombe stuff.

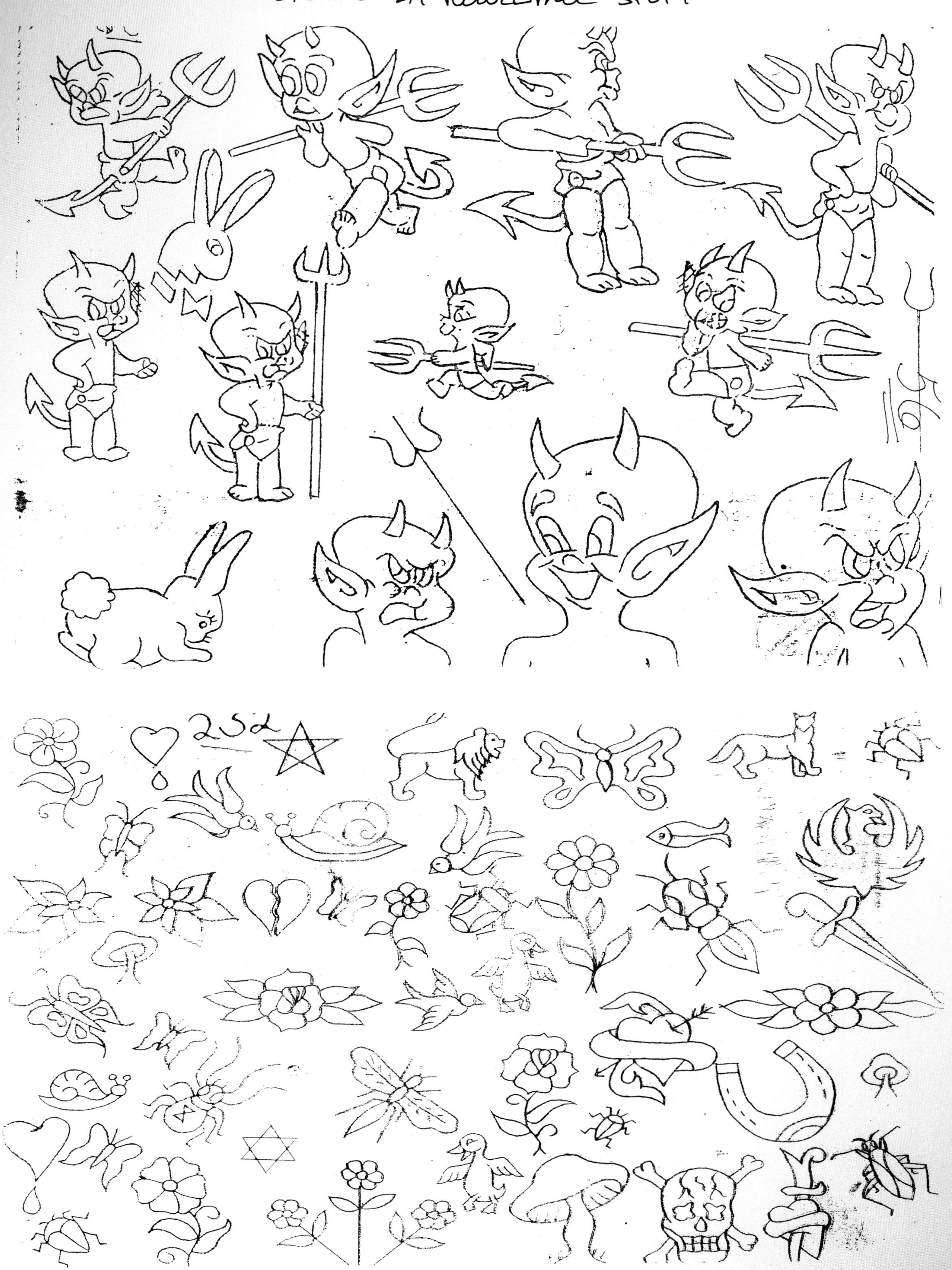

Newcombe 1950s 60s

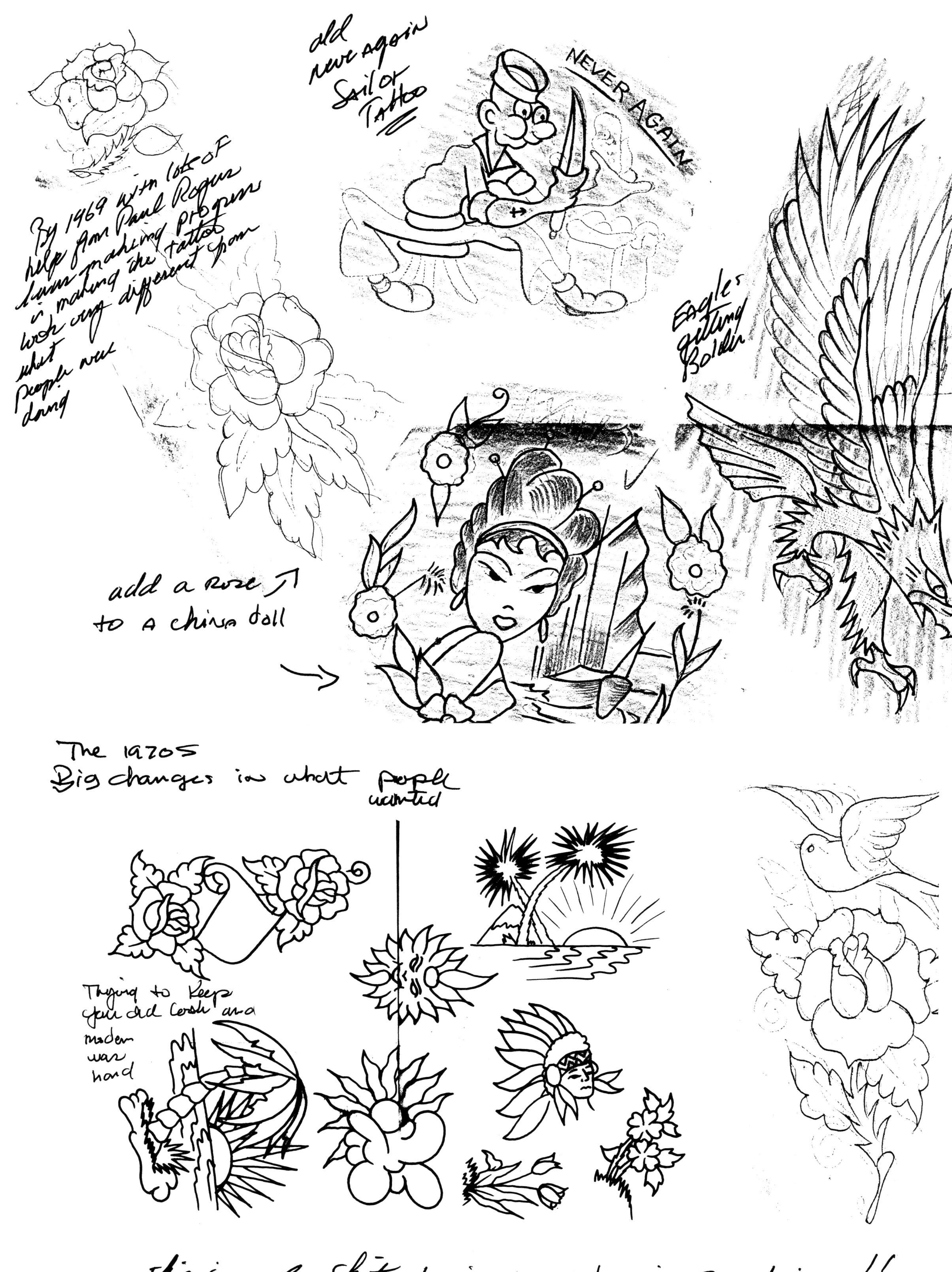

this is real shit trying to modernize the designs !!

By Al Newcombe

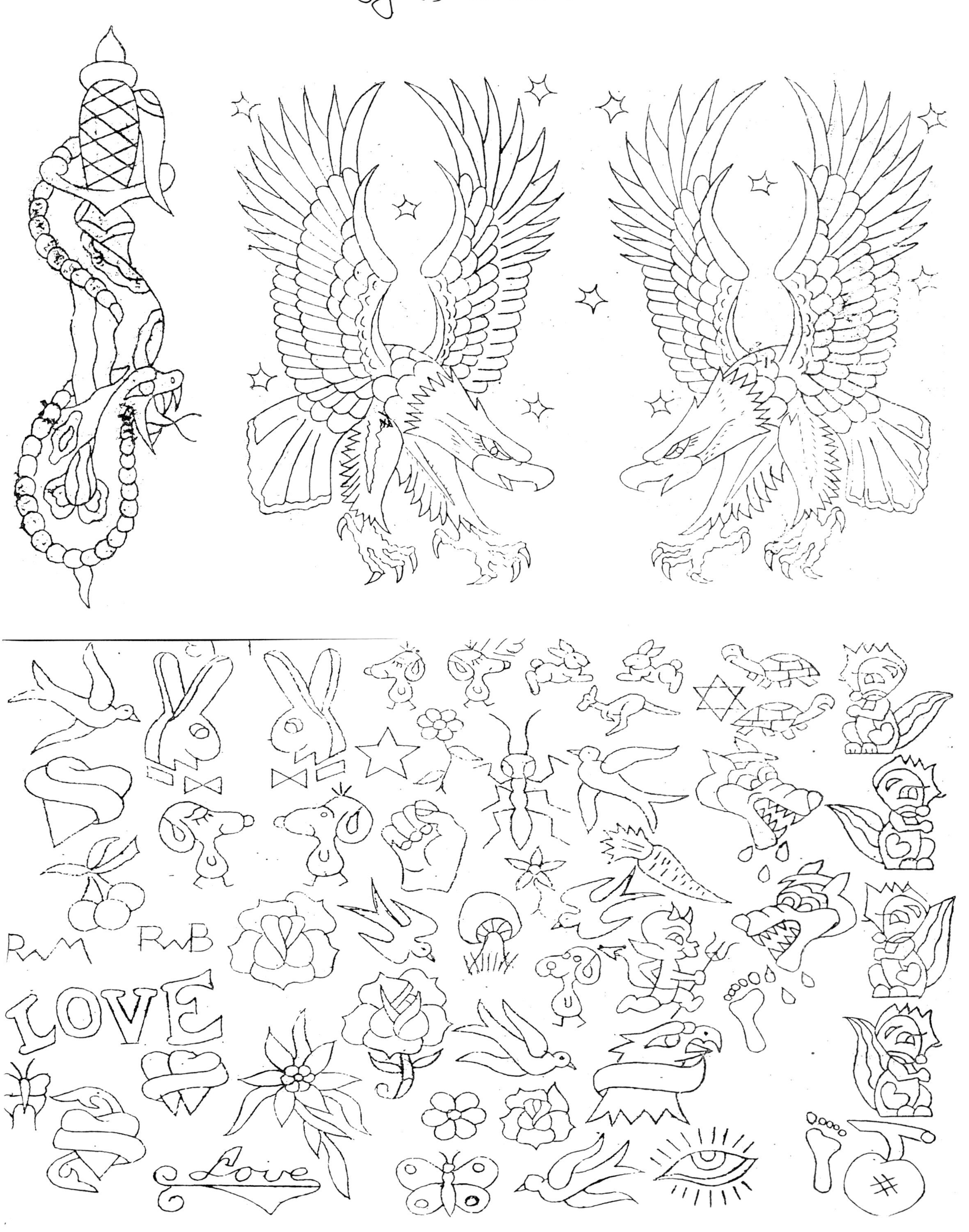

Designs by Al Newcombe. London Canada

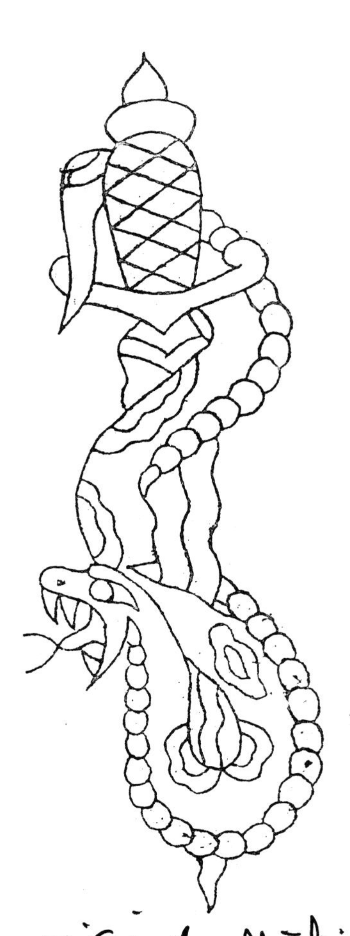

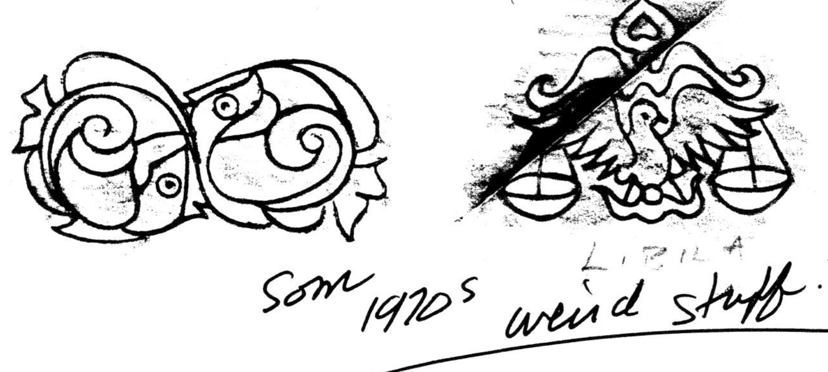

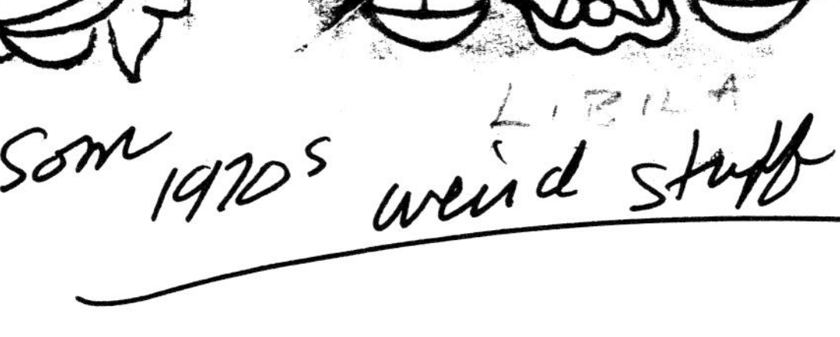

Som 1920s weird stuff!

Standard Snake Dagger by A. Newcombe

originals of this stuff was Joe Liebers.

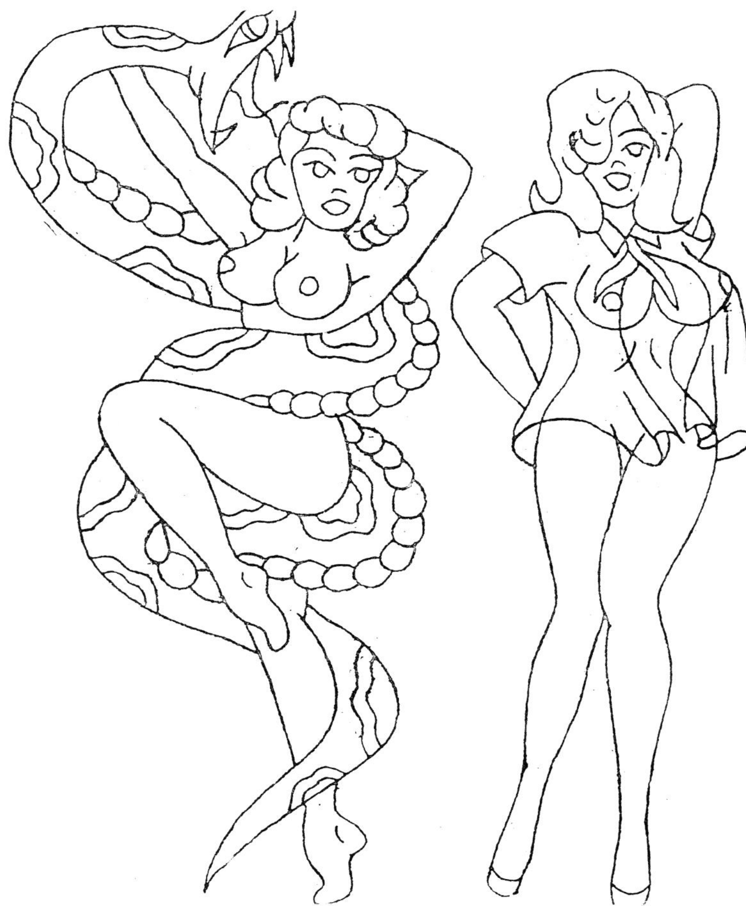

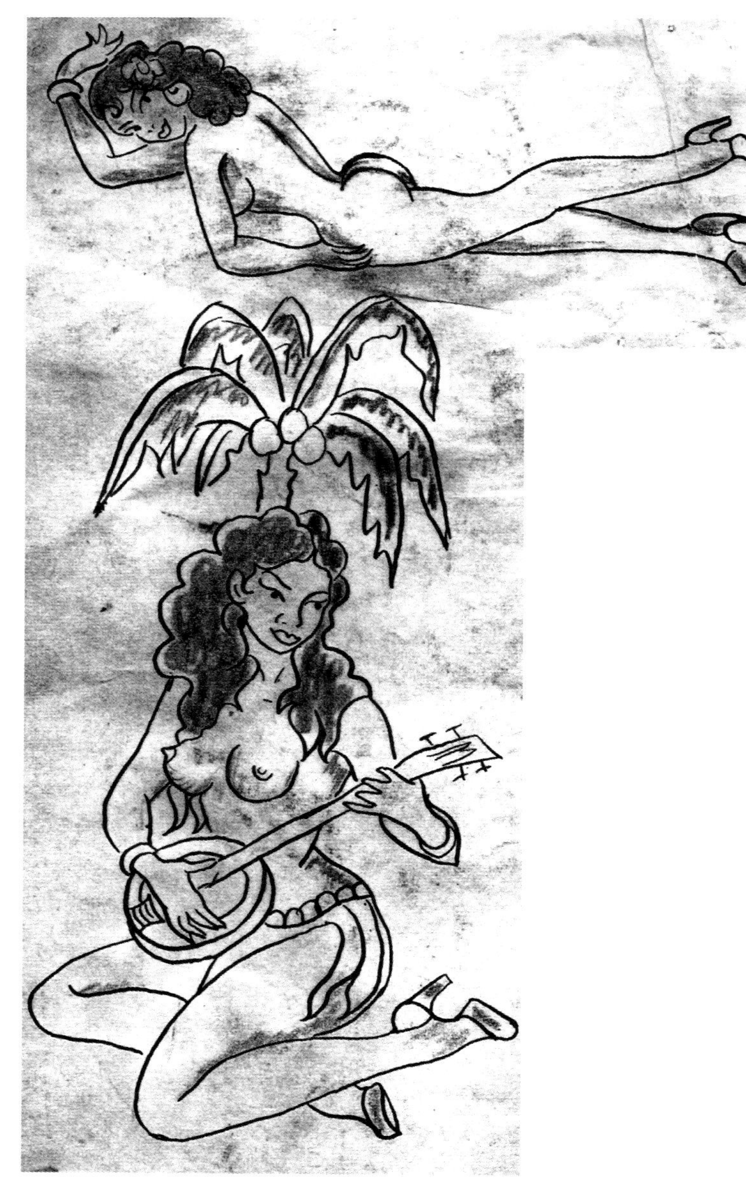

This is Original ART By Les Skuse Bristol Eng. UK. you can see the Coleman style in it every thing They no doubt ever met !! —

A. Newcombe..

my stencil prints

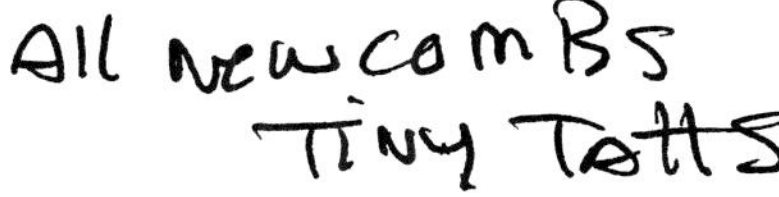

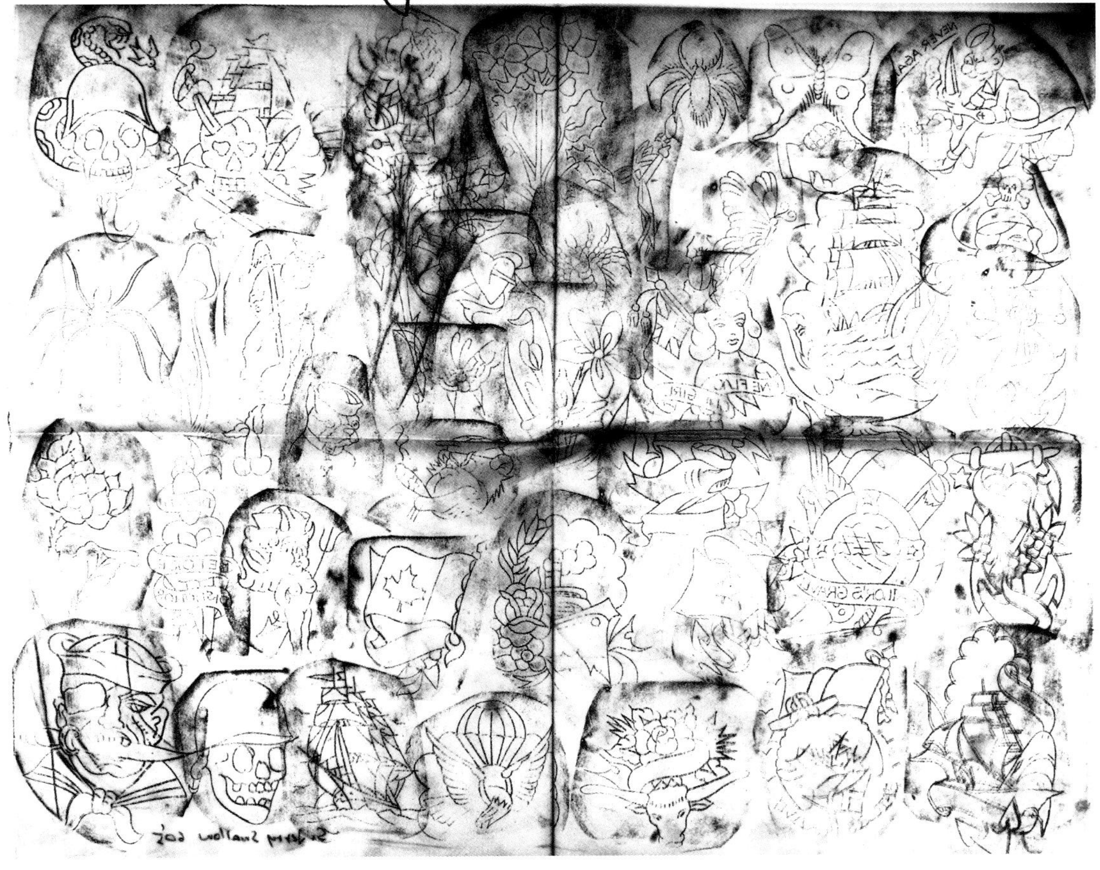

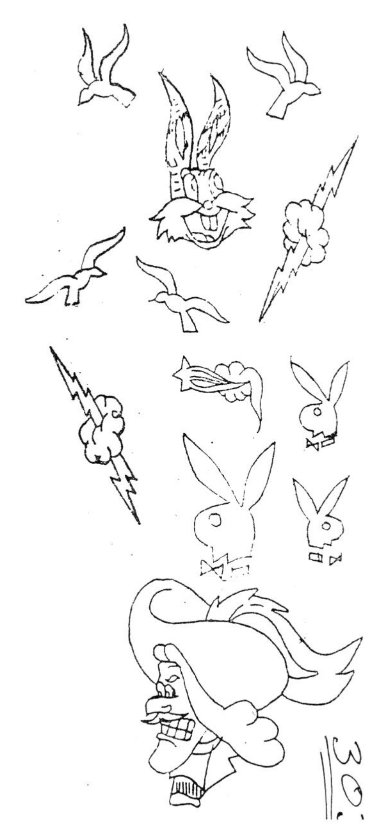

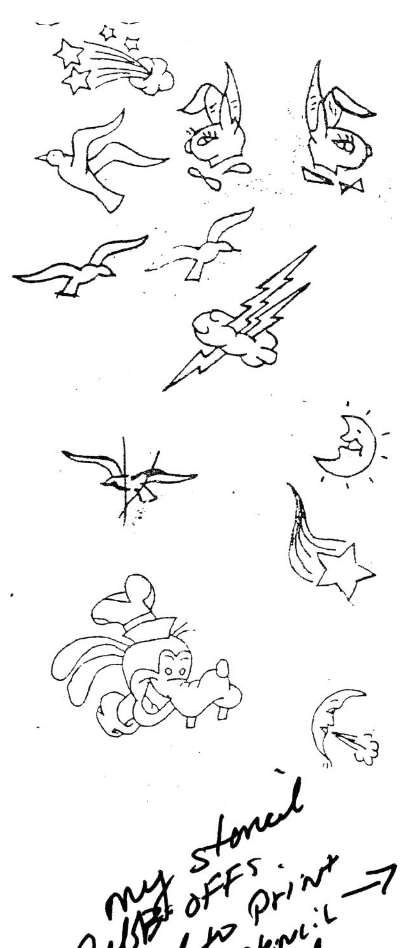

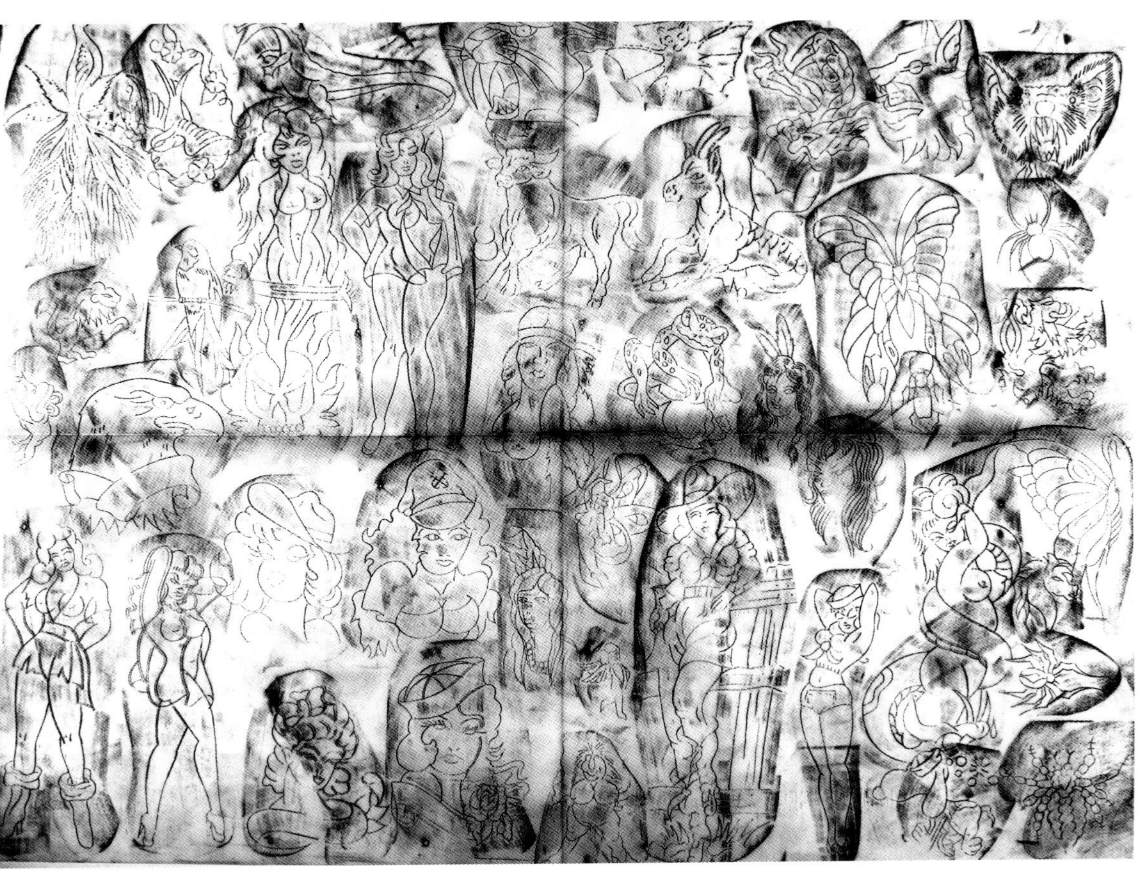

my stencil RuBBer OFFs I used to print each stencil I had on paper →

IN case Any Stole Them etc always had a copy.

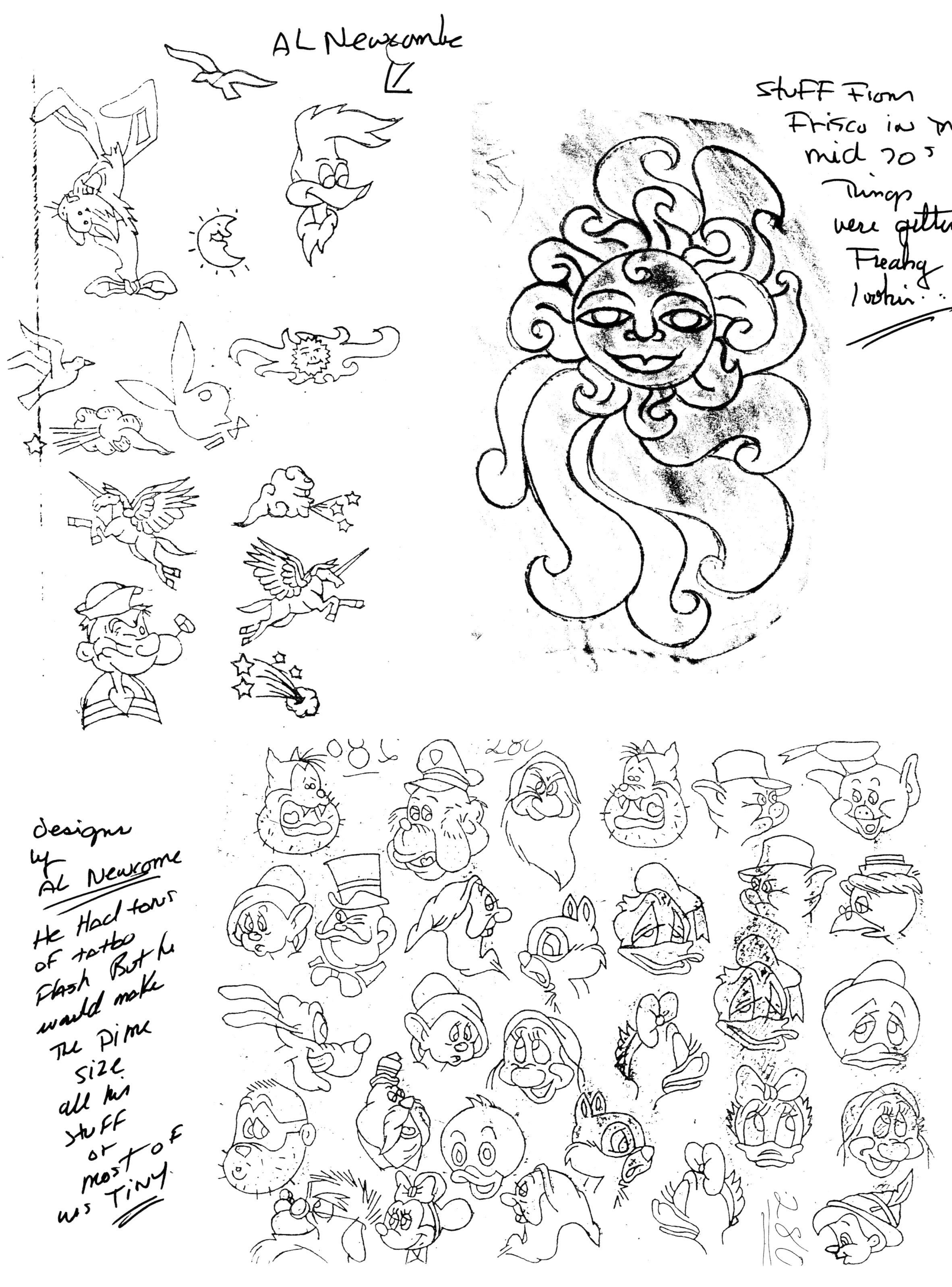
AL Newcombe
Stuff From Frisco in the mid 70's Things were gettin Freaky lookin...
designs by AL Newcome
He Had tons of tattoo Flash But he would make the Dime size all his stuff or most of was TINY

I called This Horseshoe Ribbon to add some color to this an other tattoos I'd do this to end of RiBBon And color it.

[illegible] 1960s

1951

GOOD LUCK

By C. Snow 1951

Classic old Tattoo design done by Charlie

another exampel by stuff everyone done

Cap. Coleman done The Best Examples!

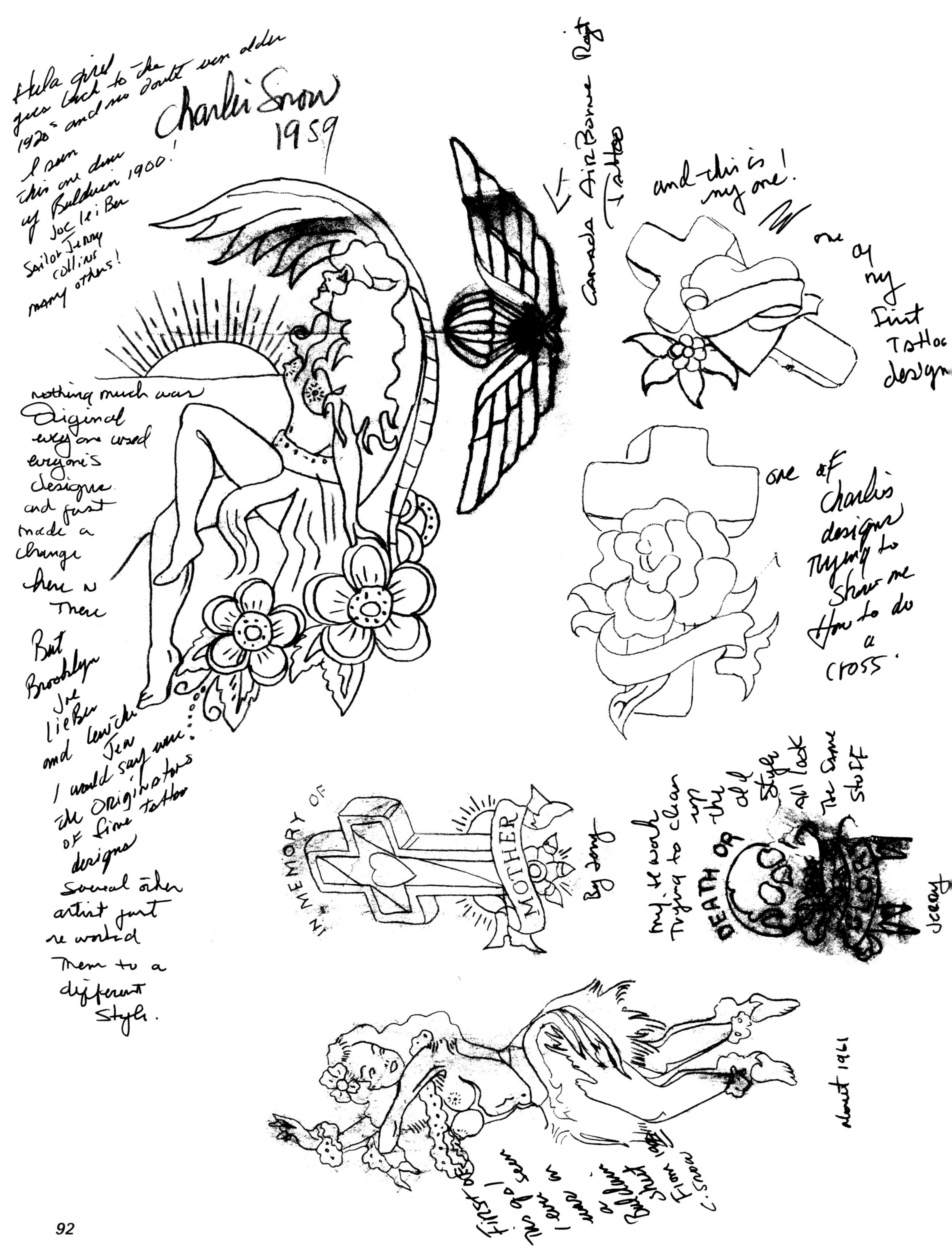
Hula girl goes back to the 1920s and no doubt even older
Charlie Snow 1959
I seen this one done by Baldwin 1900! Joe LeiBer Sailor Jerry Collins many others!
Canada AirBorne Regt Tattoo
and this is my one!
one of my first Tattoo design
nothing much was original everyone used everyone's designs and just made a change here n there
But Brooklyn Joe LieBer and Lewiston Jew I would say were the ORIGINATORS of fine tattoo designs
several other artist just re worked them to a different style.
one of Charlie's designs trying to show me how to do a cross.
IN MEMORY OF
MOTHER
By Jerry
my rework trying to clean up the old style all look the same stuff
DEATH OR GLORY
Jerry
about 1961
C. Snow

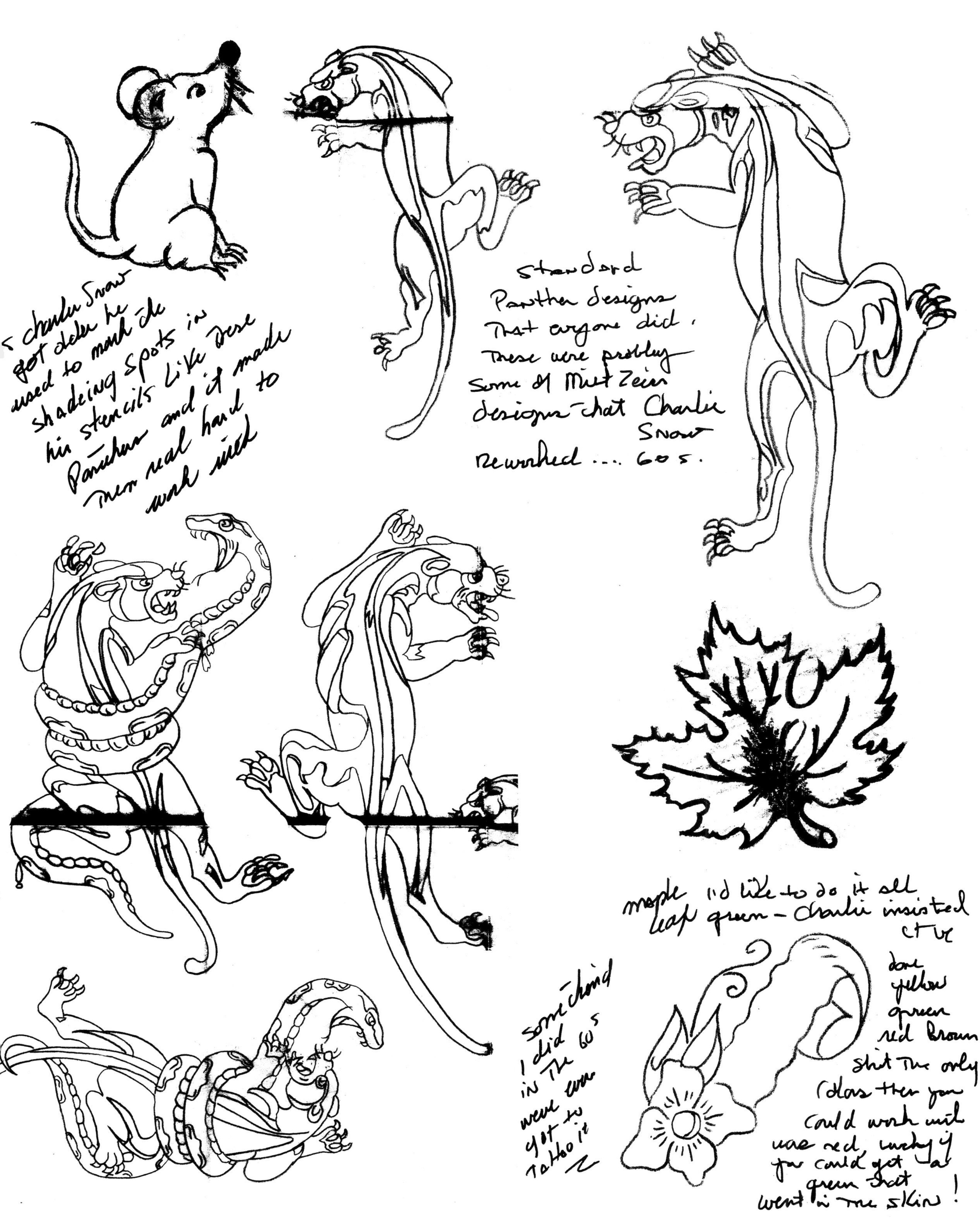

5 Charlie Snow got older he used to mark the shadeing spots in his stencils like these Panthers and it made them real hard to work with
standard Panther designs That everyone did. These were probably some of Milt Zeis designs that Charlie Snow Reworked ... 60s.
maple leaf I'd like to do it all green – Charlie insisted it be done yellow green red brown shit The only colors then you could work with was red, lucky if you could get a green that went in the skin!
something I did in The 60s

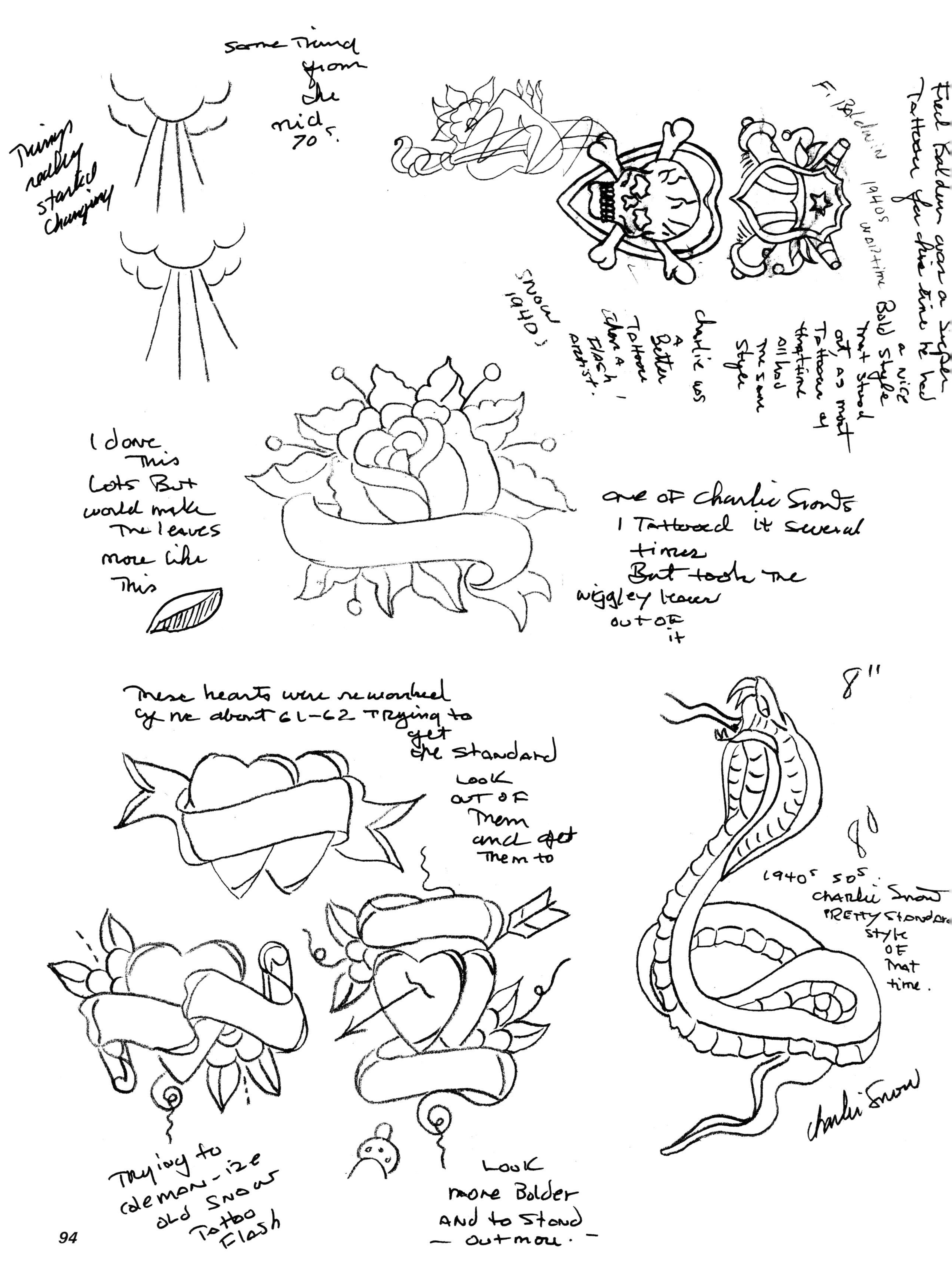
Things really started changing
same Thing from the mid 70's.
F. Baldwin 1940s wartime
Fred Baldwin was a super Tattooer for his time he had a nice Bold style that stood out as most Tattooers of that time all had the same style
Charlie was a Better Tattooer than a Flash artist.
Snow 1940's
I done This Lots But would make The leaves more like This
one of Charlie Snow's I Tattooed it several times But took the wiggley leaves out of it
These hearts were reworked by me about 61-62 Trying to get the standard Look out of Them and get Them to
Look more Bolder and to Stand — out more. —
Trying to demon-ize old Snow Tattoo Flash
8"
8"
1940s 50s. Charlie Snow Pretty Standard style of That time.
Charlie Snow

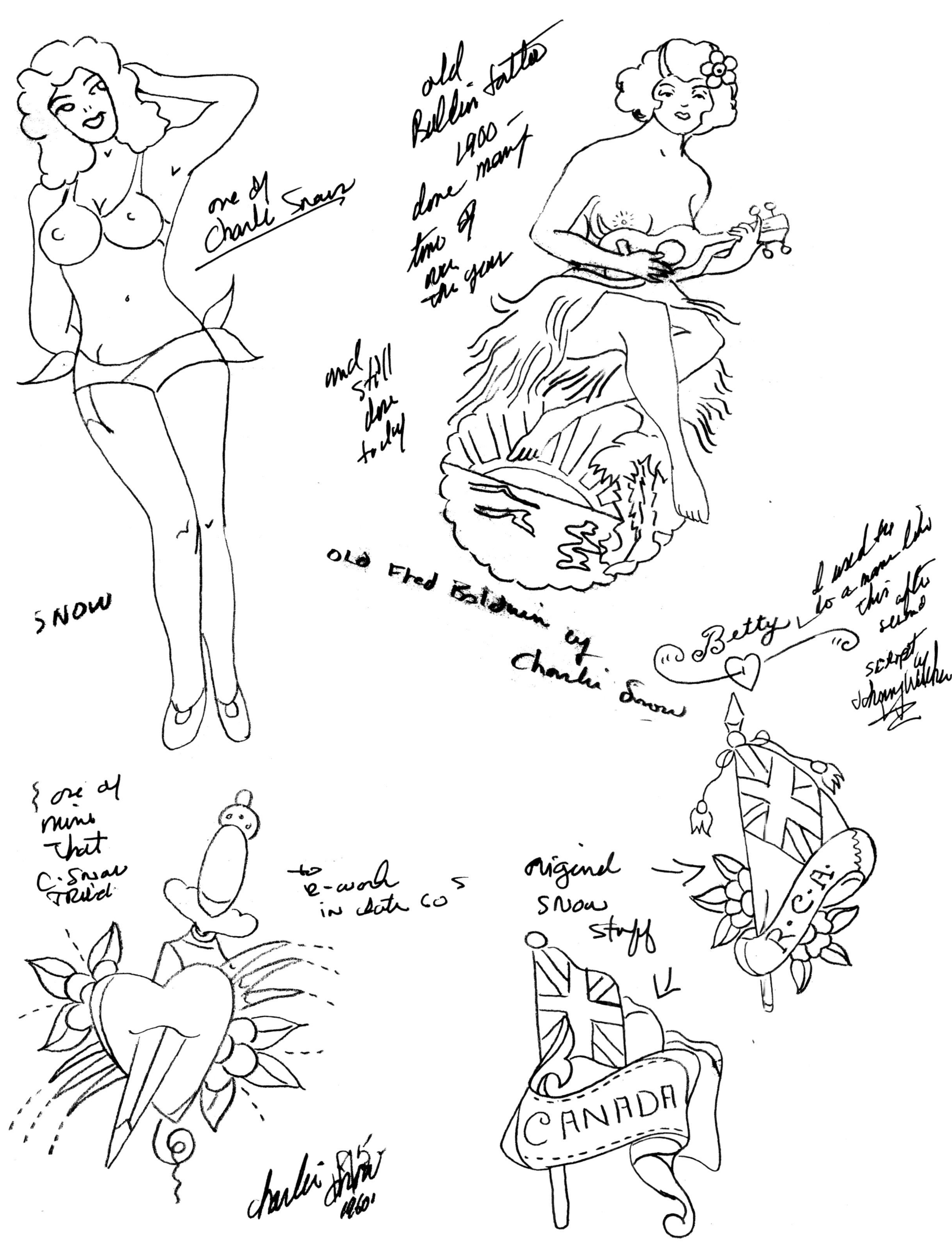
one of Charlie Snow
old Baldwin tattoo 1900 — done many times over the years
and still done today
SNOW
OLD Fred Baldwin by Charlie Snow
Betty
one of mine that C. Snow tried to re-work in late 60s
original Snow stuff
R.C.A.
CANADA
Charlie Snow
Charlie Snow 1940s

original work by Joe lieber - re drawn over by Charlie Barr, Cap Colman, Roger and myself

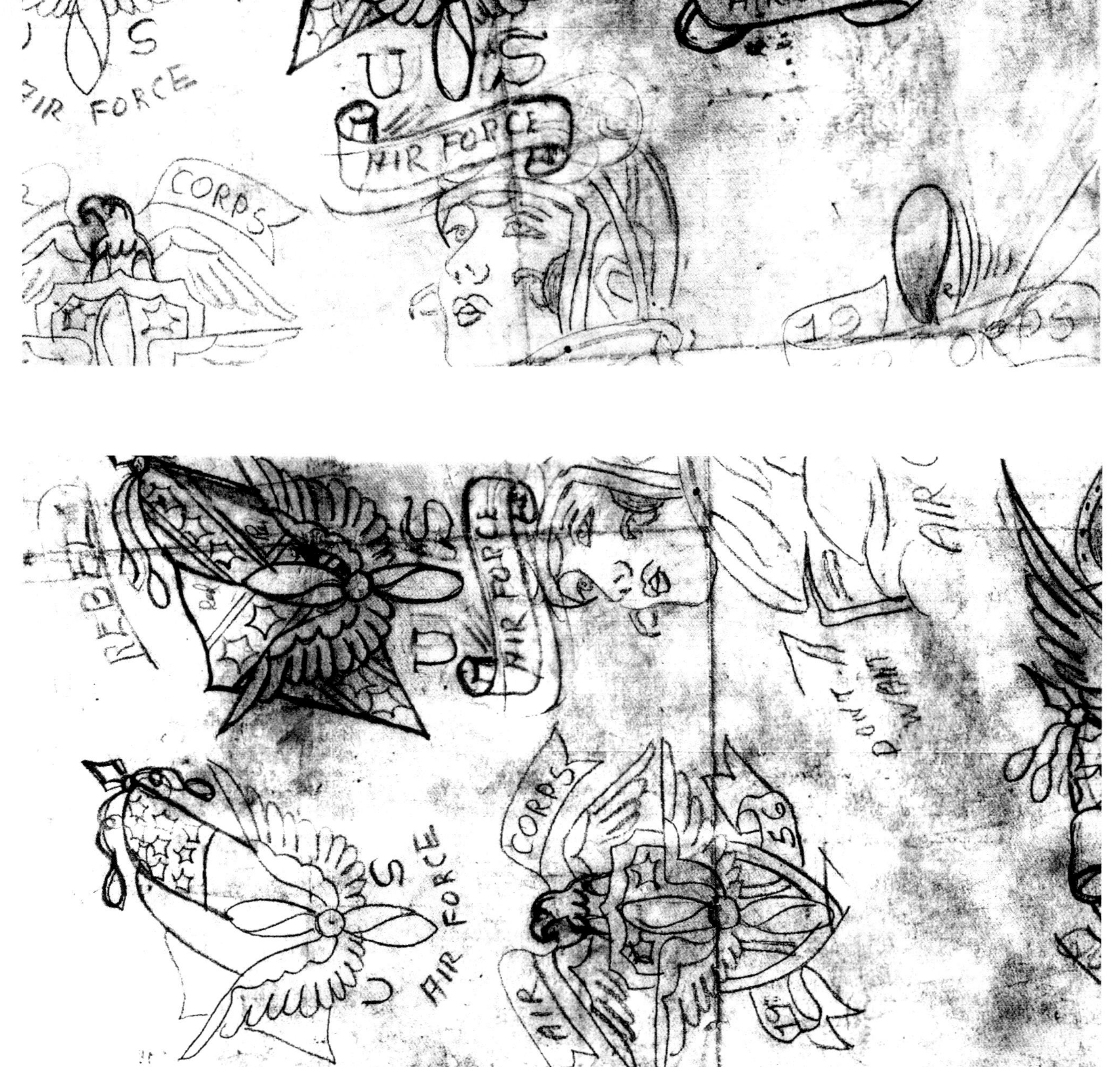

Joe lieber was probly the tattoo designer of all time
these design still being done today
Jay.